ADVANCE PRAISE FOR

# Expanding the Critical Animal Studies Imagination: Essays in Solidarity and Total Liberation

"It is rare, truly, that one finds a book that delivers on its radical and iconoclastic promise. This book does precisely that. Delinking critical animal studies from a presumed narrowness, Expanding the Critical Animal Studies Imagination is deeply intersectional, deeply committed, and deeply cutting edge—in a rigorous, robust, and genuine way. This collection goes there; it is not afraid, at all, to be Black, trans, feminist, and anarchistic in ways that we strongly need. In short, read this. Now."

—Marquis Bey
Author of Black Trans Feminism

"I am always seeking out unruly ideas and undisciplined perspectives that will unsettle the ways that we have been conditioned to think about the world we live in, and that invite us to imagine and act to realize the worlds we might co-create. This powerful collection of writings on the future of Critical Animal Studies is an exemplar of such a vision and has challenged me to expand, deepen, and sharpen my thinking about how we can and must transform our freedom dreams into lived experience."

—David Naguib Pellow
University of California Santa Barbara, author of Total Liberation and What is Critical Environmental Justice?

"A wake-up call for critical animal studies that invites us to abandon respectability politics. These imaginative essays link liberatory thought and social justice action in ways that will astound, inspire, and anger you in turn. Best read with a mind open to anarchism."

—Margaret Robinson (Mi'kmaq)
Dalhousie University, Tier 2 Canada Research Chair in Reconciliation, Gender, and Identity

"Expanding the CAS Imagination addresses new topics in Critical Animal Studies and pushes foundational ones in new directions. If you think you know what Critical Animal Studies is about, this edited collection will show you that there is always a need to unlearn through new critical tools and practices outside the traditional spaces of knowledge. If you do not know what Critical Animal Studies is about, this book will take you by the hand, rooting its principles into new perspectives for reflection and action. This book strongly highlights that oppressions are interlocked and need to be fought accordingly, to imagine a liberated life in solidarity with other social justice movements."

—Federica Timeto, Associate Professor, Ca' Foscari University

"This collection asks that we use imagination as a tool to expand ourselves and society in the direction of total liberation, to make connections, unlearn, push boundaries, challenge existing structures, and take action. Part of the work of total liberation is to bring topics into relationship in ways that may have seemed unimaginable before. This project engages in this work, becoming an effort of expansion, not simply an expansion of existing critical animal studies scholarship, but an expansion of the possibilities for solidarity with a diversity of non/human others."

—Amanda R Williams
Activist-Scholar, Institute for Critical Animal Studies, author of *The Overprivileged Human: Understanding and Eliminating Species Privilege for Total Liberation*

"The eruption of intersectional social justice advocacy, within the past decade, necessitates that theory and activism adapt to the new paradigm. Expanding the Critical Animal Studies Imagination achieves its mission of engaging with emerging social justice movements in order to reach a greater conceptualization of what total liberation can be. Readers will be introduced to a variety of ideas relevant to the future of both critical animal studies and total liberation generally."

—Dr. Richard Giles
Independent Scholar

"*Expanding the Critical Animal Studies Imagination* is a powerful, stimulating and challenging exploration of the connections between human, nonhuman, and environmental liberation. It gives voice and speaks to communities involved in intersectional struggles, promoting learning, trust-building and solidarity as critical, creative tools."

—Ruth Kinna
Author of *The Government of No One: The Theory and Practice of Anarchism*

"The turn into the 21st century is hounding humanity with revelations. The impact of a growing "human enterprise" is manifesting in epoch shifting shocks. The calamities we inhabit are consequences of a supremacist zeitgeist gone viral. This comprehensive collection of writings recognizes the singularity of the hierarchy of beings, the entangled ways in which nonhumans and humans alike are subjugated, humiliated, and annihilated. The contributors call for total liberation that heeds the lyrics: None of us are free if one of us is chained. Does the dream of total liberation sound utopian? No, it voices the revealed knowledge of our existential shattering."

—Eileen Crist
Associate Editor of *The Ecological Citizen*

"This groundbreaking volume offers timely analysis on human, nonhuman, and environmental justice that stays true to critical animal studies' radical roots while extending the discipline in exciting new directions. During a time of unprecedented global crisis, the scholar-activist contributors make important connections between diverse social movements, and illuminate the path to a new possible world. The insights to be gained from listening to this dialogue cannot be overestimated. Powerful and cutting-edge, this book is a must-read."

—Sarat Colling
Author of *Animal Resistance in the Global Capitalist Era*

"By bringing together a diverse range of international scholar-activists, who are themselves positioned at the cutting edge(s) of the interdisciplinary field of critical animal studies, ensures that this book makes a highly original, timely and powerful intervention to the existing literature. It deserves to be read widely, and I hope it achieves its guiding vision to help unleash new imaginaries and possibilities into a world that so desperately needs it!"

—Dr. Richard J White
Reader in Human Geography, Sheffield Hallam University, UK, Editor of 'Vegan Geographies: Spaces Beyond Violence, Ethics Beyond Speciesism' (2022, Lantern Press)

# Expanding the Critical Animal Studies Imagination

**RADICAL ANIMAL STUDIES
AND TOTAL LIBERATION**

Anthony J. Nocella II
*Series Editor*

Vol. 12

# Expanding the Critical Animal Studies Imagination

## Essays in Solidarity and Total Liberation

Edited by Nathan Poirier, Sarah Tomasello, and
Amber E. George

PETER LANG
New York - Berlin - Bruxelles - Chennai - Lausanne - Oxford

Library of Congress Cataloging-in-Publication Data

Names: Poirier, Nathan, editor. | Tomasello, Sarah, editor. |
George, Amber E., editor.
Title: Expanding the critical animal studies imagination: essays in
solidarity and total liberation / edited by Nathan Poirier, Sarah
Tomasello, Amber E. George.
Description: 1 Edition. | New York: Peter Lang, [2024] | Series: Radical
animal studies and total liberation, 2469-3065; Vol. 12 |
Includes bibliographical references and index.
Identifiers: LCCN 2023041970 (print) | LCCN 2023041971 (ebook) |
ISBN 9781636672236 (paperback) | ISBN 9781636672229 (hardback) |
ISBN 9781636670751 (pdf) | ISBN 9781636670768 (epub)
Subjects: LCSH: Animal rights. | Animal welfare—Moral and ethical aspects.
Classification: LCC HV4708. E97 2024 (print) | LCC HV4708 (ebook) |
DDC 179/.3—dc23/eng/20231013
LC record available at https://lccn.loc.gov/2023041970
LC ebook record available at https://lccn.loc.gov/2023041971


Bibliographic information published by the Deutsche Nationalbibliothek.
The German National Library lists this publication in the German
National Bibliography; detailed bibliographic data is available
on the Internet at http://dnb.d-nb.de.

Cover design by Peter Lang Group AG


ISSN 2469-3065 (print)
ISSN 2469-3081 (online)
ISBN 9781636672229 (hardback)
ISBN 9781636672236 (paperback)
ISBN 9781636670751 (ebook)
ISBN 9781636670768 (epub)
DOI 10.3726/b21322

© 2024 Peter Lang Group AG, Lausanne
Published by Peter Lang Publishing Inc., New York, USA
info@peterlang.com - www.peterlang.com

This publication has been peer reviewed.

# Contents

Dedication

*This book is dedicated to the animals (nonhuman and human) who have been killed due to the gross negligence of the Turkish and Syrian states during the 2023 earthquakes and the total liberationists who got straight into mutual aid to save lives and minimize suffering under dire repressive and environmental circumstances. We also dedicate it to those affected by anti-trans legislation: we love you and will fight alongside you.*

# Acknowledgments

We the editors (Nathan Poirier, Sarah Tomasello, and Amber E. George) of this book would like to thank first the contributors within this book – Charlotte Anne, Cam Whitley, Agnese Martini, Francesca Corradini, Matteo Porazzi, Nandita Bajaj, Kirsten Stade, John Tallent, Elisabeth Demitras, Ezgi Karaoğlu, Zane McNeill, Simon Springer, Will Boisseau, Jeremy Bendik-Keymer, and Seven Mattes. We would also like to thank those that wrote reviews for the book – Marquis Bey, David Naguib Pellow, Margaret Robinson, Federica Timeto, Amanda Williams, Richard Giles, Ruth Kinna, Eileen Crist, Sarat Colling, and Richard White. This book would not be possible if not for the organizations and academic departments that support our scholarship and activism such as Save the Kids, Academy for Peace Education, Journal for Critical Animal Studies, Green Theory and Praxis Journal, Transformative Justice Journal, Department of Criminal Justice at Salt Lake Community College, Peace Studies Journal, Institute for Critical Animal Studies, Academy for Critical Animal Studies, Critical Animal Studies Society, Lowrider Studies Journal, Punk Studies Journal, and Journal of Hip Hop Studies.

As the idea for this book originally arose between Nate and Sarah, we have some personal acknowledgements. Nate would like to thank my partner, Erin, who has played an indispensable role in my life. You have helped, in more ways than one, to create time and space for me to work on projects like this book. I thank my parents who encouraged my individuality without judgment since childhood. This is a privilege not everyone enjoys. Last but not least, to Marquis Bey: You have helped to majorly shift my intellectual and personal orientations for the better - you are my Fred Moten. Sarah is forever thankful for the support of my husband, Andrew, who is always available to listen and help me work through my ideas. His encouragement means the world to me. I'd also like to thank my two spunky cats, Nunu and Sprinks, for their love and companionship. They bring much joy into my life each day.

# *Foreword*

CHARLOTTE ANNE

Hello dear reader, a warm welcome to a book intent on not only fueling your fires but sparking your imaginations beyond what we have come to expect. firstly, let me introduce myself. i'm a long-term revolutionary intersectional vegan. the "revolutionary" and "intersectional" parts ought to be superfluous but very much require emphasis contemporarily considering capitalism's recuperation of, and therefore depoliticization, of veganism. i've been invested in various liberation struggles in my life which brought me to the attention of and into affinity with some of the contributors and organizers of these liberatory texts, and me to them. so, it is through what we might call comradeship, friendship, mutual respect and common ground that i was asked to prepare this foreword. i'm a white trans anti-binary feminist veganarchist race traitor living in Athens, greece. probably not the type of person regularly approached to script openings to academic works. and, as you'll hopefully see, that's partly the point.

The entries in this book work as individual but also as mosaic provocations amidst the stagnant and uninspired background of university education level engagement with animal lives. indeed, this is the aspiration of critical animal studies (CAS). Critical animal studies, as exemplified in the efforts contained in the following pages, is an intentional intervention into insincere and ineffective analysis, a captivating aberration, a molotov cocktail of seeds, water and nutrients for potentials otherwise effectively locked in the closets of public and campus libraries. what you hold in your hands isn't supposed to create the enthusiasm of an over-tested and fatigued student looking for the answers expected of them. this book wants you to care as much as the writers care. they want you to think on it. to talk about it. and to act on it.

this book emphasizes the inescapable necessity of attending to our collective needs which include our collective desires.

Considering this, it should be no surprise then that arguments laid out and subjects interrogated herein could easily be described as controversial. nevertheless, the tact, sensitivity and clarity of thought makes the ideas and proposals highly persuasive. nonhuman animals need books and co-conspirators like these. too long have human supremacist logics, forged largely in the heads of colonizing white men, sowed such deep doubts about animal liberation that scarcely a human voice is entertained that refuses to abandon some "groups" in the naive hope of protecting another. CAS is a spectacular thorn in the side of this dismal state of affairs, threatening to poison those in proximity, instilling in them an infectious drive for total liberation. the world is replete with impotent passages waxing lyrical about things that the reader senses the writer is palpably not genuinely committed to. these chapters feature people who are profoundly moved by and for total liberation and intend to cultivate in you richer understandings and capacities.

It would please them, as well as me, for you to not merely enjoy and appreciate their efforts, but for their efforts to be propellants firing you into your own total liberation efforts. treat this book with the excitement it deserves. it's neither an ornament nor sacred text, but to be swept up by. this is to be passed between lovers or gifted to likeminded strangers. so have fun, reader, because there's room left in this world for that too.

kisses to your whiskers x

# Introduction: Imagining with Abandon

NATHAN POIRIER, SARAH TOMASELLO, AND AMBER E. GEORGE

## The Emerging Context

[…] a Winchester rifle should have a place of honor in every black home, and it should be used for that protection which the law refuses to give. When the white man who is always the aggressor knows he runs as great risk of biting the dust every time his Afro-American victim does, he will have greater respect for Afro-American life.

—Ida Wells (2016, p. 80)

[I]n 1906 I rushed back from Alabama to Atlanta where my wife and six-year old child were living. A mob had raged for days killing Negroes. I bought a Winchester double-barreled shotgun and two dozen rounds of shells filled with buckshot. If a white mob had stepped on the campus where I lived I would without hesitation have sprayed their guts over the grass.

—W.E.B. Du Bois (1968, p. 286)

I keep a shotgun in every corner of my bedroom and the first cracker even look like he wants to throw some dynamite on the porch won't write his mama again.

—Fannie Lou Hamer (quoted in Cobb Jr., 2015, p. 124)

My only comment or recommendation for New Years is for people in Hawai'i to think about spending their annual New Years fireworks budget on actual arms and stockpiles in prep for the unknown. Thousands of dollars can buy a nice little collection and some paramilitary training.

—Lea Lani Kinikini, Facebook post, January 2, 2023

The stranglehold of oppression cannot be loosened by a plea to the oppressor's conscience. Social change in something as fundamental as racist oppression involves violence … because it's a struggle for survival for one and a struggle for liberation for the other. Always the powers in command are ruthless and unmerciful in defending their position and their privileges. This is not an abstract rule to be meditated upon by Americans.
—Robert F. Williams (2013, p. 72).

As it often has been throughout Black history, armed self-defense should become more of a serious consideration in the future. We will not be given a choice.
—William C. Anderson (2021, p. 136)

Self-defense is not violence, it is a means of survival.

—Zoe Samudzi and William C. Anderson (2018, p. 54)

There is a near constant slew of violent atrocities that threaten the survival of most of life on Earth. These stem from supremacist modes of thought premised on some being more worthy of life and love than others. While writing this introduction, on November 19–20, 2022, a mass shooting occurred at Club Q, a LGBTQIA nightclub in Colorado Springs, Colorado. Five people were murdered and 25 others were injured. That the shooter claimed to use they/them pronouns and be non-binary appears to be a ruse, likely a hackneyed reaction to justify their violence. A few days later, many people in the "United States" proceeded to give thanks for and celebrate their settler privilege, possessions, *their* "family," freedom, and their white nationalist pride during a "holiday" known as Thanksgiving out of some morbid faith in "America." They also prayed and ate dead animals. Thus, this introduction arose out of a violent environment. We want to be clear that the authors of this introduction do not experience violence as directly or in the same way as other marginalized and targeted populations do. The guide quotes preceding this introduction are intended as a warning and lesson that the violence that is the "United States"—and all ruling entities—brings uncomfortable realities for many who have and continue to benefit from its institutions. The quotes from Black activists above can be shocking and scary to read. White people possessing hegemonic identities will likely react differently to them than Black folks, queer folks, the disabled, people of color, etc.—and let us not forget nonhuman animals—who are much more consistently and historically placed as targets of the US state system. Those of us who haven't already, must start listening to and learning from militant revolutionaries such as those quoted above. We must start to accept the reality that we need to fight—and be willing to die—alongside the more marginalized among us.

This is also not a comfortable position for those quoted above to bring up either. Despite the fire in their words, none of them wants such a situation to exist. All prefer(ed) peace. It is the burden of those skeptical or offended by the prospect of armed self-defense to get over it. Likely it is some sense of decorum or being "civilized" that makes armed self-defense seem reprehensible. In a sense this is true: the violence of whiteness, the State, patriarchy, and militarism, capitalism, and colonialism are indeed deplorable. But it is precisely these institutions that enact violence and create the situations in which violence is used. "Civility" requires violence to be maintained and hence is a violent concept itself that must be shunned. Overcoming an apprehension to armed self-defense, engaging in it and supporting it, will not necessarily be easy and may take some time, but now is the time to begin that process. As the Black, ecowomanist, "undisciplined" scholar-activist Frances Roberts-Gregory (2021, p. 137) says, "Moving forward, emerging feminist leaders will have to decide when and where our politics exceed the confines of civility and traditional modes of political engagement. In other words, what are we willing to risk and sacrifice to bring about the change we want to see in the world?" Those who have steadfastly held to nonviolence and eschewed guns previously, must reconsider armed self-defense in preparation against the current violence and that which lies ahead. As Anderson says above, there is no choice.

## The Purpose and Mission of This Book

The central thesis of this book is that to remain relevant and effective in its mission, critical animal studies (CAS) must push its own boundaries and connect with evolving social justice movements. We believe the title *Expanding the Critical Animal Studies Imagination: Essays in Solidarity and Total Liberation* (or, *Expanding the CAS Imagination* for short) reflects our main goal of pushing CAS to new territories via building solidarity with other social justice movements that it has hitherto had little to no direct engagement with. The Institute for Critical Animal Studies (ICAS) was founded on the mission to "be in solidarity with, and be part of radical and revolutionary actions, theories, groups and movements for total liberation..." (https://www.criticalanimalstudies.org/about/). This book aims to expand the already broad conceptual horizon that makes up the organization and project of CAS. We chose this as the book's purpose for three primary reasons. One is that as times and the salience of various movements change, CAS must adapt to stay relevant. Two, for the field to remain holistic and inclusive, it must constantly push itself into new territories and ideas through dialogue. And three, making new connections stays true to ICAS's founding mission and ten principles. We cautiously accept this challenge, as any wading into new territory consists of less than solid footing. We use this introduction primarily to introduce the theory behind this project, reflect upon CAS as an organization, and consider other relevant critical texts on total liberation, veganism, and critical pedagogy. This work also acknowledges and draws inspiration from women of color activism (Taylor, 2022). Taylor (2022) speaks to how many early writings on coalitional feminism by women of color were edited collections that were political, activist, and self-reflexive. This work and CAS more generally draws on this legacy by being an assemblage of different voices coming together to contribute toward coalition building for total liberation. The goal is to build alliances across identities to deconstruct intersecting systems of domination and oppression (Taylor, 2022, p. 12).

Despite possessing different backgrounds, interests, and goals, the contributors in this volume show how we may work together to achieve total liberation. The twin themes of learning and unlearning stretch throughout the chapters, revealing how pedagogical strategies can bring CAS concepts to life both within and beyond the classroom. These observations thread each chapter while stretching the boundaries of CAS. We feel the diversity of chapters is a strength of the book. The breadth of CAS is one of its major strengths and has always been a founding tenet of the field. *Expanding the CAS Imagination* highlights this. In doing so, it emphasizes that all types of oppression must be resisted holistically; anything less is insufficient. One unknown reviewer of Nathan's co-edited *Emerging New Voices in Critical Animal Studies* (Poirier et al., 2022) said that newer CAS books must connect with other disciplines and topics. *Expanding the CAS Imagination* addresses that comment by containing chapters on new topics to CAS and pushing foundational topics (e.g., anarchism) in new directions. Part of this is a commitment to learning from the history of various social movements (Nocella II & Socha, 2022). Several chapters in *Expanding the CAS Imagination* contain historical components or even a historical focus, while remaining grounded in the more comprehensive anarchist project of CAS. They bridge theory and activism, highlight various epistemological orientations, and give space to interwoven perspectives.

*Expanding the CAS Imagination* is related to and builds on several key CAS texts. In a complimentary way, this book is similar to *Intersectionality of Critical Animal Studies* (Nocella II & George, 2019), the point of which was to reflect the diversity of CAS through noteworthy articles previously published in the *Journal for Critical Animal Studies*. We see *Expanding the CAS Imagination* as a companion volume to Nocella II and George (2019) in that it pushes CAS in new directions through new works. *Intersectionality of CAS* shows where CAS has been; *Expanding the CAS Imagination* shows where CAS can go and is going currently. Also, *Expanding the CAS Imagination* could be viewed as an extension volume of *Defining Critical Animal Studies* (Nocella II et al., 2014) which revolved around CAS's ten principles. Our book builds on those principles to extend the field of CAS with new social movements and topics. The edited book *Critical Animal Studies: Towards Trans-Species Social Justice* (Matsuoka & Sorenson, 2018) is a book intended to "chart new territory by showcasing some of the newest developments in the rapidly-growing field of Critical Animal Studies." While a superb text, it connects to academic disciplines specifically. *Expanding the CAS Imagination* makes connections to new *movements* with almost every chapter freshly combining liberation struggles, including pushing the foundational CAS principle of anarchism in multiple new directions within the field (engaging with anti-colonialism, Blackness, and vegan mutual aid). As such, *Expanding the CAS Imagination* builds from previous related works to push the field forward and outward.

## *Theoretical Grounding: Critical Pedagogy and Imagination*

This book is both informed by and promotes critical pedagogy. In particular, we take influence from Henry Giroux (2020, 2021, 2022), who, alongside Paolo Friere is considered a founding figure of critical pedagogy. Across various books, Giroux (2020, 2021, 2022) makes a number of points about critical pedagogy: (1) that it goes beyond classroom learning to include cultural teachings/practices, (2) that it must learn from history, (3) that critique must be accompanied by visions of hope, (4) it must promote massive united movements against all oppression, (5) it must provide the opportunity for people to write/speak from a position of empowerment, (6) it should translate private issues into social problems, and (7) it must make invisible systemic inequalities in power relations visible. Chapters in this volume cover all of these components, making the chapters and this book as a whole, a work of critical pedagogy. *Expanding the CAS Imagination* emphasizes the informal (outside the classroom) social education that is constantly at work in all societies. This book could be considered a companion volume to *Education for Total Liberation* (Nocella II et al., 2019) which focuses more on formal in-class critical pedagogy. Pedagogically, each chapter in this volume exemplifies actions that should be unlearned (such as how to exploit others) and actions that should be (re)learned (such as building solidarity).

An important component of learning is also unlearning, realizing that many things we "know" may not actually be true, or are off somehow, or are harmful. Practices we thought were normal, necessary, or stable (such as the police or government) may actually be highly fragile systems constructed only recently in human history. If such systems can be created, they can also be dismantled. Indeed, many current mindsets, social structures, policies, institutions, etc., must be unlearned such as any sort of hierarchical thinking. Colonialism, capitalism, white supremacy, and speciesism have indoctrinated many generations and countless individuals to think that these are the only viable or legitimate forms of life or social organization. They are hegemonic in that they dominate world systems and many people's individual thinking. Many are born into and grow up within these systems, learning their ways from our parents who likewise internalized these systems, who in turn were bombarded by propaganda from religion, media, education, and so on. In other words, many people grow up in a suffocating social environment of negative messages disguised in ways to make them seem appealing and inevitable. It is not a surprise, then, that such messages become internalized and passed down through generations. It is understandable (but never excusable) that many of us are influenced to significant extents by dominant ideologies and that it is difficult to free oneself—mentally and materially—from their confines. On the other hand, it is manifestly possible to do so as countless activists have proven. It is possible—and necessary—to learn alternate ways of thinking and being. Many chapters in this book speak to the dialectic of learning/unlearning/relearning. Contributors ask us to unlearn outmoded harmful practices and re-learn compassionate forms of praxis such as love, liberation and abolition. The original plan for this book was for chapters to imagine alternative futures in which all could safely live and thrive. In line with critical pedagogy, we wanted the book to be solutions-based, instead of mainly critique, based around the varied personal, social, and environmental desires of contributors. This is because in critical pedagogy, "[e]ducation must integrate the head, heart, and hands. It must be transformative" (Kirk & Hall, 2021, p. 8).

Our goal with the volume gradually evolved towards breaking new ground for CAS, and we are grateful for that shift. The original theme of desiring liberatory futures is still noticeable in the chapters and we retained this original impetus in the use of "imagination" in the title. We link the keyword "imagination" to Marquis Bey's (2019, 2022a, 2022b) work which is largely about pushing concepts as far as they can go to imagine and strive for modes and means of existence that seem currently unimaginable. We take influence from Bey in that we do not see life as limited by imagination. Any social world that can be imagined can be striven for—and there are other possibilities outside of what is currently conceived of as possible. We see this book as aligned with Bey's (2019) imaginative notion of fugitivity, "a kind of outlawish indiscreet disavowal of and disengagement from the project of hegemony" (p. 16). This can only be accomplished through imagining and enacting alternatives. Through constant flux motivated by both resistance to unjust systems and solidarity with social justice, CAS refuses "to sit still, [is always] refusing to settle" (p. 16). Bey beckons us to exceed categories and live unruly, anarchic lives. Likewise and linking with chapters herein on trans liberation, Bey (2022b) theorizes transness beyond a gender orientation, positing that "trans is an itch that things are not enough, a project of undoing, be it gender, institutions, the fabric of the social world" (p. 3). This goes hand-in-hand with a creative force that builds liberation.

Also influencing our use of imagination is the sociological imagination of C. Wright Mills (1959) and the edited book *The Anarchist Imagination* (Levy & Newman, 2019). Mills's term refers to realizing the social element in personal issues and vice versa. It's a different fashioning of the feminist phrase "the personal is political." The sociological imagination allows one to see what is affecting them, but it also allows one to imagine how they have an influence on the social. Through the sociological imagination, one is intrinsically connected to the social world and therefore by acting, necessarily affects others. This is important for activism as one can and should feel empowered to create change even as an individual. Activism becomes a social venture and maybe even a social movement. One person can and necessarily does make a difference. This use of imagination connects to Giroux's points on critical pedagogy above in making systemic inequality visible and making the personal social. Levy and Newman's *The Anarchist Imagination* contains chapters illustrating how anarchism has infiltrated many other realms of thought. As such, the book shows how anarchism has had a far reach and contains theory capable of organizing all spheres of life. Likewise with *Expanding the CAS Imagination*, this book reaches out to many new disciplines and movements to further integrate itself into the holistic struggle for total liberation.

Further working with the concept of imagination, the title also connects to critical pedagogy via Giroux's (2022) "crisis of the public imagination" and the need to make education beyond formal education central to politics and everyday life. The public imagination refers to what the mass of a society collectively believes is possible. Ultimately with this book, we want to encourage readers to think and live unencumbered by imagination and to constantly seek new ways to express themselves, thrive, improve activist efficacy, and build solidarity. Above all,

> we need to trust that we are not an "I" but a "We", and we need to imagine that "We" can breathe together in a different world. A world in which we dare to say "We" without fearing that in doing so the "I" will disappear. We need to trust that our imagination will take us there. (Loizidou, 2023, p. 169)

We should never limit ourselves—or anyone else—to what we think or others tell us is possible. As Loizidou (2023) discusses, any set of rules is inherently limiting. We must imagine outside of any boundary. *Expanding the CAS Imagination* imagines outside of where CAS has gone before to stretch its own boundaries. This is done for the sake of internal consistency of the movement of CAS and to show others how seriously total liberation is taken. To imagine with abandon is liberating. If anyone was thinking that CAS has stalled, or stopped making connections and pushing itself–ourselves–this book emphatically responds *absolutely not*!

### *Existing Relations and Building Connections*

All three editors have collaborated on previous projects. Sarah and Nate have been writing together since 2016 (Poirier & Tomasello, 2017), including publishing in CAS journals (Tomasello & Poirier, 2018) and a co-authored chapter (with April Piazza) in Amber's book *Gender and Sexuality in Critical Animal Studies* (Tomasello et al., 2021). Sarah and Nate have also co-organized students for critical animal studies conferences, and Sarah contributed a chapter in Nate's co-edited book on CAS (Tomasello, 2022; Poirier et al., 2022). Likewise, Amber and Nate have been editor and assistant editor, respectively, of the *Journal for Critical Animal Studies* since the spring of 2020. Thus, we thought that the collaboration of co-editing this book would be a particularly meaningful partnership based on our existing relationships.

In putting this collection together, we thought it important to extend the familiarity we have with each other to contributors. To this end and throughout the course of this book's development, the editors and contributors had multiple meetings over Zoom to get to know each other better in relationships that we hope will extend well beyond this book. The goal of this was to use this book to help form relationships. However, in reflecting on this process for the introduction, it became clear that it may have been more effective the other way around. Relationships should perhaps come first and then a book can form around shared struggle. Or, perhaps a mix of both. Regardless, relationships in one way or another underpin this text. We did come to know contributors through working with them and we are grateful for these relations. To us, a contributor is not reducible to their contribution, but a potential ally, friend, co-conspirator in activism, and writing partner.

Contributors and editors share a completed volume and the project of editing a book is a mutual process. Editors may have a vision for a book but contributors are the ones who realize that vision through their chapters. In fact, if anything, we as editors did less actual work for this book than authors.

Lastly, we commissioned an artist, Lauren Suchyta-Korany, to design the book's cover. It was a pleasure working with Ren and we are proud to have Ren's art be the face of this book. Ren's work and contact info can be found at https://renskstudio.com/ and https://www.etsy.com/shop/renskstudio. We wanted to hire an independent and queer artist to design the full cover—front, spine, and back—to subvert capitalist economies and the banality of stock images.

## *On Critical Animal Studies*

ICAS is an anarchist, theory-to-action activist organization that aims to bring together radical scholar-activists of all stripes and from all causes to dismantle all systems of domination and oppression in the pursuit of total liberation–liberation of human and nonhuman animals and the environment. This book is a work of critical animal studies (CAS). As such, we feel it incumbent upon us to point out that there are a number of misperceptions of what CAS is or stands for, some of which are even held by those who identify with CAS. In putting together this book, we were confronted with two in particular which we would like to address here to help correct them. The first is that CAS is an academic field. This is largely incorrect. We ran into this misconception through people hesitant to submit to the call for chapters because they felt their topic or writing wouldn't be academic enough. While we tried to inform such individuals that this perception is misguided, it was a bit alarming nonetheless that this appeared to be common. Academics is not the "home" of CAS. If it is even appropriate to speak of a "home" for CAS, which it may not be, CAS's home is on the streets, or in the gutter, or in the soil. It's in the hearts, minds, bodies, souls, and spirits of activists, good trouble-makers, and the oppressed–human and nonhuman. As Marquis Bey (2019, p. 14) says, "I want to move arm in arm with the misfits, the deviants, the lowlifes and imbeciles, the poor and the uneducated, because rebellious knowledge happens underground." CAS is wherever resistance and transformation exist. It is mobile and flexible. This is not to say academic insights have no place in CAS, but that CAS is not concerned with integrating itself within the academy—but in the margins, in the underground. CAS does not look for traditional academic writings with their jargon, high theory, and formal paper structures complete with the obligatory and monotonous sections of literature review, methods, results, discussion. CAS openly invites activist writings, creative writing, non-traditional and unconventional writing, structures, and styles. CAS emphatically distances itself from academic disciplines of animal studies, human-animal studies, or anthrozoology. Exactly when or under what circumstances writings become "too" academic is of course impossible to say. But we do think it is a good general rule to err on the side of activist writing and not academic. When in doubt, assume your own or another piece of writing is too academic and look for ways to sharpen its bite. Academics, civility, and a notion of being "proper" are not CAS concerns.

The other misconception is that CAS writings or presentations must include, and even center on, nonhuman animals. This misperception was evident in the content of submissions for this book, entries in the *Journal for Critical Animal Studies*, and many other conferences or book chapters that overwhelmingly focus on nonhumans. Not every CAS writing or activism needs to explicitly address nonhuman animals. That being said, CAS is a vegan organization in that it expects those involved to be vegan (in the sense that John Tallent discusses in their chapter to this book in terms of practicability). As Julia Feliz (2017) emphasizes, veganism should center nonhuman animals—but not to the detriment of humans. In the CAS perspective, all liberation is inextricably related, as stated especially in CAS's principle #6: CAS "does not concentrate solely on animal issues. Instead, it aims at making alliances with other social movements devoted to struggles against oppression." This radical openness we hope will be welcoming to intellectuals and activists unfamiliar with CAS even if they do not talk about nonhuman animals or any other given cause. We want to show that CAS welcomes anyone and any topic with open arms. The only thing CAS would ask is that no cause is denigrated for the sake of another. CAS is about total liberation. This means that all struggles for justice are intertwined, that no one can be free while any other is oppressed. This is all part of the "one struggle" mentality.

This being said, we do not blame those who think CAS is primarily academic or that it must focus on nonhuman animals. CAS does attract many scholar-activists, and admittingly it has become a bit too academic in its publications. Some deviation from principles can occur when connections are made to bring CAS to the attention of like-minded others. This is understandable, as long as attention is paid to ensure we realign ourselves to stay true to our mission and principles. Staying true to one's mission and reaching out to make connections is a balance that can be hard to keep, but we can do better by acknowledging and addressing these shortcomings. We wish to see CAS flourish alongside other similarly situated organizations. One of innumerable possible examples is Sanctuary Publishers (see sanctuarypublishers.

com) and its associated initiatives coordinated by Julia Feliz. We encourage the reader to read books by Sanctuary Publishers and to buy them through their website to support Julia's and their collaborators' work. Being reflexive is key to not going astray or deviating from original principles (as long as those principles are still relevant and helpful). We make these statements and suggestions of further engagement below, out of support for CAS and its mission, while also wanting to acknowledge that we do not adhere to CAS as if it were a religion. Here are CAS's ten principles that this book is based on (Best et al., 2007, pp. 4–5):

1. Pursues interdisciplinary collaborative writing and research in a rich and comprehensive manner that includes perspectives typically ignored by animal studies such as political economy.

2. Rejects pseudo-objective academic analysis by explicitly clarifying its normative values and political commitments, such that there are no positivist illusions whatsoever that theory is disinterested or writing and research is nonpolitical. To support experiential understanding and subjectivity.

3. Eschews narrow academic viewpoints and the debilitating theory-for-theory's sake position in order to link theory to practice, analysis to politics, and the academy to the community.

4. Advances a holistic understanding of the commonality of oppressions, such that speciesism, sexism, racism, ableism, statism, classism, militarism and other hierarchical ideologies and institutions are viewed as parts of a larger, interlocking, global system of domination.

5. Rejects apolitical, conservative, and liberal positions in order to advance an anti-capitalist, and, more generally, a radical anti-hierarchical politics. This orientation seeks to dismantle all structures of exploitation, domination, oppression, torture, killing, and power in favor of decentralizing and democratizing society at all levels and on a global basis.

6. Rejects reformist, single-issue, nation-based, legislative, strictly animal interest politics in favor of alliance politics and solidarity with other struggles against oppression and hierarchy.

7. Champions a politics of total liberation which grasps the need for, and the inseparability of, human, nonhuman animal, and Earth liberation and freedom for all in one comprehensive, though diverse, struggle; to quote Martin Luther King Jr.: "Injustice anywhere is a threat to justice everywhere.

8. Deconstructs and reconstructs the socially constructed binary oppositions between human and nonhuman animals, a move basic

to mainstream animal studies, but also looks to illuminate related dichotomies between culture and nature, civilization and wilderness and other dominator hierarchies to emphasize the historical limits placed upon humanity, nonhuman animals, cultural/political norms, and the liberation of nature as part of a transformative project that seeks to transcend these limits towards greater freedom, peace, and ecological harmony.

9.  Openly supports and examines controversial radical politics and strategies used in all kinds of social justice movements, such as those that involve economic sabotage from boycotts to direct action toward the goal of peace.

10. Seeks to create openings for constructive critical dialogue on issues relevant to critical animal studies across a wide-range of academic groups; citizens and grassroots activists; the staffs of policy and social service organizations; and people in private, public, and non-profit sectors. Through – and only through — new paradigms of ecopedagogy, bridge-building with other social movements, and a solidarity-based alliance politics, is it possible to build the new forms of consciousness, knowledge, social institutions that are necessary to dissolve the hierarchical society that has enslaved this planet for the last ten thousand years.

## Where Might Critical Animal Studies Go from Here?

In terms of entering into dialogues with social justice movements, this collection is necessarily limited by our own positionalities and abilities. We editors have our own connections we were able to draw on to include contributors to this text. We reached out to many people in order to make connections in ongoing collaborations, whether or not those new connections resulted in a chapter in this book. This means that the gaps filled with this book are still limited and so there is (always) more work to be done. We do not see it as a fault of CAS for having some areas with little to no engagement. Championing all social justice causes and resisting all oppressions all at once– while working towards alternative futures–is a monumental task. People come and go from CAS and all are limited in their knowledge, abilities, personalities, and networks. Others may disagree with our assessment above or topics covered below. This is welcome as it can lead to productive dialogue. We encourage those who may wish to add topics to the following discussion to do by becoming involved. Our vision is not monolithic and is open to ongoing evolution. The present book claims to make new connections within CAS in the following areas:

- Trans studies
- Human population
- Flight-free
- Black anarchism
- Chapters not focused on nonhuman animals

One may also ask why we feel it is important to make these connections specifically and to make them explicitly. Is not CAS's mission statement about being holistic and dismantling all forms of oppression enough? Is it not clear that CAS already supports all the causes mentioned above (and below)–in fact, all of them, even those beyond any such list? Is CAS not always and already completely inclusive by, from the get-go, not excluding anyone or any cause? Yes, CAS is all those things. Our concern has to do with people new to CAS or those skeptical of it. Not excluding is not necessarily synonymous with explicitly including. One can be not against something and also not be *for* it. Therefore, we think it is important to call out to and call in as many movements as we can reach to let them–and everyone–know that CAS is always in the process of coalition building and reflexivity. All must actually mean all and anyone struggling for liberation or abolition should see their cause represented in CAS. This ongoing process also constantly unsettles the "ground" of CAS. Taking inspiration from Nahum Chandler through Marquis Bey, CAS aims to unsettle the very ground it is built on. By covering every cause happening everywhere all the time, the aim of CAS, and by extension this book, is to dissolve the criteria for inclusion and exclusion (Bey, 2020, p. 14). CAS is not an organization that includes "everything but nothing specifically," but everything specifically. CAS is nebulous, shapeshifting, it desedimentalizes. It cannot be precisely defined or outlined because it defies all classification, notions of purity, and fixity. In the scheme of things, it is not CAS that matters but the causes of liberation and abolition. This constant shaking things up, the trembling of foundations, and elisions of rigid categorical distinctions between movements for freedom, leaves cracks in the foundation of society, of normality. Through these cracks light enters and imagination runs rampant.

CAS has numerous well-trodden themes such as anarchism, intersectionality, total liberation, and radical activism. A particularly strong, novel, and visible current in CAS has been eco-ability, a topic that brings together nonhuman, environmental, and disability liberation. Eco-ability having been founded in 2010 as a CAS project, ICAS has published books on eco-ability for over ten years (Nocella II et al., 2012; Nocella II. et al., 2022) and is still going strong. ICAS also hosts an annual eco-ability conference. This focus on combining multiple sites of oppression and highlighting those with multiple marginalized identities is a hallmark of CAS scholar-activism. So while some concepts have been well-covered in CAS, some have not. It's important to note that in making new connections, the chapters in this book are also aware of the complexities and nuances involved, especially when it comes to offering solutions. This is particularly important when discussing the topics of human population, trans studies, and Black anarchism.

It's important to note that in making these new connections, the chapters in this book are also aware of the complexities and nuances involved, especially when it comes to offering solutions. This is particularly important when discussing the topics of human population, trans studies, and Black anarchism.

Talking about decreasing the size of the human population is a very serious and sensitive issue. Throughout history, population control has been used as an excuse to perpetuate colonialism, white supremacy, classism, and anti-immigrant sentiment, among other harmful systems, and is understandably a sensitive topic for marginalized communities. Because of this, it is perhaps *the* most taboo topic, period. Many are afraid to talk about it because of the negative reputation the topic has garnered. But being afraid of controversy is not necessarily a reason to avoid a topic. CAS confronts many controversial topics but there has been no publicly declared support for lowering the human population from within CAS, perhaps understandably out of worry of alienating others. But this does not have to be the case. Indeed, chapters on this topic in this book denounce coercive population measures. Any form of coercion goes strongly against CAS's anarchist principles of dismantling structures of exploitation and championing a comprehensive politics of total liberation. Coercion is unacceptable in all its forms. Rather, authors encourage people to make the decision to have fewer (or no) children for themselves and support social structures that allow people to make these decisions for themselves. They also understand that not everyone has equal access to reproductive healthcare and education, or affordable contraception, and therefore, the choice to remain childfree is more possible for some than others. Lastly, no contributor argues for human extinction. These chapters do not place the burden of reducing the human population on the economically poor and/or marginalized. Beyond this, we allow the authors to speak for themselves and stand with them.

Similarly, while this book makes connections between Black anarchism, trans studies, and critical animal studies, it does so in a way that does not place the burden of education on Black and trans persons. Far too often, Black and transgender people, along with other marginalized groups, are expected to take on the role of educator as if it is their duty to help white, cis-gendered people to understand them. This is simply another form of oppression. Instead, these chapters encourage white, cisgendered individuals to spend time learning about and engaging with these topics on their own and to make space for them within CAS.

In addition to the topics mentioned above, there are four areas of particular interest that we notice gaps in and would like to see addressed within CAS. It is worth mentioning that these areas are not discrete but can and do all overlap. But first, there are two general remarks we wish to make about further future topics for CAS. One is that we prefer and want to seek out activist voices, and two is that we would like CAS writings to more fully center solutions over critique. In line with the major theme of "imagination" of this volume, writings that envision alternate, liberatory, hopeful futures and describe how to achieve them (or how they're already being achieved, if only partly) by activists participating in their prefiguration, help to inspire further action.

*Indigeneity.* In at least one important sense, this book should not exist because it is a product of settlers and settler descendants (the editors) working on stolen lands within the "United States." Therefore, the topic of indigeneity and decolonization are of fundamental importance to CAS and we would love to see them better represented. We are not putting the onus on indigenous people to do all of this work, nor would it be appropriate for non-indigenous people to be the only voices speaking against colonialism (and especially not speaking *for* indigenous people). Appealing to Four Arrows and Narvaez (2022), "All people are indigenous to Earth and have the right and responsibility to practice and teach the Indigenous worldview precepts. All have the responsibility to support Indigenous sovereignty, dignity and use of traditional lands" (p. 5). We suggest the essay "The Indigenization Controversy: For Whom by Whom" (Four Arrows, 2019) for a more extended discussion. Such an undertaking requires non-indigenous people to actively resist colonialism alongside indigenous people, while listening to and learning from them to follow their lead (but being able to take the lead if/when asked or needed). As Four Arrows and Darcia Narvaez (2022) reflect on this point,

One concern or question that often comes up with our recommendation to decolonize and Indigenize our minds and institutions relates to the right of "non-Indian" people to attempt to re-Indigenize themselves and their systems

> such as education. Indeed, many Indigenous people believe that non-Indigenous teachers have no right to try to teach the Indigenous worldview. They call it a cultural appropriation. Such a concern is well grounded and must be respected in light of the massive mistreatment of Indigenous peoples in the last half millennium.
>
> However, many Indigenous elders believe otherwise. They know about mis-appropriation, but they also know that with sincerity, respect and support for Indigenous rights, allies are necessary. (p. 9)

This means that connections must be formed and this takes time. Relationships cannot be rushed or forced, just like total liberation. Effort must be put into unlearning the dominant worldview and a (re)learning of the Indigenous worldview.

*Other Identities on the Gender Spectrum.* CAS has done a lot with respect to gender. It draws from and acknowledges a debt to feminists, Black feminists and ecofeminists. It has frequently linked queer liberation to animal liberation (Simonsen, 2012; George, 2021; Nocella II & George, 2019). But there is a wealth of other gender orientations out there that can still be engaged with, including gender abolition. We encourage CAS to engage more with other gender identities that are much less frequently represented in popular culture as well as in academic women's and gender studies programs. Amber George's chapter on intersex (George, 2021) as well as a Black asexual treatise (Brown, 2022) are refreshing examples of this.

*War.* This seems like one of the biggest oversights. War is easily the most significant threat to the bulk of life on this planet. While CAS has put forth critiques (and solutions) to war before, most notably in *Animals and War: Confronting the Military-Animal Industrial Complex* (Nocella II et al., 2010), this book is now over a decade old. War continues to be present, occupy a growing share of industrialized nations' budgets, and loom large as a threat of mass extinction that could happen any day at the whims of a power-hungry, selfish, violent, masculinist elite. More can and should be done to critique, but even more importantly propose alternatives to, war. Although not from a CAS perspective, a recent paper by critical sociologist Randy Laprairie (2022) has provided an updated take on U.S. militarism since World War II. We would have welcomed this paper in the *Journal for Critical Animal Studies*.

*Non-Western and Non-White Anarchisms.* CAS is an anarchist (as opposed to merely anarchic) organization. It is fundamentally premised on being non-hierarchical, purely volunteer based, with no keynote speakers and no one is ever paid to present at a CAS event or to write in a CAS book. As such, anarchism is in no short supply within CAS. However, much of the anarchism that is referred to is Eurocentric and thoroughly white. This should change. Anarchism exists to an extent in every part of the globe and always has as long as there have been people. Therefore, there is a wealth of non-western and non-white anarchisms to draw from. There is readily available anarchist theory and practice from every continent and country, and from anarchists of all genders. These voices and perspectives should be celebrated, cited, and engaged with within CAS.

## *Overview of Chapters*

We structured this book to address total liberation as a whole. Not every chapter connects human, nonhuman, and environmental liberation directly; but throughout the book, these three areas are significantly featured and connected. In this way, the book reads as a coherent whole and provides various ways these three categories are interlinked, sometimes focusing on one, two, or all three. In the chapter descriptions below, we refer to authors by their first name because it feels too distant to use surnames. We know the contributors more personally than that. Several groupings of chapters into sections were tried out but all proved unsatisfactory. We ultimately settled on a two-part organization because each part is broad enough to encompass a loose division in how each section's chapters contribute towards expanding the CAS imagination. Readers may also disregard section titles and read chapters individually without loss.

Part I "New Movement Connections: Trans Liberation and Human Population" contains the most prominent interventions into CAS. While CAS has done much in the way of gender, it has not explicitly connected to trans liberation struggles. Additionally, CAS has never engaged in this conversation of the growing human population in writing. Regarding trans liberation, in chapter 1, "Connecting Transgender Studies and Critical Animal Studies," Cameron Whitley, explicitly brings together these two radical fields for the first time within CAS. Cam points out numerous direct connections between these two fields to argue that both should include the other in their praxis, reminding the reader, once again, that all oppression is linked. Chapter 2, "Anthropogenic Monsters: A CAS and Liberating Perspective on the Contemporary Production of Human and Nonhuman Monsters," by Agnese Martini, Francesca Corradini, and Matteo Porazzi extends Cam's connection of transgender and critical animal studies with a specific application. Agnese, Francesca, and Matteo show how "monstrocity" can have both negative and positive elements and connotations. The authors show how monstrocity can be and has been claimed as a point of pride, as in Susan Stryker's famous use of it to describe transgender people.

The next three chapters focus on procreation and human population. Chapter 3, "Animal Liberation through Procreative Justice," by Nandita Bajaj and Kirsten Stade focuses on a critique of pronatalism. Pronatalism is the ideology that encourages and normalizes procreation. Their focus on pronatalism is unique among population activists and provides an excellent alternative critique of procreation, while avoiding anti-natalism. Chapter 4, "Antinatalism, Veganism, and the Imperative of a Total Liberationist Perspective," by John Tallent departs with Nandita and Kirsten by promoting anti-natalism. John argues that veganism and anti-natalism are both frequently misunderstood and this is why they are often both critiqued unfairly. They propose that veganism and anti-natalism complement each other as they share similar logic and motivations. Chapter five "Procreation and Aviation: The Elephants in the Vegan Room," by Elisabeth Dimitras brings together the idea of (not) having children and not flying in airplanes. Elisabeth exposes how being flightfree is a frequently overlooked topic in various spaces, including veganism. In addition to population, the topics of pronatalism, anti-natalism, and flightfree are new within CAS. The plurality of voices on this topic of procreation gives diversity to this fraught issue and acts not just as a formal introduction of this topic to CAS, but advances it as an initial and ongoing dialogue.

Part II, "New Convergences and Extensions" focuses on subject matters that may not be completely new to CAS but are approached in new or different ways. This may be in the connections they make or the directions they take. While disparate in subject matter, each chapter makes a particular intervention within CAS. Each chapter could also be tied together through a consistent anti-oppression take on veganism as much more than a diet (Feliz, 2017; Feliz & McNeill, 2020; Giraud, 2021). The first three chapters in this section, chapters 6–8, do not necessarily connect to CAS explicitly, but this is intentional. Their inclusion here is to say that such topics are within CAS's purview. Chapters highlight the topics of the non-West and of Blackness as a show of solidarity with populations and movements less typically or explicitly engaged with. Further integration of such topics within CAS scholar-activism can and should be done going forward. The first chapter in this section, chapter 6, "Infrastructural Approach to Urban Street Animals of Istanbul: Contestation, Violence, Affectivity, and Spatial Visibility in the Metropolis," by Ezgi Karaoğlu brings together anarchy and the non-West, something woefully uncommon within CAS. Although Ezgi doesn't refer to citizen protection of street animals in Istanbul as anarchy, their direct actions could be interpreted that way. This chapter is included because of its connection to Turkey, one of many places little engaged within CAS.

The next couple chapters reassert the influences of Black liberation for CAS, again a topic and influence that is not always readily apparent. Chapter 7, "Ida B. Wells' Historical and Contemporary Legacy, and Relevance to Critical Animal Studies," by Zane McNeill and Nathan Poirier highlights the historical and foundational influence the Black feminist body of work plays for CAS. This influence is all too often not made clear. While barely mentioning nonhuman animals, this chapter fundamentally belongs within CAS via consistent anti-oppression. This chapter looks historically at gender and racial activism through the efforts of an early and important yet understudied Black feminist. This sort of profile is unique for CAS. Chapter 8, "Listening to and Learning with African Anarchism, Black Anarchism, and Anarcho-Blackness," by Nathan Poirier and Simon Springer brings non-White and non-western anarchisms into CAS. Nathan and Simon challenge the focus on Euro-American anarchism within CAS and provide an overview of the trenchant praxis of African and Black anarchisms. This chapter is unique in its focus, both within CAS and outside of it.

The next set of four chapters, chapters 9–12, all touch on veganism in less than typical ways. "Vegan Mutual Aid: Anarchist Solidarity in Times of Crisis" by Will Boisseau (Chapter 9) brings veganism into conversations about mutual aid organizing. While mutual aid has been frequently discussed, especially since the COVID-19 pandemic, rarely is veganism part of that praxis. Chapter 10, "Create Meat Though the World May Perish: A Vegan Critique of In Vitro Meat and Clean Milk" by Nathan Poirier offers a critique of the uncritical positions of well-known scholar-activists Carol Adams and Josh Milburn on engineered meat from a vegan and total liberation perspective. Deeply skeptical of this technology, Nathan calls for the cellular agriculture space to engage with decolonization to better understand the implications that this technology could have for indigenous land and culture. The connection between in vitro meat and colonialism has almost never been made within the alternative animal product space.

Chapter 11, "The Others Called 'Humans' amidst the Many: Anthroponomy and the Planetary Problem," by Jeremy Bendik-Keymer brings anarchism and animal liberation into conversation with the anthropocene, anthroponomy, and decoloniality. Anthroponomy is an orientation that is at once personal, social, and anarchic. The final chapter, chapter 12, "Post-Scarcity Veganarchism" by Laura Schleifer, brings veganism into conversation with Murray Bookchin's post-scarcity anarchism. Abundantly imaginative yet remaining grounded in reality, Laura argues that veganism can go a long way towards creating and sharing the abundances that resound in nature so that everyone can live fulfilling lives. This, along with Jeremy's chapter, make an excellent pair of chapters with which to close the book because the praxis of anthroponomy and post-scarcity veganarchism can go a long way toward forging solidarity for total liberation.

## *References*

Anderson, W. C. (2021). *The nation on no map: Black anarchism and abolition*. AK Press.

Bayraktar, D. H. (2022). The phaeton conflict in Turkey: The C.A.S.E of animal domination in Instanbul Adalar. In N. Poirier, A. J. Nocella II, & A. Bernatchez (Eds.), *Emerging new voices in critical animal studies: Vegan studies for total liberation* (pp. 87–100). Peter Lang.

Bayraktar, D. H., & Bayraktar, O. (2022). A comparison of the local governments in terms of approaches to stray animals in Turkey. In N. Poirier, A. J. Nocella II, & A. Bernatchez (Eds.), *Emerging new voices in critical animal studies: Vegan studies for total liberation* (pp. 101–114). Peter Lang.

Bendik-Keymer, J. (2020). *Involving anthroponomy in the anthropocene: On decoloniality*. Routledge.

Best, S., Nocella II, A. J., Kahn, R., Gigliotti, C., & Kemmerer, L. (2007). Introducing critical animal studies. *Journal for Critical Animal Studies, 5*(1), 4–5.

Bey, M. (2019). *Them goon rules: Fugitive essays on radical black feminism*. University of Arizona Press.

Bey, M. (2020). *The problem of the negro as a problem for gender*. University of Minnesota Press.

Bey, M. (2022a). *Black trans feminism*. Duke University Press.

Bey, M. (2022b). *Cistem failure: Essays on blackness and cisgender*. Duke University Press.

Bilgin, A., & Ozdogan, K. (2021). "Street dogs" of Instanbul: An exemplary case for the construction and contestation of human domination over urban animals. In S. Springer, J. Mateer, M. Locret-Collet, & M. Acker (Eds.), *Undoing human supremacy: Anarchist political ecology in the face of anthroparchy* (pp. 209–234). Rowman & Littlefield.

Brown, S. J. (2022). *Refusing compulsory sexuality: A black asexual lens on our sex-obsessed culture*. North Atlantic Books.

Cobb Jr., C. E. (2015). *This nonviolent stuff'll get you killed: How guns made the civil rights movement possible*. Duke University Press.

Du Bois, W. E. B. (1968). *The autobiography of W.E.B. Du Bois: A soliloquy on viewing my life from the last decade of its first century*. International Publishers.

Feliz [Brueck], J. (2017). *Veganism in an oppressive world: A community of color project*. Sanctuary Publishers.

Feliz, J., & McNeill, Z. Z. (2020). *Queer and trans voices: Achieving liberation through consistent anti-oppression.* Sanctuary Publishers.

Four Arrows. (2019). The indigenization controversy: For whom and by whom? *Critical Education 10*(18), 1–13.

Four Arrows, Narvaez, D. (2022). *Restoring the kinship worldview: Indigenous voices introduce 28 precepts for rebalancing life on planet earth.* North Atlantic Books.

George, A. E. (Ed.). (2021). *Gender and sexuality in critical animal studies.* Lexington Books.

Giraud, E. H. (2021). *Veganism: Politics, practice, and theory.* Bloomsbury.

Giroux, H. A. (2020). *On critical pedagogy,* 2nd edition. Bloomsbury.

Giroux, H. A. (2021). *Race, politics and pandemic pedagogy: Education in a time of crisis.* Bloomsbury.

Giroux, H. A. (2022). *Pedagogy of resistance: Against manufactured ignorance.* Bloomsbury.

Kirk, G., & Hall, K. M. Q. (2021). Maps, gardens, and quilts. In L. Hall & G. Kirk (Eds.), *Mapping gendered ecologies: Engaging with and beyond ecowomanism and ecofeminism* (pp. 1–16). Lexington Books.

LaPrairie, R. (2022). Theoretical sociology of war and structural causes of the 2003 US invasion of Iraq. *Humanity & Society 0*(0). https://doi.org/10.1177/0160597622 1119997.

Levy, C., & Newman, S. (2019). *The anarchist imagination: Anarchism encounters the humanities and the social sciences.* Routledge.

Loizidou, Elena. (2023). *Anarchism: An art of living without law.* Routledge.

Matsuoka, A., & Sorenson, J. (Eds.). (2018). *Critical animal studies: Towards trans-species social justice.* Rowman & Littlefield.

Mills, C. W. (1959). *The sociological imagination.* Oxford University Press.

Nocella II, A., & Socha, K. (Eds.). (2022). *Radical animal studies: Beyond respectability politics, opportunism, and cooptation.* Peter Lang.

Nocella II, A., J., Drew, C., George, A. E., Ketenci, S., Lupinacci, J., Purdy, I., & Leeson-Schatz, J. (Eds.). (2019). *Education for total liberation: Critical animal pedagogy and teaching against speciesism.* Peter Lang.

Nocella II, A., J., Sorenson, J., Socha, K., & Matsuoka, A. (Eds.). (2014). *Defining critical animal studies: An intersectional social justice approach for liberation.* Peter Lang.

Nocella II, A.J. & George, A. E. (Eds.). (2019). *Intersectionality of critical animal studies: A historical collection.* Peter Lang.

Poirier, N., Nocella II, A. J., & Bernatchez, A. (Eds.). (2022). *Emerging new voices in critical animal studies: Vegan studies for total liberation.* Peter Lang.

Poirier, N., & Tomasello, S. (2017). Polar similar: Intersections of anthropology and conservation. *Animalia: An Anthrozoology Journal, 3*(1), 1–20.

Roberts-Gregory, F. (2021). Climate justice in the wild n' dirty south: An autoethnographic reflection on ecowomanism as engaged scholar-activist praxis before and during COVID-19. In L. Hall & G. Kirk (Eds.), *Mapping gendered ecologies: Engaging with and beyond ecowomanism and ecofeminism* (pp. 125–146). Lexington Books.

Samudzi, Z., & Anderson, W. C. (2018). *As black as resistance: Finding the conditions for liberation*. AK Press.

Shotwell, A. (2016). *Against purity: Living ethically in compromised times*. University of Minnesota Press.

Taylor, L. (2022). *Feminism in coalition: Thinking with US women of color feminism*. Duke University Press.

Tomasello, S. (2022). Nonhuman "others": A theology of hope and liberation. In N. Poirier, A. Nocella II, & A. Bernatchez (Eds.), *Emerging new voices in critical animal studies: Vegan studies for total liberation* (pp. 55–70). Peter Lang.

Tomasello, S., & Poirier, N. (2018). The intersectionality of wildlife conservation and indigenous rights. *Green Theory and Praxis, 11*(1), 18–34.

Tomasello, S., Piazza, A., & Poirier, N. (2021). Reproduction or the lack thereof: A mode of oppression, a means to liberation? In A. E. George (Ed.), *Gender and sexuality in critical animal studies* (pp. 145–162). Lexington Books.

Wells, I. B. (2016). *The light of truth: Writings of an anti-lynching crusader*. Penguin.

Williams. R. F. (2013/1962). *Negroes with guns*. Martino Fine Books.

# Part I. New Movement Connections: Trans Liberation and Human Population

# 1 Connecting Transgender Studies and Critical Animal Studies

Cameron Whitley

In 2018, a 50-year-old elephant named Happy, forced to live in the Bronx Zoo for 45 years after being born in the wild, became the center of a national push for personhood recognition and freedom for other animals like her. While Happy could not fight in court for her sovereignty or liberation, the Nonhuman Rights Project (N.R.P.) has done so, arguing that Happy has been exploited and that she "is an autonomous, cognitively complex elephant worthy of the rights reserved in law for a 'person'" (Brown, 2022, p. 1). The case was ultimately decided in 2022 when New York's top court ruled that although Happy and all elephants are "intelligent beings deserving of proper care and compassion," she should not be considered a person (Salcedo, 2022, p. 1). At nearly the same time, Texas Governor Greg Abbott issued a letter to Texas state health agencies that state law indicated that providing gender-affirming care to transgender youth is considered child abuse (Sharrow & Sederbaum, 2022). It further "stipulated that doctors, nurses and teachers are legally now required to report parents who aid their child in receiving such care to the Texas Department of Family and Protective Services (D.F.P.S.)" (Sharrow & Sederbaum, 2022, p. 1). While the A.C.L.U. and the federal government have pushed back against this proclamation, dozens of other states have initiated similar legislative measures to remove transgender agencies and limit access to gender-affirming resources. While the connections between these cases may not be immediately evident, both cases show how the rights of some humans, and all animals remain controversial and tenuous. In both cases, the health, well-being, and identity of the transgender and animal subject are deemed to need management as these "subjects" cannot function autonomously in their best interests. The instances of rights being deliberated across both populations are extensive.

Scholars argue that transgender people and nonhuman animals are connected as the transgender body has never been considered fully human (Hayward & Weinstein, 2015). The transgender body defies and challenges long-coveted ideas of gender and social roles, setting it apart as something that should be feared, controlled, and heavily managed, a cyborg walking among us. Haraway establishes the cyborg as a hybrid creature, "a disassembled and reassembled, postmodern collection and personal self [...]" (1985, p. 163). In the cyborg, nature, culture, technology, and biology combine to create a unique techno-social assemblage in flesh (Stoyanova, 2021). The transgender body becomes the ultimate cyborg, a being that is composed of both organic and biomechatronic parts seen to replicate, mimic or resemble gender identities and roles. Such a deranged interpretation of the transgender body creates avenues for delegitimating and dehumanizing that persist within and across organizations, especially within the media (Li, 2021). In fact, transgender people face numerous rights restrictions or are deemed to need management within organizational frameworks (Westbrook, 2020). Similarly, but to a greater extent, nonhuman animals continue to have limited rights and lack personhood recognition, with no court in the U.S. recognizing nonhuman personhood (Kurki, 2021). The legal and social pushback against extending rights to these seemingly different populations necessitates connecting transgender studies (T.S.) with critical animal studies (CAS) to better understand how these communities can find commonalities for advocacy.

T.S. examines gender embodiment, expression, and identity and how these factors influence support, representation, policy, and rights for transgender and nonbinary people. In many ways, the evolution of T.S. has come from a movement to critically interrogate how transgender bodies have been depicted as deviant medical anomalies and as subjects to study, profile, and control. It is a critical normative discipline, now controlled and facilitated by transgender and nonbinary people to use research to embody a liberation mindset in advocacy. Like T.S., CAS is a theory-driven, activist-oriented, interdisciplinary field that challenges how power and structure affect animal (human and nonhuman) autonomy and agency. In engaging these two seemingly divergent fields, this chapter provides an example of how connecting the material realities of different species can lead to what Nocella and colleagues (2014) term intersectional animal liberation.

## A Very Brief History of Critical Animal Studies

Among other historical activist influences, CAS can be traced back to the first animal liberation movements that emerged in the 1960s and 1970s with the publication of books such as *Animal Liberation* (Singer, 1975). Of course, concern for animals was well embedded into society before then. While CAS aims to liberate all, it has only sometimes been well received. Partly this is because individuals and other social movements are affected by speciesism and lack reflection on how all beings are connected; in this, the inclusion of animals and their liberation appears to deter from human liberation instead of supporting it. A common narrative is that working to liberate nonhumans wastes time and resources that could be better spent on humans. Additionally, CAS has recognized intersectional struggles such as how geography, access, culture, and other features situate human and non-human animal relationships. As Nocella II and colleagues write, "[...] while the animal rights movement was progressive in seeking liberation for other animals as well as humans, some of the movement's assumptions, campaigns, and rhetoric were flawed by unintended and unconscious ableism, classism, racism, and sexism" (2014, p. xix). They give an example where vegetarian and vegan advocacy often ignores food access in that access in many poverty-stricken areas is restricted to convenience stores and fast-food restaurants. In this way, structural conditions limit viable options to eating a vegetarian or vegan diet (yet, as John Tallent demonstrates in their chapter in this book, do not preclude one from still being vegan).

CAS argues that while animal studies (A.S.) has made prolific developments in contributing "to our understanding of the historical, sociological, and philosophical aspects of human/nonhuman animal relations, the discipline is strangely detached from the dire plight of nonhuman animals, human beings and the Earth" (Best et al., 2007, p. 1). A.S. is an interdisciplinary field investigating relationships between humans and nonhuman animals regarding representation, social engagement, political entanglements, and cognitive perceptions. A.S. attempts to be objective and does not directly advocate for animal liberation, although many A.S. scholars likely hold liberation views and regularly participate in animal activism. In comparison, CAS is focused on total liberation and an anarchist approach. Although some scholars are centrally located within a CAS framework, it has also become a place for A.S. scholars to engage in activism and be scholar activists. Yet, CAS has readily been critiqued for the lack of intersectional analysis and the reproduction of forms of settler colonialism with little acknowledgment of Indigenous perspectives (Montford & Taylor, 2020) and other underrepresented identities.

## *A Very Brief History of Transgender Studies*

Within various disciplines, such as sociology, feminist and queer scholars have leveraged critiques of how theory and disciplinary boundaries center the experiences of the dominant paradigm to evaluate the lived experiences of L.G.B.T.Q.I.A.+ people. Transgender studies emerged to challenge these paradigms and to critique the use and depiction of the transgender body as a medical anomaly in need of control and management (Johnson, 2015). Scholars argue that T.S. has had two distinct focal points during its tenure, both necessitated by the political culture of the time: an early focus on gender deviance and a continued centering on gender difference (Schilt & Lagos, 2017). From the 1970s to the late 1990s, T.S. centered on delineating transsexuality as a medical diagnosis and group identity to be recognized. The concept of "doing gender" was born (West & Zimmerman, 1987; Whitley, 2013). This focal point was about legitimizing and documenting the transgender identity. In the late 1990s through the early 2000s, transgender people were presented as subjects exploring how gender difference emerges and is engaged (Namaste, 2000; Vidal & Ortiz, 2008). The focus on gender difference is still a dominant focal point. A shift from defining gender differences to protecting bodily autonomy and agency in policy and medical decisions has surfaced. Much empirical research before 1970 appeared exclusively in medical and psychiatric journals. Here, transgender bodies became a subject of medical exploration, exploitation, and identification, where medical professionals held control over agency and body autonomy and where transgender bodies were defined as deviant against "normal" constructions of gender. It was only through the organization of transgender people in support groups and online forums that stories were shared, and people began to demand greater bodily sovereignty. Similar to the plight of CAS scholarship, Schilt and Lagos suggest that "[...] transgender scholarship, much like critical sexualities [...] faces disciplinary barriers in the publication process," which limits who can engage and maintain status within the community (2017, p. 427). Given that limited work has evolved to address connections across LGBTQIA+ identities with AS or CAS, this chapter seeks to connect transgender studies to critical animal studies by highlighting five key challenges as points of connection shared across species and identities. These challenges include: advocating for rights, pronoun and language use, body trafficking, experimentation and medical intervention, and teaching about the animal and transgender body.

## Shared Challenges for Connection between T.S. and CAS: Advocating for Rights

How gender has been constructed and reconstructed in society has served as a basis for limiting or extending rights to transgender bodies (Hines, 2009). Both T.S. and CAS are heavily involved in monitoring and advocating body autonomy and agency in policy development. In both communities, the rights of transgender humans and nonhuman animals are highly contentious and heavily debated, often as a means to maintain social norms and capitalist ideals (McMullen, 2015). The backlash against transgender bodies and the "transgender tipping point" is well documented (Bowers & Whitley, 2020b, 2020a; George & Goguen, 2021). In 2021, eight states passed anti-trans-gender legislation, while 29 made attempts (Barbee et al., 2022). In the first three months of 2022, over 230 anti-L.G.B.T.Q.I.A.+ bills were introduced in state legislatures, most targeting transgender people (Lavietes & Ramos, 2022). This solidified a coordinated national effort to target transgender people largely by the Evangelical Christian right (Lavietes & Ramos, 2022). Passed and proposed legislation ranged from denying transgender youth tran-sition-related services (hormone replacement and blockers, gender-affirming surgery), banning transgender people from athletics, and limiting access to bathrooms, locker rooms, and gendered facilities. These actions have known health consequences such as anxiety, depression, suicidal ideation, and induc-ing post-traumatic stress (Barr et al., 2021; Horne et al., 2022). Globally, most legal jurisdictions recognize two gender identities: man and woman, while often excluding those that do not fit within these categories, limiting rights to transgender and nonbinary people. In the U.S., legal recognition of transgender people is often determined based on gender-affirming surgeries. Many who do not engage in medical transition cannot be legally recognized as their expressed gender, and anti-transgender legislation increases barriers to legal recognition. Control of transgender bodies by the medical profession and government means that many people have inconsistent documentation setting them up for discrimination when seeking employment, medical care, or other avenues that require identification.

Although there are fewer attacks on nonhuman animal rights, this is largely because legislation has given few (if any) rights to animals in the first place. Within the U.S., the limited rights that some animals are afforded are presented in the Animal Welfare Act (A.W.A.) which is the only federal law that provides minimum standards for the treatment of animals in research, teaching, testing, exhibition, transport, and by dealers (Act, 1966). The A.W.A. is centered on cats, primates, and other mammals but excludes rats, mice, and birds. As discussed in the opening of this chapter, animals remain the legal property of humans without personhood and autonomy. Instead of attacking animals' rights, animal agriculture has sought to take away the rights of citizens to be informed about animals' lack of rights. This happens through ag-gag laws that criminalize activists who obtain undercover footage of farms or slaughterhouses. These laws are intended to keep animals as unprotected as possible. The recognition of body autonomy and the push for minimal rights remains an issue for both communities.

## Pronoun and Language Use

The extension of rights often depends on the language used to describe communities and how this language is applied in advocacy. This is especially true for transgender and nonhuman animal communities where language is often used to dehumanize or depersonify. Although language for and against these communities is extensive and complex, this section focuses on using pronouns as tools to de/humanize and de/personify. In both communities, the abandoned use of "it" applied to transgender and nonhuman animal bodies serves to delegitimize personhood in favor of promoting the individual as an object or something other than a unique individual. Numerous studies show that chronic misgendering remains a problem for transgender people and that this experience has negative mental health implications (McCann & Sharek, 2016; Whitley et al., 2022). On the other hand, while the experience of being misgendered may not directly impact the mental health of individual nonhumans, it has implications for how people perceive individual and collective groups of nonhuman animals and directly contributes to their oppression and exploitation (Merskin, 2022). In both cases, applying pronouns to transgender people and nonhuman animals is a learned behavior. Among children, using pronouns for animals correlates with parental use (Rigney & Callanan, 2011). The same is likely to be true for the use of pronouns for transgender people. Ultimately, when pronouns are not used to identify individuals, this reduces social importance, creating a space for disrespect and exploitation.

## Body Trafficking

Transgender people and nonhuman animals are trafficked at exceptionally high rates, with many of these cases leading to the untimely end of the individual. It is common to think of trafficking as sexual exploitation, but thousands of humans are trafficked yearly for domestic servitude, forced labor, and organ retrieval. Regardless of the reason, it all comes down to money and profit margins. Roughly 13 percent of transgender people report participating in the sex trafficking industry, with transgender women and transfeminine people being twice as likely to engage in the sex trade (Fitzgerald et al., 2015). Research shows that there are few resources to support transgender people who are trafficked because transgender people are viewed as less exploitable when compared to cisgender women (Fehrenbacher et al., 2020; Martinez & Kelle, 2013). While data suggests that the trafficking of transgender bodies is significant relative to the population, transgender people are often excluded from human trafficking research (Fehrenbacher et al., 2020).

Similarly, nonhuman animal trafficking is one of the most profitable illegal activities in the world, being the third most valuable illegal market globally (Kim, 2021; Bergman, 2009). Trafficked animals are used as exotic pets, traditional medicine, clothing, food, and jewelry (Tow et al., 2021). The most trafficked animal globally is the pangolin, used in traditional Chinese medicine. It is estimated that over one million pangolins have been killed for their scales in the past decade (National Geographic Photo Ark, 2022). Wildlife trafficking impacts the natural environment by decreasing biodiversity, critically endangering animals, and exposing ecosystems to the possibility of collapse (Lynch, 2020). Since the 1980s, animal trafficking worldwide has increased by 2,000 percent (IPBES, 2019). It is well documented that human trafficking is on the rise and that the COVID-19 pandemic amplified the impacts on vulnerable populations like transgender people (Tillyer et al., 2021; Todres & Diaz, 2021). Human and nonhuman animal trafficking is rising, with ineffective systems to monitor and protect trafficked bodies.

## *Experimentation and Medical Intervention*

It is well understood that CAS rejects any form of animal testing. Research shows that using nonhuman animals in experiments is often superfluous. It is time-consuming, involves a highly skilled workforce, and uses expensive protocols to only create unnecessary pain, distress, and death for millions of animals yearly (Doke & Dhawale, 2015). Alternatives to animal testing are becoming more prevalent and often provide better results than using animals as subjects (Alves et al., 2021; Huang et al., 2021). Transgender people have long been the objects of medical research (Shuster, 2021; Slagstad, 2021). Much early experimentation on transgender bodies explored psychological pathways to change gender identities. This work expanded to the experimentation of hormones and surgeries on transgender bodies. Before some insurance companies covered gender affirming surgeries, these procedures had little oversight, leaving transgender bodies as a site of medical experimentation for profit. Much of transgender medical history explores how transgender people often need to advocate for their own well-being within medical institutions, an issue that remains today (Stroumsa et al., 2019).

Transgender people may also be uniquely wrapped up in the use of products derived from nonhuman animals to sustain their gender presentation. While most people have utilized products or pharmaceuticals created through animal testing with or without their knowledge, transgender people rely on some for social, physical, and mental survival. Specifically, many transgender people use medical interventions in the form of hormones and gender-affirming surgeries developed from animal experimentation. The use of animals to assess hormone composition and effect is well documented. Studies suggest that these experiments are unnecessary and that alternatives to animal experimentation for hormonal compound research often produce more reliable results (Greek & Kramer, 2019; Penza et al., 2009). Transgender people seeking hormone replacement therapy to masculinize their bodies may seek testosterone supplementation. This is most often a plant-based synthetic product. However, transgender people seeking to feminize their bodies may seek estrogen. Premarin is the most commonly used product derived from horse urine (Reisman & Safer, 2022; Vance, 2007). In this process, mares are forcefully impregnated repeatedly to produce urine with high estrogen levels to create Premarin products. It is unlikely that many transgender people know about the composition of Premarin. With greater education, this might change how this product is produced, as plant-based and synthetic alternatives exist but are not always supported by insurance.

## Teaching about Animals and Transgender Bodies

Although historically contested, T.S. and CAS are direct responses to tangible social (human and nonhuman animal) issues that have gone unaddressed within broader, less advocacy centered fields such as animal studies and gender studies. However, teaching these subjects can be quite difficult. What academics can study and teach is often defined by instructional barriers and promotion requirements. Teaching and engaging in research that addresses controversial topics, such as those often found in T.S. and CAS, inherently involves a position of privilege (Whitley & Cherry, 2023). Because of this, doing research from a completely CAS perspective is often impossible due to organizational constraints and concerns about alienating people accustomed to exploiting animals. For instance, allowing CAS courses to be taught at agriculture institutions is counterintuitive to supporting the agriculture mission of the university. Specifically, agricultural schools that train students in animal husbandry using intensive confinement systems may worry that CAS courses would push students to think critically about this training and may demand alternatives to traditional animal agriculture.

This, among many examples, suggests that those allowed to teach and do research from a CAS perspective exclusively are few and far between. In most cases, these individuals likely carry identities that have already afforded them power (race, class, gender) and job security (tenure). Even with tenure, the institution may not support including a CAS course for fear of the animal agricultural or medical industry responding negatively, leading to challenges to the institution's reputation or reduced funding. The reality is that scholarly recognition of T.S. and CAS has been limited, although recognition of T.S. has increased. It is only within the past decade that transgender individuals have received greater public attention, which correlates with the "transgender tipping point" defined in a 2015 *Time* article about the growing visibility of transgender people (Steinmetz, 2015). Johnson (2022) argues that the lack of T.S. inclusion is concerning as greater structural competency is needed in mainstream institutions to address the harmful rhetoric and ideology attached to the proliferation of anti-transgender legislation that has surfaced since 2014, which is considered the tipping point. The same point could be said for CAS. To address biodiversity loss, we must examine how nonhuman animals are exploited for human benefit and how oppression exists and is maintained across species (Kalof & Whitley, 2021; Whitley & Kalof, 2014). Without such dialogue, the drivers of biodiversity (climate change, pollution, habitat loss, animal exploitation) cannot be addressed (Dietz et al., 2020).

Although instructors and teachers may not be able to teach CAS courses, no formal legislation dictates what can and cannot be taught about animals in the classroom. This differs from T.S., where the Florida House Bill (H.B.) 1577, the "Don't Say Gay" bill, states that school districts in Florida may not discuss sexual orientation or gender identity in primary grade levels, limiting what can and cannot be taught about transgender people. In addition, many conservative religion-based colleges do not support L.G.B.T.Q.I.A.+ identities in their institutions, again limiting what can be taught (Gjelten, 2018). Although the U.S. Department of Education confirms that Title IX protects students from discrimination based on sexual orientation and gender identity (US Department of Education, 2022), some universities still engage in promoting institutional barriers to the expression and support of transgender students (Martino et al., 2022; Whitley et al., 2022). While CAS has fewer legal limitations imposed on individual adherents, the social pushback on animal liberation and veganism are high especially in conservative rural environments (Asher & Cherry, 2015; Greenebaum, 2018). As conversations about CAS increase, we will likely see more students and community members speaking out about using animals in university settings in research and agriculture. These outcries will likely spark pushback from individuals and agribusiness.

## Conclusion

Very little published work has connected transgender studies to critical animal studies. In this chapter, I start this conversation by connecting transgender and animal communities across five areas of shared concern: advocating for rights, pronoun and language use, body trafficking, experimentation and medical intervention, and teaching about the animal and transgender body. The shared connection across these issues often exists in the dehumanization, depersonification, and desire to control the nonhuman animal and transgender body, which could best be addressed with animal standpoint theory. As Best notes in describing animal standpoint theory, "nonhuman animals have been key driving and shaping forces of human thought, psychology, moral and social life, and history overall, and that in fundamental ways, the oppression of human over human is rooted in the oppression of human over nonhuman animal" (2009. p. 18). The points of connection are clear, as there is no liberation until all are liberated. In this case, transgender people and advocates should be equally concerned with how animal populations are treated and exploited. Similarly, animal advocacy should focus more on exploited and dehumanized human populations such as the transgender community.

## References

Act, A. W. (1966). Animal Welfare Act. *Public Law*, 89–544.

Alves, V. M., Auerbach, S. S., Kleinstreuer, N., Rooney, J. P., Muratov, E. N., Rusyn, I., Tropsha, A., & Schmitt, C. (2021). Curated data in—Trustworthy in silico models out: The impact of data quality on the reliability of artificial intelligence models as alternatives to animal testing. *Alternatives to Laboratory Animals*, *49*(3), 73–82.

Asher, K., & Cherry, E. (2015). Home is where the food is: Barriers to vegetarianism and veganism in the domestic sphere. *Journal for Critical Animal Studies*, *13*(1), 66–91.

Barbee, H., Deal, C., & Gonzales, G. (2022). Anti-transgender legislation—A public health concern for transgender youth. *JAMA Pediatrics*, *176*(2), 125–126.

Barr, S. M., Snyder, K. E., Adelson, J. L., & Budge, S. L. (2021). Posttraumatic stress in the trans community: The roles of anti-transgender bias, non-affirmation, and internalized transphobia. *Psychology of Sexual Orientation and Gender Diversity*.

Bergman, C. (2009, December). Wildlife Trafficking. *Smithsonian*. https://www.smithsonianmag.com/travel/wildlife-trafficking-149079896/

Best, S. (2009). The rise of critical animal studies: Putting theory into action and animal liberation into higher education. *Journal for Critical Animal Studies, 7*(1), 9–52.

Best, S., Nocella, A. J., Kahn, R., Gigliotti, C., & Kemmerer, L. (2007). Introducing critical animal studies. *Journal for Critical Animal Studies, 5*(1), 4–5.

Bowers, M. M., & Whitley, C. T. (2020a). Assessing voter registration among transgender and gender non-conforming individuals. *Political Behavior, 42*(1), 143–164.

Bowers, M. M., & Whitley, C. T. (2020b). What drives support for transgender rights? Assessing the effects of biological attribution on US public opinion of transgender rights. *Sex Roles*, 1–13.

Brown, E. N. (2022, May 19). Are elephants people? New York's highest court hears case for animal personhood. *Reason.* https://reason.com/2022/05/19/are-elepha nts-people-new-yorks-highest-court-hears-case-for-animal-personhood/

Dietz, T., Shwom, R. L., & Whitley, C. T. (2020). Climate change and society. *Annual Review of Sociology, 46.*

Doke, S. K., & Dhawale, S. C. (2015). Alternatives to animal testing: A review. *Saudi Pharmaceutical Journal, 23*(3), 223–229.

Fehrenbacher, A. E., Musto, J., Hoefinger, H., Mai, N., Macioti, P., Giametta, C., & Bennachie, C. (2020). Transgender people and human trafficking: Intersectional exclusion of transgender migrants and people of color from anti-trafficking protection in the United States. *Journal of Human Trafficking, 6*(2), 182–194.

Fitzgerald, E., Patterson, S., Hickey, D., Biko, C., & Tobin, H. (2015). Meaningful work: Transgender experiences in the sex trade with new analysis from the national transgender discrimination survey. *Calabasas, CA: Best Practices Policy Project, Red Umbrella Project, National Center for Transgender Equality.* http://www.Transe quality.Org/Sites/Default/Files/Meaningful% 20Work-Full% 20Report_FINAL_ 3. Pdf

George, B., & Goguen, S. (2021). Hermeneutical backlash: Trans youth panics as epistemic injustice. *Feminist Philosophy Quarterly, 7*(4).

Gjelten, T. (2018, March 27). Christian colleges that oppose LGBT rights worried about losing funding. *NPR.* https://www.npr.org/2018/03/27/597390654/christian-colleges-that-oppose-lgbt-rights-worried-about-losing-funding-under-ti

Greek, R., & Kramer, L. A. (2019). The scientific problems with using non-human animals to predict human response to drugs and disease. In *Animal Experimentation: Working towards a paradigm change* (pp. 391–416). Brill.

Greenebaum, J. (2018). Vegans of color: Managing visible and invisible stigmas. *Food, Culture & Society, 21*(5), 680–697.

Haraway, D. (1985). *A manifesto for cyborgs: Science, technology, and socialist-feminism in the late twentieth century. Socialist Review.*

Hayward, E., & Weinstein, J. (2015). Introduction: Tranimalities in the age of trans* life. *Transgender Studies Quarterly, 2*(2), 195–208.

Hines, S. (2009). A pathway to diversity?: Human rights, citizenship and the politics of transgender. *Contemporary Politics, 15*(1), 87–102.

Horne, S. G., McGinley, M., Yel, N., & Maroney, M. R. (2022). The stench of bathroom bills and anti-transgender legislation: Anxiety and depression among transgender, nonbinary, and cisgender LGBQ people during a state referendum. *Journal of Counseling Psychology, 69*(1), 1.

Huang, H.-J., Lee, Y.-H., Hsu, Y.-H., Liao, C.-T., Lin, Y.-F., & Chiu, H.-W. (2021). Current strategies in the assessment of nanotoxicity: Alternatives to in vivo animal testing. *International Journal of Molecular Sciences, 22*(8), 4216.

IPBES. (2019). *The global assessment report on biodiversity and ecosystem services.* IPBES Secretariat. https://ipbes.net/global-assessment

Johnson, A. H. (2015). Normative accountability: How the medical model influences transgender identities and experiences. *Sociology Compass, 9*(9), 803–813.

Johnson, A. H. (2022). Tipping points and shifting expectations: The promise of applied trans studies for building structural competency. *Bulletin of Applied Transgender Studies, 1*(1–2), 163–177.

Kalof, L., & Whitley, C. T. (2021). Animals in environmental sociology. In *Handbook of environmental sociology* (pp. 289–313). Springer.

Kim, H. (2021, December 22). How animal trafficking became one of the most lucrative industries on the planet. *Sentient Media.* https://sentientmedia.org/animal-trafficking/

Kurki, V. (2021). Legal personhood and animal rights. *Journal of Animal Ethics, 11*(1), 47–62.

Lavietes, M., & Ramos, E. (2022, March 1). *Nearly 240 anti-LGBTQ bill filed in 2-22 so far. Most of them targeting trans people.* https://www.nbcnews.com/nbc-out/out-politics-and-policy/nearly-240-anti-lgbtq-bills-filed-2022-far-targeting-trans-people-rcna20418

Li, M. (2021). Exemplifying power matters: The impact of power exemplification of transgender people in the news on issue attribution, dehumanization, and aggression tendencies. *Journalism Practice,* 1–29.

Lynch, M. J. (2020). Green criminology and environmental crime: Criminology that matters in the age of global ecological collapse. *Journal of White Collar and Corporate Crime, 1*(1), 50–61.

Martinez, O., & Kelle, G. (2013). Sex trafficking of LGBT individuals: A call for service provision, research, and action. *The International Law News, 42*(4).

Martino, W., Kassen, J., & Omercajic, K. (2022). Supporting transgender students in schools: Beyond an individualist approach to trans inclusion in the education system. *Educational Review, 74*(4), 753–772.

McCann, E., & Sharek, D. (2016). Mental health needs of people who identify as transgender: A review of the literature. *Archives of Psychiatric Nursing, 30*(2), 280–285.

McMullen, S. (2015). Is capitalism to blame? Animal lives in the marketplace. *Journal of Animal Ethics, 5*(2), 126–134.

Merskin, D. (2022). She, he, not it: Language, personal pronouns, and animal advocacy. *Journal of World Languages, 8*(2), 391–408.

Montford, K. S., & Taylor, C. (2020). *Colonialism and animality: Anti-colonial perspectives in critical animal studies.* Routledge.

Namaste, V. (2000). *Invisible lives: The erasure of transsexual and transgendered people.* University of Chicago Press.

National Geographic Photo Ark. (2022). *Pangolins.* https://www.nationalgeographic.com/animals/mammals/facts/pangolins

Nocella II, A. J., Sorenson, J., Socha, K., & Matsuoka, A. (2014). Introduction: The emergence of critical animal studies: The rise of intersectional animal liberation. *Counterpoints,* xix–xxxvi.

Penza, M., Jeremic, M., Montani, C., Unkila, M., Caimi, L., Mazzoleni, G., & Di Lorenzo, D. (2009). Alternatives to animal experimentation for hormonal compounds research. *Genes & Nutrition, 4*(3), 165–172.

Reisman, T., & Safer, J. D. (2022). Perioperative estrogen considerations for transgender women undergoing vaginoplasty. In *A case-based guide to clinical endocrinology* (pp. 507–512). Springer.

Rigney, J. C., & Callanan, M. A. (2011). Patterns in parent–child conversations about animals at a marine science center. *Cognitive Development, 26*(2), 155–171.

Salcedo, A. (2022, June 15). Brox Zoo's Happy the elephant is not a legal person, Court Rules. *The Washington Post.* https://www.washingtonpost.com/nation/2022/06/15/happy-elephant-person-bronx-zoo/

Schilt, K., & Lagos, D. (2017). The development of transgender studies in sociology. *Annual Review of Sociology, 43*(1), 425–443.

Sharrow, E., & Sederbaum, I. (2022, March 10). Texas isn't the only state denying essential medical care to trans youth. Here's what's going on. *The Washington Post,* Monkey Cage. https://www.washingtonpost.com/politics/2022/03/10/texas-trans-kids-abortion-lgbtq-gender-ideology/

Shuster, S. S. (2021). *Trans medicine: The emergence and practice of treating gender.* NYU Press.

Singer, P. (1975). *Animal liberation. Towards an end to man's inhumanity to animals.* Granada Publishing Ltd.

Slagstad, K. (2021). The political nature of sex—Transgender in the history of medicine. *New England Journal of Medicine, 384*(11), 1070–1074.

Steinmetz, K. (2015, January 21). Why it's a big deal that Obama said "Transgender." *TIME.* http://time.com/3676881/state-of-the-union-2015-barack-obama-transgender/

Stoyanova, M. (2021). Performing the cyborg self: Explicit and implicit examples of body hacking the distributed self. *International Journal of Performance Arts and Digital Media, 17*(2), 253–270.

Stroumsa, D., Shires, D. A., Richardson, C. R., Jaffee, K. D., & Woodford, M. R. (2019). Transphobia rather than education predicts provider knowledge of transgender health care. *Medical Education, 53*(4), 398–407.

Tillyer, M. S., Smith, M. R., & Tillyer, R. (2021). Findings from the U.S. National Human Trafficking Hotline. *Journal of Human Trafficking*, 1–10.

Todres, J., & Diaz, A. (2021). COVID-19 and human trafficking—The amplified impact on vulnerable populations. *JAMA Pediatrics, 175*(2), 123–124.

Tow, J. H., Symes, W. S., & Carrasco, L. R. (2021). Economic value of illegal wildlife trade entering the USA. *PloS One, 16*(10), e0258523.

U.S. Department of Education. (2022). *U.S. Department of Education Confirms Title IX Protects Students from Discrimination Based on Sexual Orientation and Gender Identity* [Press Release]. U.S. Department of Education. https://www.ed.gov/news/press-releases/us-department-education-confirms-title-ix-protects-students-discrimination-based-sexual-orientation-and-gender-identity

Vance, D. A. (2007). PREMARIN: The intriguing history of a controversial drug. *International Journal of Pharmaceutical Compounding, 11*(4), 282.

Vidal-Ortiz, S. (2008). Transgender and transsexual studies: Sociology's influence and future steps. *Sociology Compass, 2*(2), 433–450.

West, C., & Zimmerman, D. H. (1987). Doing gender. *Gender & Society, 1*(2), 125–151.

Westbrook, L. (2020). *Unlivable lives: Violence and identity in transgender activism.* University of California Press.

Whitley, C., & Cherry, E. (2023). Environmental sociology and sociological animal studies. In S. Cabrera & S. Sweet (Eds.), *The handbook of teaching and learning in sociology.* Edward Elgar Publishing.

Whitley, C. T. (2013). Trans-kin undoing and redoing gender: Negotiating relational identity among friends and family of transgender persons. *Sociological Perspectives, 56*(4), 597–621.

Whitley, C. T., & Kalof, L. (2014). Animal imagery in the discourse of climate change. *International Journal of Sociology, 44*(1), 10–33.

Whitley, C. T., Nordmarken, S., Kolysh, S., & Goldstein-Kral, J. (2022). I've been misgendered so many times: Comparing the experiences of chronic misgendering among transgender graduate students in the social and natural sciences. *Sociological Inquiry.*

# 2 Anthropogenic Monsters: A CAS and Liberating Perspective on the Contemporary Production of Human and Nonhuman Monsters

AGNESE MARTINI, FRANCESCA CORRADINI, AND MATTEO PORAZZI

## What Is Monstrosity?

> On the basis of the continuum held by nature, the monster ensures the
> emergence of difference.
> —Foucault (2005, p. 156)

Monsters have always haunted the human imagination, "living things of anomalous shape or structure," fabulous creatures "composed of strikingly incongruous corporeal parts" (Stryker, 1994, p. 247). But what constitutes a monster in the first place? Etymologically, monster derives from the Latin *monstrum*, related to the verbs *monstrare*—to show, reveal, or signify—and *monere*—to warn. The monster of the past was a wonder and a prodigy, "a message that breaks into this world from the realm of the divine" (Beal, 2002, p. 7). During the sixteenth and seventeenth centuries, monsters inhabited the unmapped spaces beyond the known world, and in the eighteenth and nineteenth centuries, they arose from the in-between states of natural history taxonomies. In the twentieth and twenty-first centuries, "they seem to demonstrate a more explicitly political identity, fracturing the humanist assumption of the Enlightenment thought" (Davies, 2013, p. 269). Monsters still have a message to transmit. But what can they reveal? Do they have something to warn us about?

Monsters are de-constructive icons that challenge the dualistic concepts of nature and culture (Haraway, 1992), and just by existing, they question our reality and norms. They unveil a world of alterations, promises, entanglements, and unexpected frictions. They inhabit liminal spaces in which differences proliferate and transformation is possible. A monster is an abjection because it "does not respect borders, positions, rules;" instead, it represents "the in-between, the ambiguous, the composite" (Kristeva, 1982, p. 4). They problematize identity, categorization, and order from this border-line and horrifying position.

> Above all, the monstrous is that which creates [a] sense of vertigo, that which calls into question our (their, anyone's) epistemological world-view, highlights its fragmentary and inadequate nature, and thereby asks us [...] to acknowledge the failures of our systems of categorization. (Mittman, 2013, p. 8)

Therefore, and in line with critical animal studies's (CAS) mission to deconstruct binaries and intentionally blur boundaries, this chapter supports the thesis that monstrous bodies are a cultural construct that tell us more about the society responsible for their creation, rather than explaining what a monster is. Indeed, "the monster exists only to be read" (Cohen, 2020, p. 38) and for this reason, it can be considered a "biotextual being" which "marks a crossing where the real and the world of symbols" become conflated (Botting, 2003, p. 345). In this sense, monsters ask us to reevaluate our cultural paradigms and perception of differences and find the reasons behind their creation. Thus, to be a monster or a "monstricity" is not necessarily negative. Through a trans, anarchist, and CAS lens, monsters enact transformative practices, imagining and becoming new possibilities by defying the status quo. This is similar to how Stryker (1994) views the term in relation to transgender people. However, we must not overlook how humans purposefully create monsters to serve the status quo, some of which are discussed below.

This chapter focuses on the contemporary production of human and nonhuman monsters, proposing that monstrosity can be a relevant category for CAS. In this way, we bring CAS together with trans studies. Whereas Cam Whitley (this volume) shows how trans studies and CAS have much in common and offer each other mutually, this chapter presents a specific application of this connection. Doing this promotes a combined trans and animal liberation—perhaps what could be referred to as tranimal liberation (Steinbock et al., 2021)—and link this to effective activism. We take inspiration from varied literature, drawing connections among and beyond trans* studies, queer theory, and posthumanism. Moreover, the approach used takes inspiration from the "non-anthropocentric zoögogy (or animal pedagogy)," proposed by Acampora (2021), which describes interspecies encounters as co-constitutive, and therefore unstable and unfixed, able to change and actively adapt to reality. Recognizing other-than-human forms of agency creates interspecies kinship based on responsibility and solidarity. In this context, we refer to contemporary monsters as anthropogenic because humans directly produce them through their actions and indirectly through their discourse.

First, this chapter will examine the serial production of nonhuman monsters through genetic modification, both in the scientific laboratory and the meat industry. In these settings (among others), beings are created by adding, deleting, or modifying physical and mental characteristics. Then we consider the proliferation of human monsters in the cultural imaginary through the discrimination and animalization of non-conforming bodies, such as people with disabilities, Black, and trans* people. In this section, we demonstrate how to reclaim monstrosity as a means of liberation. Finally, this chapter explores the unexpected pathways and turns that monsters can reveal to overcome anthropocentrism and speciesism. This section widens the discussion from the previous one to promote more effective social movements to resist oppression, representing CAS's core themes and goals.

## The Serial Production of the Nonhuman Monster: OncoMouse and the Broiler Chicken

> To which world do the mutant hybrids of genetic engineering or the violated and deformed bodies of non-humans in factory farms belong?
> —Filippi & Dal Lago (2018, p. 9)

Our monstrous path starts with the multifaceted monstrosities societies create and reproduce through biotechnological enhancements and inventions. Such anthropogenic monsters emerge in at least two different but intertwined ways: through the logic and practice of laboratory testing and intensive animal farming. Both contribute to the serial production of monstrous animal bodies through force and without consent. Humans appropriate and alter the living bodies of nonhuman animals to the extent that they reconfigure the global biosphere in an anthropocentric manner. This logic follows two lines, namely that "improved" animals will produce "improved" food, and those test animals will also produce "improved" humans, albeit at the expense of the nonhuman animals' suffering and death (Twine, 2010, pp. 49–50). Although we do not go into detail here, we would like to point out that humans should critically examine the meaning(s) of words like "improved" regarding who defines such a term and who benefits from its use. In this context, we can conceive of livestock genetic science as a site of new and unrecognized politics, where forms of biopower control and manipulate nonhumans.

In 1983 at Harvard University, scientists Philip Leder and Timothy Stewart gave life to a posthuman child (Haraway, 1997), the OncoMouse, a genetically engineered laboratory animal model for breast cancer research. The OncoMouse, along with other anthropogenic and transgenic lab-born animals such as "cybrids, and neo-morts" (Scala, 2012, p. 40), embodies the idealized border of the natural and the artificial, of the living being and the non-living techno-being: "as a model, the transgenic mouse is both a trope and a tool that reconfigures biological knowledge, laboratory practice, property law, economic fortunes and collective personal hopes and fears" (Haraway, 1997, p. 47). The United States patented the OncoMouse on April 12, 1988, making it the first animal to receive such patent protection. From then on, mice have become the most commonly chosen animal in laboratory research precisely because they mature early and breed quickly, making them easy to reproduce in large scale and serial forms. Moreover, their genome has been fully mapped, showing similar traits to humans (Kirk, 2016, p. 131). In this sense, the mouse body becomes the perfect raw material to be "explored, colonized, and mined" (Scala, 2012, p. 41) for human purposes. Therefore, after the OncoMouse we observe a proliferation of bioengineered mice. These include "Smart mice," who with their enhanced memory imply future enhancement of human intelligence; the "Schwarzenegger mice," whose bodies grow after the injection of a gene linked to muscle growth; and finally, "fearless mice," who may be used to create new treatments for people suffering from phobias or anxieties (Davies, 2013).

The OncoMouse, genetically modified to have an active cancer gene, is a nonhuman animal with an expiration date, only created for human scientific purposes within oncological (that is, cancer) research. Like farmed animals, the OncoMouse is born to die. Donna Haraway (1997) defines the OncoMouse as a figure of secular technoscientific salvation, a promise of progress and scientific enhancement in "the biotechnical war on cancer" (p. 8). However, as Haraway explains, we should think about the OncoMouse as an object of science and a subject heavily invested with human values, goals, and desires. As Weisberg argues, transgenic animals join the ranks of the "crippled monstrosities" (2015, p. 34) that capitalism has so indifferently produced over the centuries. They represent the objects of human mental property by becoming (despite themselves) a sacrificial victim of science and casualties of the manipulative and ideologically loaded term of "sacrifice" (Haraway, 2008). Therefore, these humanized mice, as well as other modified animals—fast-growing salmons, heat-resistant Slick (TM) cows, hyper-muscled cattle, Friendly (TM) Mosquitoes, and pigs growing human organs—are only some of the many new life forms that have appeared from corporate and university laboratories around the world, all promising to "lubricate the circuits of capital accumulation" in myriad ways (Borg & Policante, 2022, p. 4).

The path in the monstrous world of industrial production continues with broiler chickens, the hopeless monsters of practical animal husbandry (Piazzesi, 2018, p. 71), representing a remarkable example of a human-centered reconfigured world. Following the Chicken-of-Tomorrow Program in the early 1950s, which aimed to encourage the development of higher meat-yielding birds, and the sequencing of chicken genomes in 2004, humans have induced radical monstrous changes in chickens. "Broilers" are indeed chickens shaped by and unable to live without intensive human intervention. Humans raise chickens for their muscular flesh so rapidly that, within weeks, the birds reach a weight that their delicate joints cannot support. Consequently, they are affected by multiple diseases, osteo-pathologies, problems related to the growth of vital organs (e.g., heart and lungs), and significant changes in their center of gravity. This decreases their life expectancy, making them more vulnerable to numerous external viruses (Twine, 2010).

It is precisely in intensive livestock farms "that the modern process of cutting out, disconnecting or simplifying life takes on monstrous dimensions" (Kuřík, 2019, p. 3). In the multiplication and simplification of industrial animal farming, monstrous figures are born to bring us messages of death and failure. However, they are not viewed this way within the industry. Products of human hubris, these farmed animals develop "numbers of parasites, drug-resistant bacteria, and more virulent diseases" (Tsing et al., 2017, p. 6), individual anomalies, and malformation, attacking even their own creators. Like Frankenstein's creature, the monster turns against them towards us with unexpected consequences. As Kuřík synthesizes, drawing from Latour, the modern human, "in his [*sic*] pursuit of purification of categories, spheres, specializations, lives, and ontological boundaries" (2019, p. 5), is often unable even to process, understand, or control the monsters that humans produce.

Since the broiler chicken industry started, chickens have been, and continue to be, rigorously and selectively bred. To maximize productivity, one must follow the logic of transforming the animal into an "organic machine" and reducing it to a level of operability, as stated by Kuřík (2019, p. 4). This process systematically erases individuality, uniqueness, and variation as they impede capitalism. Massively farmed chickens have always been selected for ease of handling, "biological plasticity, short developmental cycle, fecundity," and their temperament have made them suitable "to a degree of manipulation unrivaled among domestic animals" (Gruen, 2018, p. 27).

As Twine (2010) affirms, in the case of nonhuman domesticated animals, docility is bred through technological forces. Broiler chickens, and other nonhuman animals, are subjected to intensive farming practices that produce docile bodies mainly through spatial restriction and surveillance. In *Discipline and Punish* (1995), Foucault argues that biopower can create docile human bodies through disciplinary forces. Although biopower was not initially designed for intensively farmed animals, we can use its legacy to illustrate how the disciplining of human and nonhuman animal bodies has been intertwined with the development of capitalism. The life of nonhuman animals belongs to the sphere of biopower: we must recognize their collaborative, albeit uneven, and always situated role in structuring "the power relations in which they are brought into being and are always already enmeshed" (Kirk, 2016, p. 131). Therefore, biopower is a "heuristic tool for thinking about power relations across species" (Twine 2010, p. 89).

Treated as mere objects and reduced as things that undergo biotechnological enhancement, nonhuman animals are dismembered through multiple divisions that go beyond their body, reaching the forms of data and codes. As Weisberg argues, the biotechnologically altered animals are locked in an "unresolvable ontological paradox": they are reduced "to sheer materiality and immateriality in the form of computer-generated information/feedback systems, data, and code" (2015, p. 44). Material beings are essentially dematerialized. In fact, nonhuman animals are reduced to and assessed in terms of their transformation into a quantitative and financial statistical output known as "Estimated Breeding Value" calculated along particular performance indices such as longevity, meat, eggs, or milk yield. In this way, nonhuman animals are continually "de-materialized, re-materialized, and dematerialized again, ad infinitum as quantifiable ideality" (p. 45). They are cognitively reduced to a projection of the human mind to be used solely for human purposes.

Reading the bodies of the monstrous creations of the OncoMouse and broiler chickens, it is possible to decrypt an embedded narrative of human supremacy and exceptionalism. These monsters warn us, revealing the contradictions and contraindications of our systems. In the case of chickens, by feeding on their hormone and preservative rich meat, we unleash in ourselves the monsters we have created. Moreover, even people who work in nonhuman animal industries "face additional risks, working long hours for indecent wages and in dangerous conditions, without recourse to basic health care" (Gruen, 2018, p. 28). As far as the OncoMouse is concerned, the intertwined agency between humans and nonhuman animals occurs more intimately within fleshy bodies. To this matter, Nancy Tuana (2008) argues about the consequences of the United States relocating plastics industries to southern states, particularly the region around Mississippi and Louisiana, known as cancer alley. In particular, workers exposed to harmful substances such as P.V.C. have begun contracting extremely deadly forms of cancer. In this sense, Tuana states that the OncoMouse reflects "the flesh of workers in the plastics factories" (2008, p. 202), both victims of the choices of a corrupt elite.

As we have seen, there are entanglements between the lives of cancer patients and the "sacrifice" and death of nonhuman others. Beatriz da Costa—who died of brain cancer in 2012—highlighted this contradiction in her 2011 multimedia installation *Dying for the Other*. The awareness that she was living at the expense of other people's lives is denounced as unacceptable yet necessary. As Anna Tsing says, humans "have twisted the monstrosity against us, conjuring new threats to livability" (2017, p. 6) and new horizons of death. These monsters remind us that the lives of nonhuman animals are intertwined with those of humans, for better or worse, but intertwined nonetheless. As Tsing states, "monsters are bodies that fall into bodies," and "the art of telling monstrosity requires stories that fall into stories" (p. 10). This applies to humans as well as nonhumans.

## The Cultural Creation of Human Monsters

> Monsters are made, not born.
> —Calafell (2015, p. 1)

Having looked at how nonhuman animals can become monsters due to human interference, this section will show how humans, too, can be subjected to forms of anthropogenic monstrosity. While human activities materially produce nonhuman monsters, human monsters are ideologically created by human discourses on our differences; nevertheless, both are created in the same general anthropocentric and speciesist ideological system. To exemplify the cultural creation of human monsters, two cultural texts are analyzed: the fictional character of Animal in Indra Sinha's book *Animal's People* (2007), and the autobiographical experience of the philosopher Paul Preciado in *Can The Monster Speak?* (2021).

### Animal's People

Animal is a six-year-old orphan child who lost the ability to stand on two legs due to poisoning from a chemical leak in the city of Khaufpur, caused by a U.S. company. The name Animal is a degrading nickname given to him by his peers due to his physical condition. This process of animalization happens because Animal's body is not aligned with the Western conception of the proper human body. But why should being considered an animal be an insult? Of course, it need not be, but culturally it is derogatory because it means, for the majority of people, "to be removed of what one considers one's proper place in a speciesist hierarchical system and denied privileges associated with human status" (Matsuoka & Sorenson, 2021, p. 115).

Nevertheless, while growing up, Animal decided to reclaim his nonhumanity by renaming himself this way. By doing that, Animal wants to highlight the similarity between his own abjected condition and one of any other animal and the benefits and duties that a human with full subject status possesses (Parry, 2017, p. 49). Moreover, he also tried to forget about his past bipedal life by saying, "I used to be a human once. So I'm told. I don't remember it myself" (Sinha, 2007, p. 1). To what extent can Animal be considered an anthropogenic monster in this process of animalization?

Firstly, it's important to underline that Animal's condition is not solely based on his (perceived) disability, but it also derives from his social condition of being an impoverished child living in a colonized country (Reggio, 2018, p. 133). Because of his extreme poverty, he cannot afford the procedures to regain the ability to stand on two legs (Reggio, 2018, p. 134), and he is obliged to scavenge food from restaurant bins to survive (Parry, 2017, p. 27). Moreover, the environmental degradation from the activity of the United States corporation in Khaufpur is how his body becomes colonized so that the mutilation of his body comes from the penetration and violation by industrialized imperial forces (p. 56). Because of that, he can be considered an anthropogenic monster, whose characteristics are dictated mainly by human (ir)responsibility.

However, Animal wants to reclaim his animality and, therefore, his monstrosity by declaring: "stay four-foot, I'm the one and only Animal" (Sinha, 2007, p. 398). As Derrida asserts, when the term "animal" is used to offend, it is a word instituted by humans to give themselves the power to describe other living things (2008, p. 23). By reappropriating the term, Animal can detach from its offensiveness and create a new dimension of its meaning. In this way, monstrosity can become empowering among marginalized groups once it is recognized as a mechanism instituted by colonial discipline to Other our relative embodied differences (LeMaster, 2016, p. 184).

## Can the Monster Speak?

The second story is a speech that philosopher Paul Preciado gave in November 2019 at the *École de la Cause Freudienne*'s annual conference in Paris in front of 3,500 psychoanalysts and transcribed in the book *Can the Monster Speak?*. At the beginning of his speech about his life as a trans man, Preciado talks about his condition as the subject of an "impossible metamorphosis," deriving from clinical beliefs and practices that depict trans people as incapable of resolving an Oedipus complex and overcoming penis envy. It is precisely these discourses that have transformed him into a monster:

> It is from the position assigned to me by you as a mentally ill person that I address you, an ape-human in a new era. I am the monster who speaks to you. The monster you have created with your discourse and your clinical practices. (Preciado, 2021, p. 12)

Preciado uses two nonhuman metaphors in this statement, describing himself as both "an ape-human" and "the monster." Through these metaphors, Preciado can outline human-imposed animality and monstrosity as part of his identitarian pattern, since humans normally classify themselves using "I am" by asserting a categorial identity that refers to symbolic ways used to define themselves in relation to a group (Hart & Long, 2011).

The monstrous identity described by Preciado detaches from the concept of the gender/sex binarism: a monster is neither a woman nor a man, but "is one who lives in transition. One whose face, body and behaviors cannot yet be considered true in a predetermined regime of knowledge and power" (p. 42). Therefore, for Preciado, gender transitioning is not a static process but a continuous shift. This theory is also shared by Judith Butler, to whom the book is dedicated, in her discourse regarding the performativity of the body (1986). Preciado wants to overcome the hetero-patriarchal system, calling for a radical transformation in psychoanalysis. Mutants and monsters are the ones that can break boundaries and contribute to "the collective construction of a different epistemology of the living human body" (2021, p. 30):

> Faced with the epistemological transformation already underway, you will have to decide, ladies and gentlemen, psychoanalysts of France, what you are going to do, where you intend to place yourselves, in which "cage" you would like to be imprisoned, and how you plan to play your discursive and clinical cards in a process as important as this. (p. 30)

Therefore, the monster can appear in racist, ableist, and trans/homophobic discourses as a metaphor for the less than human, a tool to take away subjectivity and to animalize. But the monster, simultaneously threatening and promising, is an ambivalent figure that invites—begs, even—to be recognized (Shildrick, 2002, p. 5). It calls attention to itself by being outside the norm and, as such, can draw attention to societies' exclusionary dimensions and expose the frailty of Western modes of thought. Animal and Preciado have decided to embrace their monstrosity, finding strength in it. Despite the usual negative connotation of the term, marginalized groups are reclaiming their difference and appropriating monstrosity as a means of resistance, as well as a constructive political strategy able to disrupt and confound long-standing systems of power based on practices of methodical exclusion, repression, and silencing of the so-called "others" (Phillips, 2014, p. 20).

## Monstrous Alliances

> I bid my hideous progeny go forth and prosper.
> —Shelley (1831, p. 193)

In this final section, we further develop the idea of embracing monstrosity by arguing that it can provide new perspectives on achieving total liberation. Monstrosity can create new alliances and possibilities, taking us on a "monstrous turn" (Haraway, 1992, p. 304):

> The horizon where the monsters dwell might well be imagined as the visible edge of the hermeneutic circle itself: the monstrous offers an escape from its hermetic path, an invitation to explore new spirals, new and interconnected methods of perceiving the world. (Cohen, 2020, p. 40)

Monsters signify "the otherness of possible worlds, or possible versions of ourselves, not yet realised" (Shildrick, 2002, p. 129). By disrupting categories and boundaries, monsters show new versions of reality. As Butler underlines, "to intervene in the name of transformation means precisely to disrupt what has become settled knowledge and knowable reality" (2004, p. 28). When monsters enter into the domain of reality, we cannot just assimilate them into prevailing norms, "the norms themselves can become rattled, display their instability, and became open to resignification" (p. 28). This is why monsters can reveal unexpected pathways: through these monstrous turns, they create multispecies alliances, question the concept of natural/unnatural as well as other binaries, and dismantle hierarchies, leading to the liberation of both humans and nonhumans.

Trans* scholar and activist Susan Stryker epitomizes this monstrous turn in the essay *My Words to Victor Frankenstein above the Village of Chamounix* (1994). First, Stryker acknowledges that the trans* body is an unnatural body: "it is a technological construction. It is flesh torn apart and sewn together again in a shape other than that in which it was born" (p. 245). From this condition, she finds a deep affinity with the monster in Mary Shelley's *Frankenstein*: "Like the monster, I am too often perceived as less than fully human due to the means of my embodiment" (p. 245). Stryker uses the scene in *Frankenstein* in which the monster speaks back to its creator as a metaphor for the encounter between her radicalized trans* subjectivity and the normative claims of medicine which created her monstrosity. As underlined by Stef Shuster (2021), in the process of medicalization certain bodies or behaviors are labeled as nonconforming and, at the same time, placed under greater surveillance.

Nevertheless, in this dialogue, Stryker affirms the power of her monstrous body as "a site of agency that negotiates a queerly complex relationship to nature, origin narratives, and language" (Koch-Rein, 2014, p. 134). Stryker declares: "I am a transsexual, and therefore I am a monster" (1994, p. 246). In doing so, she reclaims the words "monster," "creature," and "unnatural" for the trans* community, just as the words "dyke," "fag," "queer," "slut," and "whore" have been reclaimed by other marginalized groups. Reclamation leads to empowerment: "by embracing and accepting them, [...] we may dispel their ability to harm us" (p. 246). Furthermore, this linguistic reclamation also became a tool to question the structure of society further and perceived reality itself:

> A creature, after all, in the dominant tradition of Western European culture, is nothing other than a created being, a made thing. The affront you humans take at being called a "creature" results from the threat the term poses to your status as "lords of creation," beings elevated above mere material existence. As in the case of being called "it," being called a "creature" suggests the lack or loss of a superior personhood. I find no shame, however, in acknowledging my egalitarian relationship with non-human material Being; everything emerges from the same matrix of possibilities. (pp. 246–7)

That makes monsters dangerous: they show that things can be otherwise than they are or were thought to be. They come to announce the overturning of reality and reveal and imagine a new one (or ones) in which there are no hierarchies nor categorizations: creatures are all equally made and equally un/natural. Stryker does not feel degraded in being called a creature. Indeed, by recognizing new egalitarian relationships with nonhumans, she neutralizes and even inverts the process of animalization. The system that condones and allows not only the discrimination of human minorities but also the arbitrary abuse of nonhuman animals is a direct consequence of human exceptionalism. But, once we see equality in animalization (and not degradation), we might pursue liberation for all animals—human and nonhuman—together and simultaneously.

Nevertheless, this liberation might not be peaceful. Stryker's call to her "fellow creatures" is also raging: "like the monster's as well, my exclusion from the human community fuels a deep and abiding rage" (Stryker, 1994, p. 245). She claims and re-channels the trans* rage "against a culture that naturalizes the sexual binarism and denies gendered recognition to trans* people" (Koch-Rein, 2014, p. 134). We should use this rage to speak loud and clear, to make trans* voices heard and respected. Drawing from Stryker's claim, the Italian trans* activist Filo Sottile invokes a transfeminist alliance among monstrous creatures in order to riot:

> We monstrous creatures do not want to tell you that everything is fine, nor to reassure you; we are not going to heal, normalize, redeem ourselves; we are not harmless and we do not guarantee you from poisoning, contagion, contamination [...]. We are heralds and tambourines: we come to announce the subversion of nature, the fall—under furious blows of tails, legs, fangs, trunks, tentacles— of the heteropatriarchy. (2020, p. 16)

Like Haraway's vampires (1997, p. 215), monsters contaminate and pollute; they are vectors of transfection and transformation. The idea of poisoning and contagion threatens oppressive phantasies of order, purity, and categorization. Thus, monsters make taxonomies impossible and boundaries leaky. They exist within entangled, sticky, messy, and turbid relationships. (Timeto, 2018). In this way, monsters disrupt the dichotomy of natural/ unnatural because nature itself is already inappropriate/d and monstrous (Timeto, 2019): "the same anarchic Womb has birthed us both" (Stryker, 1994, p. 247).

Once we realize that we already are in "the womb of a pregnant monster" (Haraway, 1992, p. 295) and our world is made of "companion monsters" (p. 300), we can start making inappropriate/d kin and alliances, entering multispecies conversations. In fact, Sottile uses—not by chance—zoomorphic language when talking about the subversion of nature. The fall of this heteropatriarchal, anthropocentric, speciesist society—that oppresses both human and nonhuman animals—can happen only if we include nonhuman agencies and subjectivities in our alliances (Martelli, 2021; El Khoury & Jacquemin, 2022). Therefore, we envision a total liberation based on multispecies care and solidarity practices, becoming-with other-than-humans in monstrous, "non-natalist and off-category" (Haraway, 2016, p. 209) relationships.

## References

Acampora, R. (2021). Zoögogy of the oppressed. *Journal for Critical Animal Studies*, *18*(1), 4–18.

Beal, T. (2002). *Religion and its monsters*. Routledge.

Borg, E., & Policante, A. (2022). *Mutant ecologies: Manufacturing life in the age of genomic capital.* Pluto Press.

Botting, F. (2003). Metaphors and monsters. *Journal for Cultural Research, 7*(4), 339–365.

Butler, J. (1986). Sex and gender in Simone de Beauvoir's *Second sex. Yale French Studies, 72*, 35–49, https://doi.org/10.2307/2930225.

Butler, J. (2004). *Undoing gender.* Routledge.

Calafell, B. M. (2015). *Monstrosity, performance, and race in contemporary culture.* Peter Lang.

Cohen, J. J. (2020). Monster culture (Seven Theses). In J. J. Cohen (Ed.), *Monster theory: Reading culture* (pp. 37–56). University of Minnesota Press.

Davies, G. (2013). Writing biology with mutant mice: The monstrous potential of post genomic life. *Geoforum, 48,* 268–278.

Derrida, J. (2008). *The animal that therefore I am (Perspectives in Continental Philosophy).* M. Mallet (Ed.); D. Wills (Trans.). Fordham University Press.

El Khoury, M., & Jacquemin, K. (2022). Agency and suffering in animal studies and in animal liberation. In N. Poirier, A. J. Nocella, & A. Bernatchez (Eds.), *Emerging new voices in critical animal studies: Vegan studies for total liberation* (pp. 29–38). Peter Lang.

Filippi, M., & Dal Lago, A. (2018). Premessa. *aut aut, 380,* 6–12.

Foucault, M. (1995). *Discipline & Punish: The birth of the prison.* Vintage Books.

Foucault, M. (2005). *The order of things: an archaeology of the human sciences.* Routledge.

Gruen, L. (2018). *Critical terms for animal studies.* University of Chicago Press.

Haraway, D. J. (1992). The promises of monsters: A regenerative politics for inappropriate/d others. In Grossberg, L., Nelson, C. & Treichler, P.A. (Eds.), *Cultural studies* (pp. 295–337). Routledge.

Haraway, D. J. (1997). *Modest witness.* Routledge.

Haraway. D. J. (2008). *When species meet.* University of Minnesota Press.

Haraway, D. J. (2016). *Staying with the trouble: Making kin in the chthulucene.* Duke University Press.

Hart, K. R., & Long Jr., J. H. (2011). Animal metaphors and metaphorizing animals: An integrated literary, cognitive, and evolutionary analysis of making and partaking of stories. *Evolution: Education and Outreach, 4*(1), 52–63, https://doi.org/10.1007/s12052-010-0301-6

Kirk, R. G. (2016). Knowing sentient subjects: Humane experimental technique and the constitution of care and knowledge in laboratory animal science. In *Humans, animals and biopolitics* (pp. 121–137). Routledge.

Koch-Rein, A. (2014). Monster. *TSQ, 1*(1–2), 134–135. https://doi.org/10.1215/23289252-2399821

Kristeva, J. (1982). *Powers of horror: An essay on abjection.* Roudiez L. S. (Trans.). Columbia University Press.

Kuřík, B. (2019). Monster farm: Parameters of life in the plantationocene. In *Large-Scale Lifestock Farming Series*, Institute of Anxiety. http://www.institutuzkosti.cz/events/velkochovy?src=cz

LeMaster, B. (2016). Monstrosity, performance, and race in contemporary culture. *Text and Performance Quarterly, 36*(2–3), 182–186. https://doi.org/10.1080/10462937.2016.1223874

Martelli, M. (2021, March 3). Critical pedagogy beyond humanism after Paulo Freire. *just-wondering.* https://www.justwondering.io/critical-pedagogy-beyond-humanism/

Matsuoka, A., & Sorenson, J. (2021). Like an animal: Tropes for delegitimization. In N. Khazaal, & N. Almiron (Eds.), *Like an animal: Critical animal studies approaches to borders, displacement, and othering* (pp. 101–124). https://doi.org/10.1163/9789004440654_005

Mittman, A. S. (2013). Introduction: The impact of monsters and monster studies. In A. S. Mittman (Ed.), *The Ashgate research companion to monsters and the monstrous* (pp. 1–14). Ashgate.

Parry, C. (2017). *Other animals in twenty-first century fiction.* Palgrave Macmillan.

Phillips, R. (2014). Abjection. *TSQ, 1*(1–2), 19–21. https://doi.org/10.1215/23289252-2399821

Preciado, P. (2021). *Can the monster speak? Report to an Academy of Psychoanalysts.* Faber and Faber.

Piazzesi, B. (2018). 'Dans des voies insolites.' Il mostro zootecnico nella prima metà dell'Ottocento. *aut aut, 380,* 65–82.

Reggio, M. (2018). A quattro zampe. Note su animalizzazione, disabilità e colonialismo. *aut aut, 380,* 132–145.

Scala, W. M. (2012). *Fairy tales, the monster, and the genetic imagination.* Vanderbilt University Press.

Shelley, M. (1831/2017). Introduction to *Frankenstein.* In D. H. Guston, E. Finn, & J. S. Robert (Eds.), *Frankenstein: Annotated for scientists, engineers, and creators of all kinds* (p. 189–194). Mit Press.

Shildrick, M. (2002). *Embodying the monster: Encounters with the vulnerable self.* Sage.

Shuster, S. M. (2021). *Trans medicine: The emergence and practice of treating gender.* New York University Press.

Sinha, I. (2007). *Animal's people.* Simon and Schuster.

Soper, K. (1999). Of OncoMice and female/men: Donna Haraway on cyborg ontology. *Capitalism Nature Socialism, 10*(3), 73–80.

Sottile, F. (2020). *La mostruositrans.* Eris.

Steinbock, E., Szczygielska, M., & Wagner, A. C. (Eds.). (2021). *Tranimacies: Intimate links between animal and trans\* studies.* Routledge.

Stryker, S. (1994). My words to Victor Frankenstein above the village of Chamounix: Performing transgender rage. *GLQ, 1*(3), 237–54.

Timeto, F. (2018). Donna Haraway e la teratotropìa degli altri in/appropriati. *aut aut, 380,* 127–139.

Timeto, F. (2019, September 24). *Dizionario per lo Chthulucene*. Not. https://not.neroe
ditions.com/dizionario-lo-chthulucene/

Tsing, A. L., Bubandt, N., Gan, E., & Swanson, H. A. (Eds.). (2017). *Arts of living on a damaged planet: Ghosts and monsters of the Anthropocene*. University of Minnesota Press.

Tuana, N. (2008). Viscous porosity: Witnessing Katrina. *Material Feminisms*, 188–213.

Twine, R. (2010). *Animals as biotechnology: Ethics, sustainability and critical animal studies*. Routledge.

Weisberg, Z. (2015). Biotechnology as end game: Ontological and ethical collapse in the "biotech century." *Nanoethics, 9*(1), 39–54.

# 3 Animal Liberation through Procreative Justice

Nandita Bajaj & Kirsten Stade

As the current era of the Anthropocene witnesses the sixth great extinction event and domesticated animals confront institutionalized terror in expanding farms, laboratories, and commercial breeding facilities, it is clear that both our voracious consumption and our rapidly growing population have placed us in severe imbalance with nonhuman communities (Bradshaw et al., 2021). Yet coercive population control efforts in the past and present have made overpopulation a taboo subject. The silencing of discourse and suppression of action surrounding overpopulation, the vast majority of which has been rights-based family planning efforts, have undermined the effectiveness of animal advocacy and conservation efforts (Bajaj & Stade, 2023).

A humane education framework, which links human rights, animal protection, and environmental sustainability and seeks to replace inhumane and unsustainable systems with solutions that enable people, nonhuman animals, and nature to thrive (Institute for Humane Education, 2021), is essential to the advancement of critical animal studies (CAS). By acknowledging that systems of oppression are multipronged (one system harms multiple communities), and intersectional (multiple systems harm various communities), this approach generates change through education and advocacy. Humane education lets us understand that the institutions that subjugate and destroy the nonhuman world are also responsible for the forces that drive overpopulation and compel people to bear children. These forces combine and are collectively known as pronatalism, the ideology that sanctifies procreation through social structures and expectations.

First, it is essential to acknowledge the legacy of institutional racism, ableism, sexism, classism, and nationalism that has driven centuries of injustice, including reproductive abuses, against traditionally marginalized communities. Echoes of that legacy are unfortunately still present and continue to undermine many communities' personal and reproductive self-determination. At the same time, however, these same forces are also responsible for perpetuating heteronormative and oppressive pronatalist pressures. Such pressures constitute a form of reproductive coercion just as egregious but more pervasive and prevalent as those that sought to restrict reproduction. Using humane education as a framework, we show how human population pressures undermine the rights and well-being of humans and nonhumans alike. We rely on a growth-based model of expansionism that thrives on the reproductive and social exploitation of those already marginalized.

Pronatalism is often a coercive societal pressure to procreate. It is a fundamental component of the world hegemonic growth model that seeks to reinforce and expand the myriad power structures ranging from religious, tribal, ethnocentric, and nationalistic identities to the military, and capitalism, all of which benefit from population growth. Underlying this growth model is human supremacy, a belief that Earth and its natural abundance and processes exist for human consumption, exploitation, management, and domination. Human supremacy and the pronatalism that stems from it contribute to the cascade of current social, ecological, and intergenerational crises. A shift from anthropocentrism to ecocentrism requires critically examining pronatalism as incompatible with nonhuman rights. We urge resolution not in the form of anti-natalism that argues humans should not reproduce but rather from a position of anti-pronatalism (Purdy, 2019). Anti-pronatalism differs from anti-natalism in that it liberates people from patriarchal social norms and allows for autonomous and responsible reproductive choices to emerge while not being against all reproduction.

## Gains by Vegan and Vegetarian Movements Offset by Population Growth

In the past half-century, as the contemporary animal rights movement has gained traction and made strides toward the uptake of vegan diets, the number of land animals slaughtered globally increased from 12 billion to 80 billion (Ritchie et al., 2017). Global fish and seafood production has quadrupled (Alexandratos & Bruinsma, 2012). These trends existed in parallel to the world's population more than doubling. Meanwhile, ecosystems, wildlife, and ecological support services have declined because entire biomes have been replaced by a few species of animals and plants that humans in predominantly industrialized countries hold captive to feed humans or other animals. The largest producers of seafood—China, Indonesia, India, Vietnam, and the United States (Ritchie & Roser, 2021)—are among the highest-population countries in the world. Asia, which is home to some of the highest-population countries as well as the fastest growth in per-capita income, has become the center for global meat production, accounting for up to 45 percent of the estimated over 70 billion land animals killed for food in 2018 (Ritchie et al., 2017).

Suppose these trends continue as projected to where the human population reaches 10 billion by 2050. In that case, restoring balance to arrive at a state where other life forms can thrive will require altering consumption patterns and restoring balance to our human population (Crist et al., 2017). While the world's population grows by roughly 80 million annually, the middle class is the most rapidly growing segment. This growing class accounts for two-thirds of overall household consumption (Kharas & Hamel, 2018), making it a major contributor to the direct consumption of animals killed for food, the environmental impacts of the industries that kill them, and the crops grown to feed them (Crist et al., 2017).

Shifting consumption patterns by redistributing wealth, reducing consumption, and converting wholesale to vegan diets, while helpful and necessary, still leaves the globe in an overshoot. This impedes our ability to cultivate and preserve a basic standard of thriving for all communities. Overshoot, defined as human demands that exceed the Earth's regenerative capacity, has left us in a state where we consume 70 percent more than the Earth can provide sustainably (GFN, 2022). It is important to note that this represents the Earth as a whole, and various regions contribute more or less to this result. As John Tallent shows in their chapter in this volume, only a handful of countries contribute to the gross inequality in resource use. It also produces real and manufactured scarcity. Overshoot stems from large populations consuming locally and high-consumption industrialized powers exploiting distant vulnerable people by extracting their natural capital. Overshoot has led to the current ecological meltdown and widespread inequality, food insecurity, poverty, and conflict (Bradshaw et al., 2021).

## *Human Expansion Has Brought Enormous Animal Suffering*

Meat consumption impacts animals far beyond the apparent suffering and loss of life of the individuals consumed. The vast and growing extent of farmed animal agriculture, its consequent destruction or alteration of most of the Earth's land area, and the cataclysmic overfishing of marine environments have pushed global biodiversity to the point of collapse. The magnitude of the biodiversity crisis is apparent from the biomass of terrestrial vegetation diminishing by half and wild animals by 83 percent since the advent of agriculture (Rees, 2020). Of the total biomass of terrestrial vertebrates, 59 percent is represented by livestock, 39 percent by human beings, and about 5 percent by wild mammals, birds, reptiles, and amphibians (Bar-On et al., 2018; Bradshaw et al., 2021).

A foremost driver of this tremendous loss of biodiversity is deforestation and habitat destruction, primarily for agriculture which is the primary threat to 86 percent of the species at risk of extinction (Benton et al., 2021). Roughly 40 percent of the planet's ice-free land area has been overtaken by crop production and livestock grazing (Crist et al., 2017), much of it attributable to large-scale, commercial agriculture used to grow meat, animal products and processed foods for wealthy populations. Cattle ranching and oil palm, soy, and cocoa production account for 40 percent of global deforestation (Brondizio et al., 2019). In the Western United States, ranching causes widespread and well-documented impacts on native biodiversity, water quality, soil and watershed health, and climate (Poff et al., 2011). Ranching also harms native wildlife through the fences that obstruct wildlife migration. The government-subsidized annual killing of millions of native species deemed a threat to the farmed animals whose short, brutal lives generate profits for a politically favored industry (USDA APHIS, 2021; Grazing Facts, 2022.

This tremendous modification of native ecosystems and habitats by extensive, land-based food systems calls into question the current enthusiasm for the potential of smallholder farming and agroecology to preserve biodiversity and ecosystem services (Brondizio et al., 2019). The continued growth of the human population and its expected concentration in cities will mean that demand for food cannot be met except through intensified agricultural operations that demand greater fossil fuel and nutrient inputs, including concentrated animal feeding operations (C.A.F.O.s) or factory farms (Crist et al., 2017). This practice originated in the United States and is increasingly being adopted worldwide to meet the needs of the growing middle class. Globally, livestock operations contribute approximately 16.5 percent of greenhouse gases—at a minimum—as a major contributor to climate change (Twine, 2021).

The vast numbers of commercially farmed and ranched animals in the (over)developed world have made these animals the focus of the animal rights movement and their environmental impacts the focus of conservation efforts. Much of the devastation of native wildlife populations in the Global South is driven not by the food needs of local human populations but by export markets serving the (over)developed world. However, subsistence agriculture to grow crops and graze livestock by local people in "developing" countries has immensely impacted wildlife, especially in tropical regions that house the Earth's biodiversity. Astonishingly, globally, local subsistence agriculture is responsible for 33 percent of deforestation while large-scale commercial agriculture is responsible for 40 percent (Brondizio et al., 2019).

Another serious but seldom discussed impact on biodiversity is the bushmeat trade. Bushmeat hunting occurs primarily in the Global South. While bushmeat hunting primarily allows humans to acquire meat for human consumption, it also encourages the acquisition of live animals for the pet trade and animal parts used in traditional medicine or ornamentation. Bushmeat hunting threatens the greatest number of species in Asia and Africa. The loss of these species has cascading effects throughout their ecosystems, impacting their functioning and other species' survival (Ripple et al., 2016). Bushmeat hunting is a subset of direct overexploitation of species via hunting and fishing. It also results from pressures imposed by overdeveloped countries participating in a global capitalist economy.

Roughly six million wild ungulates are killed by game hunters yearly in the Northern Hemisphere; hunting and poaching, driven by the growing human population, are placing extraordinary pressure on large mammals worldwide (Brondizio et al., 2019). Meanwhile, overfishing, driven largely by population increase, is the most significant force of marine biodiversity loss (Ritchie & Roser, 2021), with small fisheries accounting for over 90 percent of commercial fishers and nearly half of the fish caught globally (Brondizio et al., 2019).

## Population Denialism Undermines Progress toward Environmental and Animal Justice

As noted above, these trends have only intensified over the past fifty years with new hunting and fishing technologies, new markets for animal products opened by globalization, the growth of the middle class, and the human population explosion. After spending the first 10,000 years as a species with a population of well under one billion, our population grew exponentially to eight billion in 200 years thanks to fossil fuels and medical advances that increased life expectancy. Nevertheless, seldom is human population growth acknowledged as a primary factor in animal and ecological harm. In recent decades any effort to address human population growth has been met with outright hostility from many in the conservation, development, and animal rights arenas (Kopnina & Washington, 2016; Coole, 2021). This aversion is understandable but often stems from an uncritical overgeneralization of previous measures.

Admittedly, many past efforts to control human fertility were coercive in nature and stemmed from a legacy of institutional racism, ableism, sexism, classism, and nationalism. Eugenics campaigns in the United States and Europe in the first third of the twentieth century used forced sterilization to control the reproduction of targeted groups for racist, ableist, and classist ends. China's one-child policy, and forced sterilization in Puerto Rico and India, used similar coercive means to "control" their population swiftly, victimizing the most marginalized in these societies (Briggs,1998; Potts, 2014). These programs were gross violations of reproductive rights and tainted all future population efforts, no matter how rights-based and voluntary, with the blemish of coercion. This association dismisses the vast majority of international family planning efforts that have been rights-based and voluntary and that have played a dramatic role in elevating the status of women and girls by affording them control over their own fertility (Sinding, 2008; Campbell & Bedford, 2009; Potts, 2014). This dismissal of all population stabilization efforts, arising from fear that they would inevitably lead to reproductive abuses, gave way to a different kind of reproductive coercion—pronatalism.

Pronatalism is the social and institutional bias to have children and leads to unrelenting pressures experienced by individuals to bear children in pursuit of certain agendas. Pronatalism is a ubiquitous force across societies that militates against authentic reproductive decisions that allow us to create the relation(ship)s we truly want, in harmony with the web of life. It ranges from religious commandments to "be fruitful and multiply," to political mandates to bear children for economic, nationalistic, and tribal ends to the cultural exaltation of biological parenthood (Bajaj & Stade, 2023). While pronatalism has been a background assumption for centuries, silencing population discourse has allowed it to surface more strongly.

## The Animal Rights Movement Must Recognize Intersectional Population-Driven Injustices

The framework of humane education requires us to maximize our advocacy efforts toward justice for people, nonhuman animals, and the planet by connecting the dots among different systems of oppression and addressing them collectively. The systems of growth that benefit the most from animal exploitation are the same ones that also rely on continual population growth and as such, turn to coercive pronatalism to realize that goal. This framework demonstrates that a vegan way of life includes not just our consumptive choices, but forces a much larger, existential conversation about the impact of human expansionism on other species. It includes a continuum of individual and collective choices, including procreation, that seek to minimize suffering while maximizing individual and collective freedom. The thrust of such transformative change must include critiquing, deconstructing, and replacing the ideology of pronatalism, which constitutes a form of oppression that institutions use to exploit reproductive capacity as a means to ends beyond mere reproduction. It has spurred human population growth that has more than undone limited (but still meaningful) progress made by environmental activism, animal rights, and vegan movements while also obstructing progress toward planetary balance and equity between humans and other species. An intersectional examination of the forces that have held back the realization of animal liberation, gender equality, and elevating the most vulnerable and marginalized human and nonhuman communities requires that we address the ubiquitous forces of pronatalism that operate at every level human society.

## *Pronatalism Exerts Its Influence in Many Forms*

Pronatalism's influence is most strongly experienced by women within the family structural unit and stems from a desire to maintain a genealogical legacy or to conform to cultural traditions. The inability or refusal to bear children can lead to disownment, domestic violence, divorce, social stigmatization, and economic marginalization (Purdy, 2019; Wells & Heinsch, 2019). In lower- and middle-income countries where birth rates are the highest, the influence of pronatalism may be best captured because over 200 million women have an unmet need for contraception. While often assumed to result from a lack of contraceptive availability, this phenomenon is largely a product of harmful pronatalist norms ranging from stigmatizing contraceptive use by family members or health authorities to sexual violence and reproductive coercion (UNFPA, 2022). We wish to emphasize that anti-pronatalism is concerned with meeting the needs of people as stipulated by themselves, not coercing people into making choices against their will.

Cultural pressures exerted by peer groups, popular media, and celebrity figures to conform to family choices presented as ideals of personal and creative fulfillment also play an enormous role in childbearing decisions (Barrett et al., 2020). Popular media incessantly promotes parenthood as the ultimate life choice through glorified depictions of pregnancy and parenthood and the perpetuation of myths surrounding the "biological clock" and virility. The capitalist notion that women can "have it all" that is sympathetically perpetuated by a select group of elite women classified as neoliberal feminists strengthen the grip of pronatalism, whose harmful effects are most experienced by those on the margins of society who cannot afford to "have it all"

(Rottenberg, 2017). In addition, this fixation on "family" as defined by the presence of biological children results in the marginalization of those who do not fit the dominant narrative, such as single adults, childfree people, L.Q.B.T.Q.I.A.+ relationships, adoptive families and other "nonnormative" relations (Bajaj & Stade, 2023).

One perspective largely missing from these cultural narratives until recently is that of parents who regret having children. While women without children are frequently warned of the possibility of regretting their absence, our cultural narrative has only begun to break through the powerful taboo on parental regret. Such regret is much more common than people think it is (or want it to be). Though highly stigmatized and fraught with guilt and shame, parenthood regret is as unequivocal as regret accompanying other major life decisions (Donath, 2015). This is not something to be ashamed of, and it does not mean that regretful parents do not love their children.

Pronatalism also has sympathetic alliances within the medical establishment. The inability to bear a child, whether due to infertility or other medical reasons, can be a source of immense grief and loss for those who authentically wish to experience biological parenthood. These feelings of inadequacy are not only compounded by the cultural stigmatization of childlessness. However, they are also capitalized on by the growing multi-billion-dollar fertility industry aided by neoliberal feminism. Despite opening the possibility of biological parenthood for those unable to conceive, assisted reproductive technologies have their own issues. A growing body of evidence is showing that the proliferation of these largely unregulated technologies across the globe, often of dubious clinical validity and mixed results, has brought about a set of heavy financial, psychological, physical, and emotional burdens on infertile individuals that remain largely unreported (Rottenberg, 2017; Patrizio et al., 2022).

When the fertility industry financially exploits those experiencing a sense of "biological fault," pronatalism likely lurks in the shadows. Pronatalism is also expressed through the medical industrial complex in several other ways. From suggestions by physicians about the "biological clock" and surgeons refusing to perform tubal ligations on women without any children (or vasectomies on young men), to the medicalization of postpartum depression that minimizes any true feelings of pain, grief, ambivalence, or regret, medicalized pronatalism contributes to the lack of reproductive agency for even those living in relatively liberal societies (Lalonde, 2018).

Religious dogma pervades most cultures, with many religious teachings being strongly pronatalist. Stemming from the moral imperative to procreate to fulfill a religious duty, these pressures across the world's largest religions are expressed as exalting parenthood and large families while shaming those who do not or cannot have biological children. Through mandates such as "Be fruitful and multiply and fill the Earth," these traditions deliberately disseminate misinformation about the use of contraceptives and abortion procedures and even impose more coercive measures such as active restriction of contraceptives and family planning services (Carroll, 2012). At their foundation, such narratives promote harmful and rigid notions of gender, such as a "natural" gender binary with each gender's attendant "roles," fueling the oppression of women and L.G.B.T.Q.I.A.+ communities. With a growing trend toward feminism and lowering fertility rates in some countries, right-wing populism has increased globally, reinforcing religion's perpetuation of gender inequality and pronatalist cultural norms that fuel the demographic growth of desired (white) ethnic groups (Bajaj, 2022; Gökarıksel et al., 2019).

Economy-driven pronatalist pressures are exerted through alarmist narratives about a "baby bust" that threatens the economy if women do not fulfill their duty of producing the next generation of workers and taxpayers. Through tactics ranging from offering lump-sum baby bonuses and tax credits for having large families, to sanctions on reproductive health care services and outright bans on abortions, nations reduce individuals to reproductive vessels in order to stave off threats of a "demographic winter" or to grow the Gross Domestic Product (G.D.P.)—a strategy that has been appropriately referred to as a pyramid scheme (McMahon, 2019; Bajaj, 2022). Advertising and media apply their own pressures by selling pregnancy, babies, and families as desirable—messages that are so ubiquitous they cannot help but influence many women and couples, even if their end is simply to sell more diapers or minivans (Carroll, 2012).

Adding to the omnipresent cultural pressures to reproduce are pressures by political leaders propagated directly or through sympathetic media. Political leaders, driven by a perceived need to grow the tax base, pressure from the military-industrial complex to maintain a strong military, or ethnocentric motivations to win a "demographic war" over a competing ethnicity or tribe, may resort to a range of pronatalist policies. These policies, ranging from bans on abortion or contraception to stigmatization of nontraditional families or queer communities, to subsidies for assisted reproductive technologies for politically preferred ethnic groups, exert an enormous influence on the fertility decisions women and families feel compelled to make (Donath et al., 2022; Bajaj & Stade, 2023). More than 50 countries have policies to increase birth rates for religious, nationalistic, or economic reasons. Indeed, countries with explicitly pronatalist policies rose from 10 percent in 1976 to 28 percent in 2015 (UNDESA, 2021).

The essence of pronatalism is that it uses reproduction to realize external agendas. It exerts a form of reproductive coercion whose strongest impacts are often experienced by the most vulnerable. The coercion that in the past forced women to give up their reproductive autonomy in the name of population control has given way to pronatalist messages that promote an overcorrection to past injustice as a way to reclaim reproductive freedom. These messages fail to deconstruct how deeply and fundamentally pronatalism shapes reproductive decisions and undermines women's genuine autonomy. These seemingly liberated countermeasures, championed among others by feminists and sexual and reproductive health and rights advocates, are being conveniently wielded by patriarchal leaders who benefit from population growth. (Briggs, 1998; Donath et al., 2022).

The social impacts of pronatalism are also heavily borne by those in societies (often women) with little to no personal or reproductive autonomy. These communities are often the most oppressed by patriarchal social structures and imperialist powers that rely on exploiting their natural and human capital. They also suffer the most from degraded natural environments, depleted ecosystem services, and strained human infrastructure that result from unchecked human population growth (Potts, 2014; Kopnina & Washington, 2016).

In countering pronatalism, we are not embracing an antinatalist perspective that no humans should be born. Instead, we embrace anti-pronatalism to promote societal conditions where people are neither pressured into having children nor scorned for having them. We wish for a world in which people can decide to procreate (or not) with maximum autonomy, education, and informed responsibility. A humane education framework allows us to see that this approach addresses multiple intersecting injustices that afflict women, marginalized communities, nonhuman animals, and the planet. Nullifying pronatalism will lead us to a more liberated relationship with our own reproductive choices and a more sustainable population.

### Conclusion: Elevating Anti-Pronatalism and Ecocentrism for Total Liberation

Given the staggering impact of our food systems upon the planet and the growth of that impact along with the size and wealth of the world's population, vegan and animal liberation movements have made relatively little—albeit fundamental—headway in reducing the number of animals killed for food. Additionally, regularly convened international biodiversity summits have done little to improve the fate of wildlife obliterated by these industries. Our efforts toward liberating human and nonhuman animal communities and conserving a rich and diverse global ecosystem—collectively known as total liberation—will always fall short until we address human overpopulation and the pronatalism that drives it.

We have all seen projections, like that of the United Nations, that our population may by the end of this century reach 11 billion or more and that food production will need to double or triple (Crist et al., 2017). These projections have inspired endless conjecture on food systems that may be employed to meet this staggering demand. However, they only sometimes prompt serious discussion of how we may reduce that demand. Likely this is because of the taboo surrounding the topic of human population and a misplaced conflation of all family planning efforts with reproductive coercion.

Family size decisions are currently the product of pronatalist coercion and are enormously responsive to changes in social norms and policies. Full contraceptive access, free health care, and reproductive norm-shifting that counters pronatalist pressures can bring our human population to sustainable levels at which every human can be fed without exterminating most other forms of life (Tucker, 2022; Bajaj & Stade, 2023). This entails a systemic transformation of current world systems.

For far too long, the animal liberation and ecological conservation movements have avoided directly (or at least publicly) addressing human overpopulation, harming the marginalized women who stand to benefit the most from pronatalism's demise. The reason for this absence or silence is often the opposite: people fear further stigmatizing historically maligned groups. This fear is indeed something to be aware of and is understandable but often misplaced. Success depends upon moving beyond this misplaced and damaging self-censorship toward an understanding of ecological and planetary boundaries and a regard for uplifting the human and ecological communities that suffer most from the excesses of our unsustainable population.

From a humane education perspective that draws the links between human rights, animal protection, and environmental sustainability, it is clear that human expansionism is not only a source of the many social and ecological crises we face, but is also premised on social and reproductive injustice. We are advocating a shift to an ecocentric perspective that demands a radical shift in our relationship to our ecosphere—from dominion to reverence and stewardship. In addition to curbing our voracious appetite for carbon, this shift will require shifting from industrial agriculture to genuinely sustainable and humane (vegan) food systems, a planned and gradual shrinking of the world's economies, and a transition to a far smaller human population. Such a transition largely depends upon our concerted effort to neutralize pronatalism so we can make authentic and responsible reproductive decisions that bring us into ecological balance with the entire web of life.

## *References*

Alexandratos, N., & Bruinsma, J. (2012). World agriculture towards 2030/2050: The 2012 revision (Vol. 12, No. 3). *FAO*, Rome: ESA Working paper. http://www.fao.org/docrep/016/ap106e/ap106e.pdf

Bajaj, N. (2022, June 7). Abortion Bans Are a Natural Outgrowth of Coercive Pronatalism. *Ms. Magazine.* https://msmagazine.com/2022/06/07/abortion-bans-coercive-pronatalism-forced-birth/.

Bajaj, N., & Stade, K. (2023). Challenging pronatalism is key to advancing reproductive rights and a sustainable population. *The Journal of Population and Sustainability*, 7(1), 39–70. https://doi.org/10.3197/JPS.63799953906861

Bar-On, Y. M., Phillips, R., & Milo, R. (2018). The biomass distribution on Earth. *Proceedings of the National Academy of Sciences*, 115(25), 6506–6511. https://doi.org/10.1073/pnas.1711842115

Barrett, S., Dasgupta, A., Dasgupta, P., Adger, W. N., Anderies, J., van den Bergh, J., Bledsoe, C., Bongaarts, J., Carpenter, S., Chapin, F. S., Crépin, A.-S., Daily, G., Ehrlich, P., Folke, C., Kautsky, N., Lambin, E. F., Levin, S. A., Mäler, K.-G., Naylor, R., ... & Wilen, J. (2020). Social dimensions of fertility behavior and consumption patterns in the Anthropocene. *Proceedings of the National Academy of Sciences*, 117(12), 6300–6307. https://doi.org/10.1073/pnas.1909857117

Benton, T. G., Bieg, C., Harwatt, H., Pudasaini, R., & Wellesley, L. (2021, February 3). *Food system impacts on biodiversity loss.* United Nations Environment Programme. https://www.unep.org/resources/publication/food-system-impacts-biodiversity-loss

Bradshaw, C. J., Ehrlich, P. R., Beattie, A., Ceballos, G., Crist, E., Diamond, J., Dirzo, R., Ehrlich, A. H., Harte, J., Harte, M. E., Pyke, G., Raven, P. H., Ripple, W. J., Saltré, F., Turnbull, C., Wackernagel, M., & Blumstein, D. T. (2021). Underestimating the challenges of avoiding a ghastly future. *Frontiers in Conservation Science*, 1. https://doi.org/10.3389/fcosc.2020.615419

Briggs, L. (1998). Discourses of "forced sterilization" in Puerto Rico: The problem with the speaking subaltern. *Differences*, 10(2), 30–66. https://doi.org/10.1215/10407391-10-2-30

Brondizio. E. S., Settele, J., Díaz, S., & Ngo, H. T. (Eds.). (2019). *Global assessment report on biodiversity and ecosystem services of the Intergovernmental Science-Policy*

*Platform on Biodiversity and Ecosystem Services*. IPBES secretariat, Bonn, Germany. https://doi.org/10.5281/zenodo.3831673

Campbell, M., & Bedford, K. (2009). The theoretical and political framing of the population factor in development. *Philosophical Transactions of the Royal Society B: Biological Sciences, 364*(1532), 3101–3113. https://doi.org/10.1098/rstb.2009.0174

Carroll, L. (2012). *The baby matrix: Why freeing our minds from outmoded thinking about parenthood & reproduction will create a better world*. LiveTrue Books.

Coole, D. (2021). The toxification of population discourse. A genealogical study. *The Journal of Development Studies, 57*(9), 1454–1469. https://doi.org/10.1080/00220 388.2021.1915479

Crist, E., Mora, C., & Engelman, R. (2017). The interaction of human population, food production, and biodiversity protection. *Science, 356*(6335), 260–264. https://doi. org/10.1126/science.aal2011

Donath, O. (2015). Regretting motherhood: A sociopolitical analysis. *Signs: Journal of Women in Culture and Society, 40*(2), 343–367. https://doi.org/10.1086/678145

Donath, O., Berkovitch, N., & Segal-Engelchin, D. (2022). "I kind of want to want": Women who are undecided about becoming mothers. *Frontiers in Psychology, 13*. https://doi.org/10.3389/fpsyg.2022.848384

Global Footprint Network (GFN). (2022, July 29). *Measure what you treasure*. https:// www.footprintnetwork.org/

Gökarıksel, B., Neubert, C., & Smith, S. (2019). Demographic fever dreams: Fragile masculinity and population politics in the rise of the global right. *Signs: Journal of Women in Culture and Society, 44*(3), 561–587. https://doi.org/10.1086/701154

Grazing Facts. (2022). *Grazing facts*. https://grazingfacts.com/

Institute for Humane Education. (2021, July 1). *What is humane education?* https:// humaneeducation.org/graduate-programs/what-is-humane-education/

Kharas, H., & Hamel, K. (2018, September 27). A global tipping point: Half the world is now middle class or wealthier. *The Brookings Institution*. https://www.brooki ngs.edu/blog/future-development/2018/09/27/a-global-tipping-point-half-the-world-is-now-middle-class-or-wealthier/.

Kopnina, H., & Washington, H. (2016). Discussing why population growth is still ignored or denied. *Chinese Journal of Population Resources and Environment, 14*(2), 133–143. https://doi.org/10.1080/10042857.2016.1149296

Lalonde, D. (2018). Regret, shame, and denials of women's voluntary sterilization. *Bioethics, 32*(5), 281–288. https://doi.org/10.1111/bioe.12431

McMahon, J. (2019, April 5). The World Economy Is A Pyramid Scheme, Steven Chu Says. *Forbes Magazine*. https://www.forbes.com/sites/jeffmcmahon/2019/04/05/ the-world-economy-is-a-pyramid-scheme-steven-chu-says/?sh=3bb9b90b4f17

Patrizio, P., Albertini, D. F., Gleicher, N., & Caplan, A. (2022). The changing world of IVF: The pros and cons of new business models offering assisted reproductive technologies. *Journal of Assisted Reproduction and Genetics, 39*(2), 305–313. https:// doi.org/10.1007/s10815-022-02399-y

Potts, M. (2014). Getting family planning and population back on track. *Global Health: Science and Practice*, 2(2), 145–151. https://doi.org/10.9745/ghsp-d-14-00012

Poff, B., Koestner, K. A., Neary, D. G., & Henderson, V. (2011). Threats to riparian ecosystems in western North America: An analysis of existing literature. *JAWRA Journal of the American Water Resources Association*, 47(6), 1241–1254. https://doi.org/10.1111/j.1752-1688.2011.00571.x

Purdy, L. M. (2019). Pronatalism is violence against women: The role of genetics. *Library of Public Policy and Public Administration*, 113–129. https://doi.org/10.1007/978-3-030-05989-7_9

Rees, W. E. (2020). Ecological economics for humanity's plague phase. *Ecological Economics*, 169, 106519. https://doi.org/10.1016/j.ecolecon.2019.106519

Ripple, W. J., Abernethy, K., Betts, M. G., Chapron, G., Dirzo, R., Galetti, M., Levi, T., Lindsey, P. A., Macdonald, D. W., Machovina, B., Newsome, T. M., Peres, C. A., Wallach, A. D., Wolf, C., & Young, H. (2016). Bushmeat hunting and extinction risk to the world's mammals. *Royal Society Open Science*, 3(10), 160498. https://doi.org/10.1098/rsos.160498

Ritchie, H., Rosado, P., & Roser, M. (2017). Meat and dairy production. *Our World in Data*. https://ourworldindata.org/meat-production.

Ritchie, H., & Roser, M. (2021). Fish and overfishing. *Our World in Data*. https://ourworldindata.org/fish-and-overfishing

Rottenberg, C. (2017). Neoliberal feminism and the future of human capital. *Signs: Journal of Women in Culture and Society*, 42(2), 329–348. https://doi.org/10.1086/688182.

Sinding, S. W. (2008). What has happened to family planning since Cairo and what are the prospects for the future? *Contraception*, 78(4). https://doi.org/10.1016/j.contraception.2008.03.019

Tucker, C. (2022). Bending the curve by 2030. *The Journal of Population and Sustainability*, 6(2), 51–61. https://doi.org/10.3197/jps.63788304908977

Twine, R. (2021). Emissions from animal agriculture—16.5% is the new minimum figure. *Sustainability*, 13(11), 6276. https://doi.org/10.3390/su13116276

United Nations Department of Economic and Social Affairs (UNDESA) (2021). *World Population Policies 2021: Policies related to fertility*. https://www.un.org/development/desa/pd/sites/www.un.org.development.desa.pd/files/undesa_pd_2021_wpp-fertility_policies.pdf.

USDA APHIS. (2021). *Program Data Reports*. https://www.aphis.usda.gov/aphis/ourfocus/wildlifedamage/sa_reports/sa_pdrs

United Nations Population Fund (UNFPA). (2022). *Nearly half of all pregnancies are unintended—a global crisis, says new UNFPA report* https://www.unfpa.org/press/nearly-half-all-pregnancies-are-unintended-global-crisis-says-new-unfpa-report.

Wells, H., & Heinsch, M. (2019). Not yet a woman: The influence of socio-political constructions of motherhood on experiences of female infertility. *The British Journal of
Social Work*, *50*(3), 890–907. https://doi.org/10.1093/bjsw/bcz07

# 4 Antinatalism, Veganism, and the Imperative of a Total Liberationist Perspective

JOHN TALLENT

> Who can know how many people or living beings he or she will have killed without knowing it in the course of a lifetime? Without knowing it at all or without knowing it consciously, all the while knowing it unconsciously?
> —Jacques Derrida (2000/2017)

We currently live in a time when humans routinely kill trillions of nonhuman animals for food. These incomprehensible human-caused numbers don't just represent individual nonhuman animal deaths, which, of course, they do, and these are extremely important. But they also have profoundly negative effects on the environment and humans, whose numbers are growing yearly. According to current research, the best ways for people to lessen their ecological footprints are to reduce or stop using nonhuman animals and avoid having children. To this end, this chapter aims to bring these two effective and feasible tactics together in conversation with(in) critical animal studies.

The vegan and anti-natalist movements attempt to use the momentum created by environmental research, which frequently encourages reductions in "meat" consumption and, less frequently, procreation, to move societies further than environmental arguments alone. They seek to provide a deeper ethical dimension to the discussion to create more significant and long-lasting change for the world. Promoting veganism or anti-natalism separately or together, however, is frequently criticized as "racism," "classism," "colonialism," "eco-fascism," and even as ultimately leading to "genocide." The criticisms are based on concerns about how there have been and still are instances of human population control and dietary colonialism aimed at vulnerable human groups. The unfair usage of veganism and anti-natalism undermines these noble concerns.

In this chapter, I refute that veganism and anti-natalism are necessarily negative and assert that they can be used to positively achieve total liberation. Both veganism and anti-natalism suffer from being misunderstood and generalized by proponents and detractors alike. As a result, discussions about veganism and anti-natalism are bogged down and dominated by inaccurate claims. I will also suggest how everyone with moral agency can equitably practice these two movements when theorized from a total liberationist perspective. This means that anyone who can make the appropriate choices in their lives can be vegan and anti-natalist.

To make this essay as accessible and concise as possible, I actively avoid the jargon-laden language typically prominent in academic circles. Thus, this essay follows the tradition of the critical animal studies (CAS) practice of eschewing the abstract, pretentious, and inaccessible writing that often presents an obstacle to comprehension for some people. Additionally, I will be utilizing other principles within CAS, especially by making my political commitments explicit, acknowledging that all forms of oppression interlock and tie together to form a system of domination, rejecting apolitical and reactionary ideas, and ultimately endeavoring with this work to bring various theories into universally reasonable practices. To read more about how critical animal studies differ from mainstream and traditional fields of study, see Best et al. (2007). As for my political commitments, I am an anarchist that views human liberation, nonhuman animal liberation, and Earth liberation as inherently entangled and inseparable when dismantling all forms of oppression. It is important to pursue the goal of total liberation as well.

## Background and Discussion

### Holistic Harm

In November of 2022, Earth's population reached eight billion humans (United Nations, 2022). World human population growth peaked between 1962 and 1963. Since then, however, it has halved. In the late 1980s, the population growth rate, in absolute terms, reached a peak of almost 90 million new humans annually. But up until recently, it remained high. The U.N. anticipates a decrease in the yearly growth rate of around one million going forward (Roser et al., 2013). Necessarily, a certain amount of consumption increases with each additional person, as every living being must consume to survive, which impacts the environment and other people. However, depending on location and income, each person's consumption and environmental impact vary. For instance, the world's wealthiest half of countries are responsible for 86 percent of global CO2 emissions, while the poorest half is only

14 percent (Ritchie, 2018). The inequality in emissions is even more striking when we consider that "[t]he very poorest countries (home to 9 percent of the global population) are responsible for just 0.5 percent" (ibid.). Ritchie continues by stating that there can be just as much inequality within nations as between them. In essence, overall country wealth and individual wealth within countries strongly influence emissions and consumption.

Each year, as the human population grows, so does the consumption and exploitation of nonhuman animals. Production of "meat" from nonhuman animals has "more than quadrupled since 1961," with China and the United States contributing the majority of the growth; additionally, higher income tends to increase consumption of nonhuman animals (Ritchie et al., 2019). By 2050, it is predicted that the total annual global consumption of eggs, sheep, goats, cows, buffalo, pigs, and chickens will increase to 557 million tons from 2013's total of 368 million tons (Our World in Data, n.d.). The environment, nonhuman animals, and humans are all adversely affected by this. Seventy billion nonhuman animals live on land; one-half and over two trillion nonhuman animals are aquatic. Humans kill an incomprehensible number of insects yearly (fishcount.co.uk, 2019; Our World in Data, 2020; Sebo, 2021). Since there is compelling evidence that nonhuman animals are sentient, including compelling evidence for insects, each of these deaths represents a being who experiences pain and suffering and has an interest in not being exploited or killed by humans (Baracchi & Baciadonna, 2020; Gibbons et al., 2022; Lambert et al., 2022). However, the harms of nonhuman animal agriculture are not just compartmentalized to nonhuman animals alone.

Nonhuman animal agriculture is one of the leading agents of anthropogenic climate change (IPCC, 2022). Making pasture for cows in "beef" production accounts for 41 percent of the world's deforestation (Ritchie & Roser, 2021). Demand for nonhuman animal "meat" is a primary culprit in biodiversity loss across the planet (Machovina et al., 2015). Nonhuman animal production is also a leading cause of water scarcity and pollution and has an extensive water footprint (Mekonnen & Hoekstra, 2012). Of all the habitable land on Earth, 50 percent of it is agriculture, and 77 percent of this agricultural land is used specifically for nonhuman animal agriculture. Going into 2022, current evidence states that nonhuman animal agriculture accounts for approximately 16.5 percent of global greenhouse gas emissions (Twine, 2021). Methane from this type of agriculture accounts for only 20 percent of the greenhouse gases emitted, but it "is more than 25 times as potent as carbon dioxide at trapping heat in the atmosphere" (Environmental Protection Agency, 2022). Topics that are often left entirely out of these discussions are the physical dangers and psychological harms that slaughterhouse workers routinely experience—especially those who are disproportionately "[p]eople of color, immigrants, and people in relatively low-income families" (Center for Economic and Policy Research, 2020; Ursachi et al., 2021).

So far, I have attempted to draw a path from human population growth to the harms of nonhuman animals, the environment, and humans. What follows is not a call for poorer and more marginalized countries and human groups to end or limit their procreation and nonhuman animal consumption and use. That would only be a call to alleviate these pressures on the wealthier countries and privileged individuals. You will also not find a call for privileged individuals to focus on veganism and anti-natalism on marginalized groups and lower-income countries; European and North American colonialism has shown how oppressive cultural imperialism is. Instead, what follows is a nuanced appeal to anyone with the means and ability to limit these behaviors, with more of the burden of change falling on the wealthier and more privileged groups. But first, let's take a look at two movements that seek to change the politics and beliefs about procreation and nonhuman animal exploitation. Both have had little success so far and face abundant criticism. Afterward, I will suggest that the only way veganism and anti-natalism make any sense, or promote any consistent form of justice, is to theorize and practice them from a total liberationist perspective. This perspective views all oppressions—nonhuman animal, human, and Earth—as inherently linked and, therefore, they can only be addressed together and holistically.

## Veganism

If someone who is not a vegan ("non-vegans") wanted to know what veganism is and Googled "what is veganism," they might be overwhelmed with the amount of contradictory information there is on its definition and practices. The first answer that showed up when I Googled it was an automated definition from Oxford Languages that defined "veganism" as "the practice of eating only food not derived from animals and typically of avoiding the use of other animal products" (Google, n.d.). A little further down, Cambridge Dictionary defines it as "the practice of not eating or using any animal products, such as meat, fish, eggs, cheese, or leather" (Cambridge Dictionary, 2019). Consider also the first result that I saw from a vegan source, The Vegan Society:

> Veganism is a philosophy and way of living which seeks to exclude—as far as is possible and practicable—all forms of exploitation of, and cruelty to, animals for food, clothing or any other purpose; and by extension, promotes the development and use of animal-free alternatives for the benefit of animals, humans

and the environment. In dietary terms it denotes the practice of dispensing with all products derived wholly or partly from animals. (The Vegan Society, n.d., para. 1)

This "official" definition goes further than the dictionary definitions by adding that veganism entails a rejection of "exploitation" and "cruelty." Its second sentence, which seems to clarify things by focusing on the "dietary terms" of veganism, may confuse people who want to learn more about the philosophy. To further complicate matters by possibly contradicting the previous sources, The Vegan Society's definition continues with,

> There are many ways to embrace vegan living. Yet one thing all vegans have in common is a plant-based diet avoiding all animal foods such as meat (including fish, shellfish and insects), dairy, eggs and honey—as well as avoiding animal-derived materials, products tested on animals and places that use animals for entertainment. (para. 2)

From these differing definitions, it seems as though veganism could potentially be split into at least two categories of vegans: those who practice the philosophy of veganism as a rejection of all exploitation of animals ("nonhuman animals") and those who practice a form of veganism based solely in a consumerist and "dietary terms" embodied as an abstention from eating nonhuman animals and (depending on who you ask) avoiding buying products made from their bodies. Yet, the most confusing part of seeking information about veganism from these online spaces is that media and commentary outlets often mention "vegan diets" rather than any philosophical understanding of the concept. It is common for "veganism," "vegan diet," "vegetarianism," "strict vegan," and "plant-based diet" to be used interchangeably (see Allen, 2022; Gatti-Santillo, 2022).

Beyond the contradicting and ambiguous definitions from various websites, many, if not most, individuals have conflicting beliefs about how veganism is theorized and practiced. Some people who identify as "vegan" follow a strict plant-based diet not out of concern for nonhuman animals' rights or quality of life but rather for their own health reasons. Conversely, many people who identify as "vegan" do so solely or primarily for nonhuman animal welfare or rights reasons and even take issue with the aforementioned so-called "health vegans." It's also the case that some people who identify as "vegan" do not adhere completely to not eating or wearing nonhuman animals (Greenebaum, 2012). North et al. (2021) compiled a list of several studies involving vegans in which each study's research methods defined veganism differently, but most studies focused mostly or exclusively on food aspects. As the article's authors noted, this could impact the accuracy of the research findings about vegans and veganism. Ultimately, the authors discovered that when comparing the views of vegans, vegetarians, and so-called "omnivores," vegans believed that veganism was focused on social justice and included more than just dietary considerations; however, vegetarians and "omnivores" were more in agreement with one another when describing veganism as a diet.

## The Left and Veganism

As someone who does a lot of writing, thinking, and outreach on behalf of veganism, non-vegans, in my opinion, frequently have misconceptions about the actual variations that exist in both the vegan community and the "official" definition of veganism. It is also clear that many vegans need to understand the finer points of the definition. Still, many others need to be made aware of how different life situations can result in barriers that may make it difficult for some people to follow the dietary terms of veganism. While the vegan movement often finds some of its biggest support on the political Left, many reject it for various reasons.

I focus on the Left in this essay because of the common criticism (overwhelmingly found on social media platforms) that veganism is impossible for everyone to practice. This criticism often leads to the suggestion that if vegan advocates believe that everyone should go vegan, they are "classist" and "ableist." That is to say, these critics of veganism do not necessarily believe that no one should be vegan if an individual chooses to be vegan, but rather that advocacy of veganism should not demand *everyone* go vegan because of each person's circumstances. These criticisms reflect the reality and prevalence of poverty, which may make it difficult for some people to buy food consistent with the dietary terms of veganism and disability, making it difficult for some people to thrive on a wholly plant-based diet. These criticisms cannot simply be disregarded because if veganism is as harmful to lower-income people and people with disabilities as its detractors claim, calls for veganism on a global scale would indeed be insensitive and ignorant of oppression already in existence. If behavior is beyond a person's control to change, insisting that they change that behavior is an oppressive endeavor that leads to unnecessary ethical judgments leveled at vulnerable and marginalized people. This is unacceptable and not part of the veganism I describe, adhere to, and promote.

This analysis now examines how anti-natalism is frequently misunderstood. Using total liberationist principles, I'll propose a framework for veganism and anti-natalism that avoids oppressing some groups while purporting to aid others.

## Anti-Natalism

It is important to remember that "anti-natalism" and the idea of being "child-free" are not synonymous. One can be childfree—that is, be without children by choice (as opposed to being "childless," which is being without children not by choice)—for many reasons, such as personal preferences, environmental concerns, or because they are anti-natalists. On the other hand, anti-natalism is the idea that bringing someone into the world causes more suffering. This includes the suffering of the child, the suffering of human children who could have been adopted but weren't, and the suffering of other sentient beings around the world who will be affected by the birth of a new large land mammal that needs resources, space to roam, and will add to greenhouse gas emissions. Anti-natalism is essentially a stance against procreation. But, like veganism, anti-natalism has varying definitions. Exploring the concept's history, Morioka generalizes the definition as "the thought that all human beings or all sentient beings should not be born" (2021, p. 2). Hereth and Ferrucci define anti-natalism as "the view that it is morally impermissible to bring a child into existence" (2021, p. 14). And perhaps the most well-known figure in the anti-natalist movement, David Benatar, describes anti-natalism as "the view that coming into existence is always a serious harm" (2006, p. 8). As quoted, these characterizations have two slightly different foci. The first two definitions concentrate on an act of (not) having children, whereas Benetar focuses on the result of that act. Yet it becomes apparent by reading anti-natalist literature that anti-natalism essentially views reproduction as harmful to at least one person—the child—and may also extend to others who may suffer *as a result of* that person's conception. However, like almost every other philosophy and social movement, one cannot reduce anti-natalism to a single, all-encompassing definition. Morioka puts it more eloquently, saying that "antinatalist activists' activities are diverse, and it is impossible to define them from a single perspective" (2021, p. 13).

There are many critics of anti-natalism, with a variety of counterarguments. Some of those counterarguments include disagreeing that life inherently constitutes suffering and bizarre and morally suspect notions that more humans existing mean fewer free-roaming nonhuman animals who suffer (Benatar & Wasserman, 2015; Tomasik, 2016). Beyond these counterarguments, more serious criticisms must be considered, such as the belief that anti-natalism discriminates against marginalized people (McLeod, 2022).

## Total Liberationist Veganism

In this discussion, I want to convince the reader of a bold and controversial statement: *every single human on the planet with moral agency can go vegan*. I do not mean this claim in any exaggerated way, and I also am not saying this to exclude particular groups of vulnerable and marginalized people, such as those in poverty or those with disabilities. If someone has moral agency, they can go vegan. Let me explain how this statement need not be controversial.

Let's start with the "official" definition of veganism that we saw earlier in this essay by The Vegan Society: "Veganism is a philosophy and way of living which seeks to exclude—*as far as is possible and practicable...*" (The Vegan Society, n.d., para. 1). The short phrase that I italicized is not a well-known part of this definition, but I think it is one of the most important parts because it provides nuance. Merriam-Webster Dictionary (2022) defines the word "practicable" as "capable of being put into practice or of being done or accomplished," and it offers as a synonym "feasible." If veganism is viewed as (from this definition) a philosophy and way of life where we don't consume nonhuman animals and we also do not exploit or use them for clothing, entertainment, or hygienic and cleaning products—as far as we are capable—what exactly would keep anyone from going vegan?

Some people may be in such extreme poverty that what they choose to buy and eat is whatever is cheapest at the grocery store. Some people may not have abundant choices of nutritious food within miles from where they live, a circumstance known as "food deserts" or "food apartheid" (Burrell, 2022). There are also concerns over whether some disabilities could prevent people from going vegan. Some people have food allergies or health conditions that make consuming some (or enough) plant-based foods difficult. However, would any of these issues actually prevent someone from being vegan? My answer to this is a resounding "no" for two reasons.

The definition of veganism above explicitly states that one engages in veganism if one refrain from consuming or exploiting nonhuman animals "as far as is possible and practicable." This definition does not say that veganism is when people do not consume or exploit nonhuman animals, *no matter what*. It gives people who are in difficult situations and cannot change certain concrete and social conditions as much nuance as they require. Therefore, the definition of veganism contains the language necessary for specific accommodations to be made to be still considered "vegan" if someone is in extreme poverty, lives in a food desert, or possibly has a disability that prevents them from thriving on a completely plant-based diet. It's crucial to keep in mind, though, that just because some people might need to practice veganism a little bit differently than others, that does not give anyone license not to practice veganism at all. It merely provides workarounds to the practices in which one cannot reasonably engage in.

The second reason why having certain disabilities, being in poverty, and living in a food desert does not preclude anyone with moral agency from going vegan is the understanding within ethics that "ought implies can." This ethical formula, which most moral philosophers accept, means that someone has an ethical obligation to do something only if that person can do it (Kurthy et al., 2017). In the context of veganism, I think this view is encapsulated in the hackneyed "gotcha" question to vegans, e.g., "Would you kill an animal and eat them if you were on a desert island with no other food?" Disregarding such ridiculous questions, total liberation, or the hopes of achieving just a taste of it depends on these nuances of our obligations to others. People living in poverty and disabled folks cannot be left out of veganism for reasons they have no control over. Likewise, the oppressions of classism and ableism cannot be dismantled while ignoring the reasonable obligations to nonhuman animals. We cannot blame someone who cannot avoid eating animal products for doing so out of social necessity (even if physically they theoretically can go without eating animal products, or vice versa).

## Total Liberationist Anti-Natalism

Anti-natalism, as a social movement and moral philosophy, should also be seen through the condition of "ought implies can." Most privileged people have no reason to have children other than a desire to do so. Although I do not dwell on this point, it is central to anti-natalism. Many who are vegan assert that there is no reason for anyone to eat animal products who has a choice not to. The same can be said of procreation. This is important to realize and accept. And desire alone is not a sufficient reason to do something if that act negatively affects others. Conversely, suppose some people have justifiable reasons to have children, which stem from a lack of access to family planning or reasons that might affect their survivability. In that case, those reasons cannot obligate them not to procreate. For that reason, like my discussion of veganism, it is true that every single human on the planet with moral agency can become anti-natalist. But are anti-natalist practices discriminatory?

Anti-natalists do not all agree on the best actions to prevent these harms created by procreation. One notable population scholar, Trevor Hedberg (2021), who does not claim to be an anti-natalist but has advocated for population declines and is critical of procreation, believes that procreation should not be dealt with in a way that impinges upon any person's right to autonomy. For him, negatively affecting someone's autonomy leads to the human rights abuses that many people conflate with anti-natalism, such as eugenics, genocide, forced sterilization, and colonialism. For Hedberg, non-coercive policies can achieve the goal of population declines and even bolster the rights of many currently denied their full rights. For instance, rights of autonomy are enhanced when people have greater access to contraception and family-planning services, increasing sexual and environmental education, dismantling patriarchal social structures, and empowering women and other marginalized genders. Others have suggested that adoption should become a moral priority for those who can (Rulli, 2016). These non-coercive policies can easily apply as a basis for anti-natalist practice based on total liberation.

It should be clear at this point that, according to the various definitions of anti-natalism and the arguments behind it, as well as the diverse ways in which it is practiced, anti-natalism should not support practices or policies that utilize coercion, eugenics, forced sterilization, or genocide. Could a person that believes in anti-natalism believe in supporting actions like those? Absolutely. However, just as with any other social movement or philosophy with individuals who hold problematic beliefs, the people who support those coercive government actions cannot be generalized to all other anti-natalists. Indeed, many anti-natalists support education, autonomy, free medical care, and adoption.

### Answering Some Possible Counterarguments

One objection is that anti-natalism is unnecessary if we push for veganism. In other words, if the human population continues increasing, negative effects arising from the consumption and use of nonhuman animals could be solved if we succeed in vegan advocacy, lessening the overall burden of so many humans. Furthermore, it might be claimed that it is not that an increase in the human population is the source of these problems, but rather that nonhuman animal exploitation's prevalence (and capitalism) is the problem. These arguments contain partial truths but ignore a few things, mostly because any sizable increase in the human population will entail more resources and environmental harm. Hedberg explains,

> Although ongoing environmental impacts such as climate change and biodiversity collapse are often viewed as solely the result of excess consumption (especially by inhabitants of the developed world), a significant factor driving the ecological crisis is the sheer numbers of people engaged in consuming activities. (2021, p. 49)

Similarly, the opposite is also claimed, that veganism is unnecessary if we push for anti-natalism. But this version of the objection ignores our moral obligation toward nonhuman animals, given their sentience. Thus, veganism and anti-natalism should be practiced *simultaneously* and not treated as disparate and unrelated movements. Using a total liberationist perspective, how non-veganism and pro-natalism overlap, interact, and negatively affect nonhuman animals, humans, and the environment makes them essential and consistent beliefs and practices.

Another common objection, especially from the Left, says that "blame" and "pressure" should not be put on individuals; instead, they should be put on corporations and capitalism because the overwhelming harm from pollution and greenhouse gas emissions comes from those sources. This is not a disingenuous concern, and it is true that individuals, especially those who are marginalized, should not be blamed and pressured *more* than the larger structures of society. This concern goes together with the larger debate, much of it in sociology, about the relative influence of social structures versus individual agency. This subject is beyond what could be adequately captured in this essay, but I want to give one general idea that I think is the best compromise in this discussion. Rather than choosing a "side," many sociologists, including Pierre Bourdieu (1972/2001), Anthony Giddens (1986), and many others, see social structures as influential factors on individuals, and individuals as influential on social structures. In the context of this essay, I think that this "compromise," by which individual agency and social structures co-constitute (mutually influence) one another, compels and empowers everyone to engage in change making. Individuals can choose to become vegan (as described above) and not procreate within their power. The mutual relations between individual choice and social structure promote the idea that we are not helpless against capitalism and assume that larger systems are not blameless. It gives me some hope, but it does not encourage me to simply "wait" for the world to change.

## Conclusion

Problems and their solutions are too often discussed in binary manners. Nonhuman animal exploitation and population growth are often dismissed as "not as important" as various other issues. For instance, Chris Williams (2010), author of the book *Socialism and Ecology: Solutions to Capitalist Ecological Crisis*, attempts to debunk concerns about population size and growth by claiming that these things are not "the leading cause" or "the main cause" of environmental destruction. Instead, Williams lays the blame on capitalism and the wealthy elites. Williams's criticism only applies to those anti-natalists who are not determined to dismantle capitalism. I do not believe many of us on the Left disagree with the idea that capitalism and the wealthy are largely to blame for many undesirable things in the world. While not entirely off base, Williams, in effect, perceives only one culprit and one solution. But why does it have to be like that? Can't we work to limit the destruction of the environment and the pain and suffering of all sentient beings in the world by seeking the end of capitalism *and* reducing the population *and* going vegan all at the same time? Shouldn't we apply all effective methods rather than focusing on a single issue?

This chapter has argued that we can, and as far as is practicable, we should. Such a holistic approach is something critical animal studies support, and therefore, it should also support anti-natalism and veganism as mutually beneficial forms of praxis. While many points still need to be addressed in this chapter, such as additional arguments for anti-natalism and debunking counter arguments against it, many existing works already provide some additional points along this general topic.

As we have examined, total liberation demands the end of single-issue politics and practice (together, these become praxis). None of the world, oppressions, or ecosystems live in a vacuum; they are all interconnected in complex and constantly changing ways. Capitalism is not the root cause of all oppression in the world; therefore, its abolition will not end all oppression. Capitalism is one pillar of many that support the existence of oppression and domination; consequently, we must smash multiple pillars simultaneously as a collective group of radicals to reach a better future for more than just ourselves. Veganism and anti-natalism are two additional ways to root out oppression at its source. They alone will not end all oppression but are important components in the total liberation effort.

## *References*

Allen, V. (2022, August 27). *Should vets be vegan? Nurse argues it is contradictory to tr.* Mail Online. https://www.dailymail.co.uk/news/article-11151149/Should-vets-vegan-Nurse-argues-contradictory-treat.html

Baracchi, D., & Baciadonna, L. (2020). Insect sentience and the rise of a new inclusive ethics. *Animal Sentience*, 5(29). https://doi.org/10.51291/2377-7478.1604

Benatar, D. (2006). *Better never to have been: The harm of coming into existence.* Oxford Oxford University Press.

Benatar, D., & Wasserman, D. (2015). *Debating procreation: Is it wrong to reproduce?* Oxford University Press.

Best, S. (2007). The killing fields of South Africa: Eco-Wars, species apartheid, and total liberation. *Fast Capitalism*, *2*(2), 1–29. https://doi.org/10.32855/fcapital.200 701.001

Best, S. Nocella, A. J., Kahn, R., Gigliotti, C., & Kemmerer, L. (2007). Introducing critical animal studies. *Journal for Critical Animal Studies*, *5*(1), 4–5.

Bourdieu, P. (2001). *Outline of a theory of practice*. Cambridge University Press. (Original work published 1972)

Burrell, D. N. (2022). Food apartheid and food insecurity. *International Journal of Public and Private Perspectives on Healthcare, Culture, and the Environment*, *6*(1), 1–11. https://doi.org/10.4018/ijppphce.306209

Cambridge Dictionary. (2019). *VEGANISM | definition in the Cambridge English dictionary*. Cambridge.org. https://dictionary.cambridge.org/us/dictionary/english/veganism

Center for Economic and Policy Research. (2020, April 29). *Meatpacking workers are a diverse group who need better protections*. CEPR. https://cepr.net/meatpacking-workers-are-a-diverse-group-who-need-better-protections/

Derrida, J. (2017). *The death penalty, volume II* (E. Rottenberg, Trans.). University of Chicago Press. (Original work published 2000)

Environmental Protection Agency. (2022). *Importance of methane | US EPA*. US EPA. https://www.epa.gov/gmi/importance-methane

Fishcount.co.uk. (2019). *Fish count estimates | fishcount.org.uk*. Fishcount.org.uk. http://fishcount.org.uk/fish-count-estimates-2

Gatti-Santillo, C. (2022, February 15). *New York City students push back against vegan lunches: "I like meat more."* Fox News. https://www.foxnews.com/lifestyle/new-york-city-students-vegan-lunches-meat

Gibbons, M., Versace, E., Crump, A., Baran, B., & Chittka, L. (2022). Motivational trade-offs and modulation of nociception in bumblebees. *Proceedings of the National Academy of Sciences*, *119*(31). https://doi.org/10.1073/pnas.2205821119

Giddens, A. (1986). *The constitution of society: Outline of the theory of structuration*. University of California Press.

Google. (n.d.). *What is veganism – google search*. Google.com. Retrieved October 19, 2022, from https://www.google.com/search?q=what+is+veganism

Greenebaum, J. (2012). Veganism, identity and the quest for authenticity. *Food, Culture & Society*, *15*(1), 129–144. https://doi.org/10.2752/175174412x13190510222101

Hedberg, T. (2021). The moral imperative to reduce global population. *The Ecological Citizen*, *5*(1), 47–54. https://www.ecologicalcitizen.net/article.php?t=moral-imperative-reduce-global-population

Hereth, B., & Ferrucci, A. (2021). *Here's not looking at you, kid: A new defence of anti-natalism*. South African Journal of Philosophy, *40*(1), 14–33. https://doi.org/10.1080/02580136.2020.1871566

IPCC. (2021). *Climate change 2021: The physical science basis*. Ipcc.ch. https://www.ipcc.ch/report/ar6/wg1/

Kim, C. J. (2015). *Dangerous crossings: Race, species, and nature in a multicultural age.* Cambridge University Press.

Kurthy, M., Lawford-Smith, H., & Sousa, P. (2017). Does ought imply can? *Plos One, 12*(4), e0175206. https://doi.org/10.1371/journal.pone.0175206

Lambert, H., Cornish, A., Elwin, A., & D'Cruze, N. (2022). A kettle of fish: A review of the scientific literature for evidence of fish sentience. *Animals, 12*(9), 1182. https://doi.org/10.3390/ani12091182

Machovina, B., Feeley, K. J., & Ripple, W. J. (2015). Biodiversity conservation: The key is reducing meat consumption. *Science of the Total Environment, 536,* 419–431. https://doi.org/10.1016/j.scitotenv.2015.07.022

McLeod, C. (2022). The right to reproduce. In *Routledge handbook of feminist bioethics* (pp. 451–462). Routledge.

Mekonnen, M. M., & Hoekstra, A. Y. (2012). A global assessment of the water footprint of farm animal products. *Ecosystems, 15*(3), 401–415. https://doi.org/10.1007/s10021-011-9517-8

Merriam-Webster Dictionary. (2022). *Practicable definition.* Merriam-Webster.com. https://www.merriam-webster.com/dictionary/practicable

Morioka, M. (2021). What is antinatalism?: Definition, history, and categories. *The Review of Life Studies, 12,* 1–39.

North, M., Kothe, E., Klas, A., & Ling, M. (2021). How to define "vegan": An exploratory study of definition preferences among omnivores, vegetarians, and vegans. *Food Quality and Preference, 93,* 1–8. https://doi.org/10.1016/j.foodqual.2021.104246

Our World in Data. (2020). *Yearly number of animals slaughtered for meat, world, 1961–2020.* Our World in Data. https://ourworldindata.org/grapher/animals-slaughtered-for-meat

Our World in Data. (n.d.). *Global meat consumption, world, 1961 to 2050.* Our World in Data. https://ourworldindata.org/grapher/global-meat-projections-to-2050

Ritchie, H. (2018, October 16). *Global inequalities in CO2 emissions.* Our World in Data. https://ourworldindata.org/co2-by-income-region

Ritchie, H. (2019). *Half of the world's habitable land is used for agriculture.* Our World in Data. https://ourworldindata.org/global-land-for-agriculture

Ritchie, H., & Roser, M. (2021, February 9). *Forests and deforestation.* Our World in Data. https://ourworldindata.org/drivers-of-deforestation

Roser, M., Ritchie, H., Ortiz-Ospina, E., & Rodés-Guirao, L. (2013, May 9). *World population growth.* Our World in Data. https://ourworldindata.org/world-population-growth

Rulli, T. (2016). The ethics of procreation and adoption. *Philosophy Compass, 11*(6), 305–315.

Sebo, J. (2021, July 27). *On the torment of insect minds and our moral duty not to farm them.* Aeon Essays. Aeon. https://aeon.co/essays/on-the-torment-of-insect-minds-and-our-moral-duty-not-to-farm-them

Tomasik, Brian. (2016). *Strategic considerations for moral antinatalists*. Reducing-Suffering.org.

Twine, R. (2021). Emissions from animal agriculture—16.5% is the new minimum figure. *Sustainability, 13*(11), 6276.

United Nations. (2022). *World population to reach 8 billion on 15 November 2022 | United Nations*. United Nations; United Nations. https://www.un.org/en/desa/world-population-reach-8-billion-15-november-2022

Ursachi, C. Ş., Munteanu, F.-D., & Cioca, G. (2021). The safety of slaughterhouse workers during the pandemic crisis. *International Journal of Environmental Research and Public Health, 18*(5), 2633. https://doi.org/10.3390/ijerph18052633

Williams, C. (2010). *Ecology and socialism: Solutions to capitalist ecological crisis*. Haymarket Books.

# 5 Procreation and Aviation: The Elephants in the Vegan Room

ELISABETH DIMITRAS

People choose to be vegan for many reasons, including concerns for the well-being of nonhuman animals, to improve their health, to live more sustainably, and to challenge the status quo. Interestingly, however, people who choose to refrain from animal exploitation for social and environmental ethical concerns continue to make other lifestyle choices that are arguably just as damaging. For example, the choice to procreate or travel by plane is extremely detrimental to the environment.

The analysis argues that living a child-free and flight-free life can significantly impact the environment and the other animals with whom Homo Sapiens share this planet. Thus, procreation and aviation—two major parts of (some) people's lives in the global North—must be challenged and re-evaluated by ethical vegans and plant-based environmentalists if they wish to align their life choices with their values.

The author obtained much of the information on aviation for this chapter by attending an online month-long seminar by the advocacy network Stay Grounded in November 2022 titled *Aviation & Climate Justice*. Stay Grounded works to educate the public on the link between aviation and climate change through science.

## Aviation

Aviation is the most climate-damaging form of transportation (Cohen et al., 2016), accounting for approximately 5.9 percent of all anthropogenic global heating (Stay Ground Fact Sheet, 2022). The carbon footprint of a single roundtrip transatlantic flight is around 3.4 tCO2e, which is significantly higher than the 1.6 tCO2e that many carbon calculators estimate (Atmosfair,

2022). The issue is that many calculators look only at the CO2 warming effects when aircraft emit high amounts of non-CO2 while burning jet fuel. Nitrous gases and contrail-induced cirrus clouds (consisting mainly of ice crystals that trap infrared rays) produced during flights warm the climate at approximately three times the rate associated with aviation CO2 emissions alone (Stay Grounded, 2022a). Thus, a flight's CO2 impact must often be tripled in footprint calculators, GHG reporting systems, and national emissions inventories (Stay Grounded, 2022a). This discrepancy is problematic as it causes the public to perceive air travel as being a much smaller environmental concern than it is.

## Biofuels, E-Fuels, Hydrogen and Carbon Offset—All Just Greenwashing

Unfortunately, despite its large carbon footprint, the aviation industry works hard to create "green" advertisements which mislead people who care about the environment. As the Climate Social Science Network explains, Greenwashing is "an umbrella term for a variety of misleading communications and practices that, intentionally or not, induce false positive perceptions of an organization's environmental performance" (CSSN, 2021). This is the case for all alternatives presented as "green" solutions by the aviation industry. While they may seem promising at first, they each have their limits.

An example of greenwashing is biofuels, which reports suggest are sustainable and renewable aviation fuels produced from biological sources such as fats, greases, algae, and waste (Office of Energy Efficiency & Renewable Energy, 2022). While biofuels are supposed to be more sustainable than traditional jet fuel, biofuel made from crops is produced in large monocultural fields and has negative environmental consequences (Stay Grounded, 2021b). For example, crop-based biofuels contribute to deforestation and biodiversity loss due to using fertilizers, pesticides, and herbicides (Transport & Environment, 2019). Furthermore, although biofuel is meant to reduce CO2 emissions, several countries utilize palm oil plantations (known to be a significant contributor to CO2 emissions) specifically to create biofuels (Transport & Environment, 2019).

Another example is E-fuels, synthetic fuels made from electricity. They are produced by combining hydrogen with carbon to create a liquid hydrocarbon (Ueckerdt et al., 2021). One must extract hydrogen from water using electrolysis powered by renewable energy and remove carbon from the air through direct air capture to reduce emissions. These can then be combined to form a hydrocarbon fuel powered by renewable energy (Stay Grounded,

2021b). If all jet fuel used today were to be replaced by E-fuels, it would require two and a half times the renewable electricity available globally in 2019. Additionally, E-fuels are incredibly expensive, costing approximately six to nine times the price of kerosene (Stay Grounded, 2021b). At this price point, flying with E-fuels would be reserved for the wealthiest members of society and therefore is not an accessible and realistic alternative.

Hydrogen is another option considered a sustainable alternative to traditional jet fuel. However, it would only be suitable for short to medium flights. What's important to understand as well is that hydrogen can be produced by methane or coal ("grey" hydrogen) or with carbon capture and storage (this method combined with grey hydrogen gives "blue" hydrogen). The only hydrogen produced from the water via sustainable electricity is green hydrogen, which is only about 0.5 percent of all hydrogen energy produced (Stay Grounded, 2021b).

Carbon offset is a reduction or removal of carbon dioxide or other greenhouse gas emissions in one location to compensate for emissions made elsewhere. Carbon offsetting, however, is not a solution because although land-based offsets (capturing carbon through forests and soils) are suitable for the environment, they should be considered solely as an opportunity for removal. They should not be perceived as an offset to justify further fossil fuel emissions, as this will not help stabilize temperatures or reduce emissions released into the atmosphere. In other words, we cannot keep digging up, extracting, and burning fossil fuels while thinking we will remove these emissions by planting trees because this does not reduce atmospheric emissions or atmospheric concentrations over a millennium. When extra carbon is absorbed through the planting of trees, this stays in the fast carbon cycle (continuous carbon cycles between the atmosphere, ocean, and land), cycling back into the atmosphere. It doesn't return to geological storage on timescales relevant to humans—meaning that carbon moving from the fast carbon cycle to the effectively permanent geological reserves (e.g., fossil fuel) does not happen in less than a thousand years (Brinknews, 2021, 2022).

These "green" alternatives are tricky because they cause people to think it is okay to continue flying. That is the danger of greenwashing advertisements, as most people will not research how biofuels are not what they are claimed to be or what a carbon offset actually involves. In truth, there is no way for carbon offsetting, biofuels, or e-fuels to sugar-coat the selfish need to fly to exotic locations. Instead, these "sustainable flights" feel more akin to eating "humanely slaughtered" animals after deciding to go vegetarian. Just as there is no way to slaughter anyone who wants to live humanely, there is also no way to travel by plane without harming the environment.

## Bullshit Flights and Ghost Flights

Preliminary disclaimer: The term "bullshit" is speciesist, and it should instead be "humanshit" because bulls and their feces have nothing to do with our wrongdoings. Although it is impossible to fly sustainably, admittedly, some flights are unavoidable or even lifesaving. An example might include flying to a different city or country to receive medical treatment, or when an animal advocate flies somewhere to escort rescued nonhuman animals to a new home or sanctuary. Other flights that may be labeled legitimate include those for disaster relief, safe escape routes for refugees, or visiting family in another continent for a considerable amount of time (when there is no alternative transport mode). However, more often than not, people book tickets for so-called "bullshit flights." Bullshit flights are similar to the concept of "bullshit jobs," jobs that feel meaningless or are harmful to society (Graeber, 2019). They include flights that are "unnecessary, frivolous and unfair" (Stay Grounded, 2021a).

Such flights include those booked for weekend trips (especially domestic ones), private jets, and cheap international flights. This term will likely annoy the majority of people, as these spontaneous trips give birth to feelings of excitement and fun (and also privilege and superiority). But at a cost. There are other more environmentally friendly ways to have fun. As the relevant article of Stay Grounded network rightfully expresses:

> The idea is to link [the notion of bullshit flights] with the institutional and societal structures behind them—with the economy and power relations that lead to bullshit flights. The power of the aviation industry exists both through a broad consensus that flights are fun, or could be fun if one could afford it, as well as through state subsidies, effective lobbying and greenwashing. It exists due to a lack of alternatives to travel, due to globalized trade, and a growing gap between rich and poor. (Stay Grounded, 2021a)

Therefore, the problem is, at its core, systemic. Few people have the practical ability or can even afford slow travel (travel by other means), as grind culture has people overworking and unable to take more than a few weeks off work. Flying is romanticized and glorified through the mentality of "go big or go home," especially among millennials. Nevertheless, it is still surprising how often and easily plant-based environmentalists and ethical vegans use airplanes.

Another astonishing type of flight unknown by many is "ghost flights." These flights have no passengers or less than 10 percent of passenger capacity. Such flights exist because airlines must run 80 percent of their flights, empty or not, to retain their landing slots. In the U.K. alone, an average of 500 climate-damaging ghost flights occurred each month in 2021 (Carrington, 2022). Thankfully, a parliamentary petition was set up in 2022, calling for an end to such flights, and 16,968 people have signed it. In response, the government issued a statement saying airlines would be freed from strict landing slot rules to prevent regular ghost flights. However, it is unclear whether this has made a difference.

Ghost flights and bullshit flights represent the epitome of human greed and selfishness. Only in the last 120 years has air flight been possible. Humanity (and other species) got along just fine without it.

## *Aviation and Social Justice*

Flying is not simply a matter of environmental justice but raises many social concerns. Although air travel is one of the most environmentally damaging modes of transportation, less than 10 percent of the human population has even set foot in an aircraft (Scott et al., 2012, p. 109). A recent study estimates that only two percent to four percent of the world's population had the opportunity to fly internationally in 2018, and it concludes that just one percent of the global population is responsible for half of all commercial aviation emissions (domestic and international) (Gossling & Humpe, 2020). This small percentage of wealthy individuals is responsible for producing an incredible amount of greenhouse gases, which will impact all life on earth, both human and nonhuman. Sadly, humans who have historically been mistreated and marginalized often are the first to experience this environmental degradation's negative impacts.

Omega Green Biofuel Refinery, South America's first advanced biofuel refinery, exemplifies aviation's interrelated social and environmental impacts. This refinery is located in Villeta, Paraguay, and is a foreign project owned by a 43-year-old Brazilian businessman with political ties between the former president of Brazil, Jair Bolsonaro, and Paraguayan president, Mario Abdo. He is the son of Brazilian farmers and known as "the king of biodiesel," who aspires to become the world's third-largest producer of biofuels by 2030. E.C.B. Group, owned by this businessman, has been reported to the Federal Public Ministry in Brazil for undermining the interests of the Brazilian people. Most of the fuel produced at this refinery is purchased by BP and Shell companies, which consumers will use in the United States and Europe (Safelanding.org).

According to its environmental impact report, the raw materials that Omega Green will require are oilseeds from the Indigenous Ayoreo peoples' territory who live in voluntary isolation. This area is already considered one of the world's highest deforested areas, with approximately 40 percent of its natural forest cover already lost before the creation of this refinery. The Omega Green Biofuel only intensifies this issue (Safe-landing.org). According to Coraina de la Plaza from the Global Forest Coalition, monoculture plantations that produce biofuels will lead to deforestation, groundwater contamination, and plant life with pesticides, and reduce the amount of arable land for the Ayoreo people to grow food (Safe-landing.org). This project is already threatening the survival of the Ayoreo people, who only have about 50 members left and are losing access to their own territory (Stay Grounded, 2022b).

Who wants to fly on planes which use biofuels with such a nasty background? Ethical vegans and plant-based environmentalists surely must consider this reality. Besides, when people and nonhuman animals are starving due to a select global few hoarding resources, consuming biofuels from crops for some privileged people to keep flying is unacceptable.

## Procreation

The decision to procreate is the largest contribution a human could make to climate change. Research shows that living childfree or at least having one less child, is the best thing someone can do for the environment since every additional child accounts for an average of 58.6 tonnes of $CO_2$-equivalent (tCO2e) emissions per year (Wynes & Nicholas, 2017). While we are in the midst of the sixth mass extinction, doesn't it sound a little bit paradoxical to procreate, especially from a vegan perspective? Our species today occupies, or has at least transformed, almost 90 percent of Earth's land (Latham et al., 2014). As our population grows, environmental degradation grows along with it, generating pollution and fragmentation of wildlife habitat. Additionally, this growth of our population disrupts the communication and mating behaviors of nonhuman species and, as a result, negatively impacts their reproductive success (Candolin & Wong, 2013).

Some people blame capitalism, consumption, and the industrial revolution, not humans. Indeed, large corporations and wealthier Western countries certainly lead to environmental destruction. The problem of overpopulation and how it affects the planet is based primarily on something other than the global South, as many want to believe or falsely propagate. Although people in this part of the world give birth to many children, the problem lies in the global North because that is where people have incredibly high carbon footprints. For example, the carbon footprint of the average person in the United States is as much as 172 Somalis, and the carbon footprint of the average person in Greece is as much as 71 Somalis (Worldometer, 2016). Yet, humans in many locations and over tens of thousands of years have been the culprit to extinctions, which demonstrates how we are the deadliest animal ever to have existed on Earth. The issue certainly resides within the collective known as humanity, yet not within all humans.

## *Homo Sapiens—The Ecological Serial Killer*

It all started with the arrival of homo Sapiens in Australia around 45,000 years ago. During this time, the Earth was experiencing a period of climate change, which it would have been able to recuperate from if it were not for humans. However, the combination of climate change and hunting devastated the Australian megafauna, which did not have enough time to evolve a fear of humankind (Harari, 2014).

Twenty-three of the twenty-four Australian animal species weighing more than 50 kilograms became extinct. Furthermore, a considerable number of smaller species also disappeared at that time and as a result, food chains throughout the entire Australian ecosystem were broken. For millions of years, this was the most important transformation of the Australian ecosystem, and the appearance of Homo Sapiens at that moment was not a coincidence. Consider also that oceanic species did not disappear because Homo Sapiens did not yet know to conquer the seas. If this massive extinction were a consequence of climate change, sea animals would have also disappeared (Harari, 2014).

Harari (2014) gives several other examples of similar ecological disasters in many different areas (as evidenced by fossil records), and the narrative is always the same:

- New Zealand: Within a couple of centuries after the arrival of the Maoris in New Zealand, most of the local megafauna and 60 percent of all bird species became extinct.
- The Americas: Around 16,000 years ago, within 2,000 years of humans' arrival, North America lost 34 out of 47 large animal species while South America lost 50 out of 60.
- Wrangel Island, north of Siberia: The last mammoths disappeared about 4,000 years ago, right after the first humans reached the island, despite having flourished for millions of years. They had already retreated from Eurasia and North America, where they disappeared 10,000 years ago.
- Madagascar: Most of the large animals of Madagascar vanished about 1,500 years ago—precisely when the first humans arrived on the island.

Solomon Islands, Fiji and New Caledonia, Samoa and Tonga, the Marquis Islands, Easter Island, the Cook Islands, and Hawaii: A similar wave of extinction occurred in these places, with hundreds of species being killed off by humans, directly or indirectly.

There is no question why more and more people who care about the Earth and other animals decide to live child-free nowadays. Even if everyone could live off the grid, the same manufacturing of solar panels and batteries is highly destructive for the environment (adding to the fact that batteries do not live forever and must be replaced). There are also no environmentally friendly vehicles (other than wooden bicycles, possibly). Only one company manufactures ethical and sustainable smartphones (which do not meet the needs of many people), and no parallel computers yet exist.

Plant-based environmentalists and ethical vegans who travel by plane and/or procreate may suffer, unbeknownst to them, from cognitive dissonance. This mental conflict occurs when a person's behavior and beliefs do not align. So, there is no way around the truth: It is not possible for humans to not be destructive to other animals and the environment, no matter how hard they try (see Shotwell, 2016). The more ethical vegans and plant-based environmentalists realize it, the better choices we can make and the better we can deal with our necessarily "messy" ethical situations.

## A Note on Parenthood and Adoption

There is nothing wrong with parenthood. It's natural for some people to feel this need. Not everyone feels this need, though; neither does everyone who feels ready to become a parent, and many who do procreate come to regret it (Donath, 2017). However, with so many kids born to irresponsible parents or people who cannot properly care for them, as well as the unfortunate kids who lose their parents while young, it would be better to give them a chance to grow up in a family rather than in orphanages, hospitals, or foster homes. Noting that sometimes being raised in an alternative family structure may be better than living within one's bio family, still staying with the family of origin may be preferable. For many nonhuman animal advocates against pro-creation, the thinking is similar to "adopt, don't shop." As long as there are kids with no parents, people should consider adopting instead of procreating.

Admittedly, adoption itself is often problematic. There is an insidious problem within many adoption agencies in which agencies persuade parents to give up their children so they can have better lives. Furthermore, adoptions conducted ethically are, in most cases, quite costly, which has only become an option for privileged people. The complicated bureaucratic adoption procedure can also create an unbearable emotional toll on prospective parents. Once again, the problem lies in the system and needs to be addressed with a multi-disciplinary approach so that more people can access ethical adoption.

## Conclusion

As explained thoroughly in this essay, flying and procreating should be considered environmental harms. Ethical vegans and plant-based environmentalists who care deeply about their non/human relations should reconsider their desire to fly or become a parent. Family is not limited to having human kids, but should be reframed to normalize adopting rescued nonhuman animals and taking care of them along with the Earth. These decisions pave the way to building a more liveable future and minimizing our environmental footprint.

## References

Atmosfair. (2022). *Emissions Calculator.* https://www.atmosfair.de/en/standards/emissions_calculation/emissions_calculator/

Brinknews. (2021, March 7). Carbon offsets do not reduce carbon emissions, only delay them. *Brinknews.com.* https://www.brinknews.com/carbon-offsets-do-not-reduce-carbon-emissions-only-delay-them/

Brinknews. (2022, March 1). Carbon offsets are not carbon reductions. *Brinknews.com* https://www.brinknews.com/carbon-offsets-are-not-carbon-reductions/

Candolin, U., & Wong, B. B. M. (2013) *Behavioural responses to a changing world: Mechanisms and consequences.* Oxford University Press.

Carrington, D. (2022, March 31). Ghost flights from UK running at 500 a month, data reveals. *The Guardian.* https://www.theguardian.com/environment/2022/mar/31/ghost-flights-from-uk-running-at-500-a-month-data-reveals#:~:text=during%20the%20period.-,Ghost%20flights%20are%20defined%20as%20those%20with%20no%20passengers%2C%20or,arrivals%2C%20or%20any%20domestic%20flights.

Cohen, S. A., Higham, J., Gössling, S., Peeters, P., & Eijgelaar, E. (2016). Finding effective pathways to sustainable mobility: Bridging the science–policy gap. *Journal of Sustainable Tourism, 24*(3), 317–334. https://doi.org/10.1080/09669582.2015.1136637

CSSN Working Paper. *2021:1 An Integrated Framework to Assess Greenwashing* CSSN. org https://cssn.org/wp-content/uploads/2021/09/CSSN-Working-Paper-2021-on-Assessing-Greenwashing-1.pdf

Donath, O. (2017). *Regretting motherhood: A study.* North Atlantic Books.

Gössling, S., & Humpe, A. (2020). The global scale, distribution and growth of aviation: Implications for climate change. *Global Environmental Change*. (1). https://doi.org/10.1016/j.gloenvcha.2020.102194

Graeber, D. (2019). *Bullshit jobs: A theory*. Simon & Schuster.

Harari, Y. N. (2014). *Sapiens: A brief history of humankind*. Random House Group Limited.

Latham, J., Cumani, R., Rosati, L., & Bloise, M. (2014). *Global land cover share*. Food and Agricultural Organization. http://www.fao.org/uploads/media/glc-share-doc.pdf

Scott, D., Gössling, S., & Hall, C. M. (2012): *Tourism and climate change: Impacts, adaptation and mitigation*. Routledge.

Shotwell, A. (2016). *Against purity: Living ethically in compromised times*. University of Minnesota Press.

Stay Grounded. (2021a). *"Bullshit flights": A debate on legitimate air traffic*. Stay-grounded.org. https://stay-grounded.org/bullshit-flights-a-debate-on-legitimate-air-travel/

Stay Grounded. (2021b). *Greenwashing fact sheet series*. Stay-grounded.org. https://stay-grounded.org/greenwashing/#factsheet

Stay Grounded fact sheet. (2022a). *It's about more than just CO2 – Aviation must reduce its total impact on climate*. Stay-grounded.org. https://stay-grounded.org/fact-sheet-climate-impact/

Stay Grounded. (2022b). *Producing fuel for other people's planes. A case study on the Omega Green Biofuel Refinery in Paraguay*. Stay-grounded.org. https://stay-grounded.org/agrofuel-case-study/

Transport & Environment. (2019, January 24). *Palm oil and soy oil for biofuels linked to high rates of deforestation—new study*. transportenvironment.org https://www.transportenvironment.org/discover/palm-oil-and-soy-oil-biofuels-linked-high-rates-deforestation-new-study/

Worldometer. (2016). *CO2 Emissions*. https://www.worldometers.info/co2-emissions/

Wynes, S., & Nicholas, K. A. (2017). The climate mitigation gap: Education and government recommendations miss the most effective individual actions. *Environmental Research Letters, 12*(7).

# Part II. New Convergences and Extensions

# 6 Infrastructural Approach to Urban Street Animals of Istanbul: Contestation, Violence, Affectivity, and Spatial Visibility in Metropolis

Ezgi Karaoğlu

## Introduction

Gli was a resident of Hagia Sophia in the very heart of the metropolis of Istanbul, though she was not a human; she was a cat. Built in 537 during the Roman Empire, Hagia Sophia served as a church and museum over the years and reopened as a mosque in 2020. Gli witnessed the transformation and recent history of Hagia Sophia until she passed away at the age of 16 on November 8, 2020 (TrtWorld, 2020). The governor of Istanbul announced her death via his Twitter account. Yet, the other 130,000 dogs and 125,000 cats who roam free alongside the over 16 million human denizens of the city of Istanbul (*The New York Times*, 2019) have received different attention and care from the state.

Since the Ottoman Empire, animals in Istanbul have been subject to several failed or absent regulations. With the Animal Welfare Act, No. 5199 in Misdemeanor Law in 2014, torture, abuse, and general mistreatment of all nonhuman street animals became a misdemeanor subject to fines until 2021 (Fortuny, 2014). Since the Act emerged in Misdemeanor Law instead of Turkish Criminal Law, no abuser can be sued, judged, and fined in the court system. In 2021, the Turkish Parliament amended the New Code of Animal Protection under Turkish Criminal Law, improving animal rights on paper. The violence against animals became subject to imprisonment

(CNNTurk, 2021). However, the law is speciesist by solely addressing street animals' rights and still fails to hold people accountable with no enforcement mechanism (Haytap, 2021). Therefore, without robust animal welfare laws to protect street animals, they are protected by the will of the residents and individual efforts through informal sheltering, feeding, and watering facilities. Beyond the informal resident-made infrastructures, which may be viewed as a form of interspecies mutual aid, the value of street animals is visibly evident in statues and graffiti throughout the landscape of Istanbul. Nonetheless, while the close interspecies relations in Istanbul might seem spectacular from a distance and can be interpreted as a form of altruism on behalf of individual city residents, ultimately, the cause(s), conditions, and continuation of the negative reality of street animals are deeply rooted in structural state-sponsored violence.

I argue that failed laws and shelters are state-sponsored animal welfare urban infrastructures that essentially abandon nonhuman animals and place the responsibility of their care on the (human) residents of the metropolis. This displacement is not communicated formally through law or policy but indirectly through indifference by the state to the animals' situation. Consequently, interactions between different species in the urban landscape can be observed through the informal structures created by residents and artistic expressions that serve as integral components of the city's infrastructure. Hence, as a city whose landscape and streets are decorated with visual work depicting street animals, Istanbul is a contested space of animal exclusion and inclusion. I pursue this scrutiny by holding an anthropological lens to the quotidian components of metropolis life: Animal shelters as formal infrastructures built by the state; sheltering, feeding, and hydration facilities as informal resident-made infrastructures; and the statues and graffiti of beloved street animals scattered around the city. Several of my own photographs of these urban elements (not featured) inform this chapter.

This chapter contains two main parts. One critiques the failure and absence of protective laws for street animals. The other is an examination of the human creations in the urban scene that illustrate the positive affective human and nonhuman interactions. The central part of this story is a dialectic between state-sponsored infrastructural harm against animals and the private citizen efforts to help them. To set this dialectic up, a discussion of the failures of the law regulating street animals and state-run animal shelters is provided. This is related to how residents take animal protection into their own hands. The artistic representations show both the infrastructural violence and the worth of animals and their role in the city, i.e., they raise awareness of the violence and promote human effect toward the animals.

I begin by reviewing how infrastructural violence is described and studied in anthropology. Then I discuss how structural violence impacts street animals in Istanbul through failed animal welfare laws, shelters as state-run formal infrastructures, and resident-made informal infrastructures. Following the discussion on infrastructural violence, I analyze the significance of artistic productions in the urban landscape in defining affective interspecies relationships and draw attention to the mismanagement of street animals in the city. In the final section, I explain the findings concerning the theories discussed.

## *An Anthropological Approach to Infrastructural Violence*

Infrastructures are a very well-studied topic in anthropological literature. Yet, most of this research focuses on the relationship between humans and infrastructures rather than nonhuman animal needs and interest in this relationship. Hence, in this section, I present an overview of different approaches to infrastructures to provide an avenue to discuss the infrastructural violence that street animals of Istanbul are exposed to.

Larkin (2013) describes infrastructures as:

> Built networks that facilitate the flow of goods, people, or ideas and allow for their exchange over space. As physical forms they shape the nature of a network, the speed and direction of its movement, its temporalities, and its vulnerability to breakdown. They comprise the architecture for circulation, literally providing the undergirding of modern societies, and they generate the ambient environment of everyday life. (p. 328)

Infrastructures are promising when they provide hope and facilitate ease of life, but detrimental when they form exclusionary apparatuses (Appel et al., 2018; Larkin, 2013). They can cause harm and grief when they serve as tools of state-sponsored neglect and abjection (Anand, 2012; Farmer, 2004) that exacerbate the inequalities, discrimination (Appel, 2012), and violence that manifest in slow, structural ways (Nixon, 2011). Various spaces can be locations of infrastructural violence, from detention centers and camps to entire cities (Gordillo, 2019; O'Neill, 2012). Artistic production can provide avenues for making violence visible and affectively felt (Murphy, 2019).

Infrastructural violence is often embodied in slow and structural ways. Slow violence occurs gradually with longitudinally constant destruction, yet it is not viewed as violence according to traditional definitions. Nixon (2011) argues that the human-made disaster in Bhopal, India, where a massive gas leak from a factory destroyed the human and nonhuman animals living there, was not an instantaneous act. Yet, the leaking gas has impacted the environment and the non/human residents, gradually allowed by the international companies, the state, and the ignorance of the Western corporate media (Nixon, 2011). Farmer (2004) describes these intentional acts of structural, slow, yet subtle violence as "sinful" social structures. He draws on his research in Haiti, investigating the roots of the ongoing poverty, tuberculosis, and HIV/AIDS epidemics. Farmer concludes, "The distribution of AIDS and tuberculosis–like slavery in earlier times—is historically given and economically driven (2004, p. 317)."

Similarly, infrastructures can be tools for state-sponsored exclusion, discrimination, denial of citizenship for certain groups, and marginalizing others. For instance, in Mumbai, the abjection of the state for specific groups is translated into tenuous and contentious infrastructural connections between Muslim settlers and the government (Anand, 2012). As Anand (2012) demonstrates, for years, the Muslim immigrants of Mumbai were denied access to clean and consistent water resources. Similarly, Appel (2012) illustrates how infrastructures draw a bold line between the neglected poor Equatoguineans and affluent private oil compounds. As the local communities of lower income cannot access infrastructures that connect them to safe water and necessary electricity systems, jeopardizing their health, the collaboration between the Equatoguinean government and the corporate oil companies could be called "sinful."

An oil compound in Equatorial Guinea, Communist-era Romanian gulags, and extraordinary rendition camps are also tools for capturing and managing the "bare life" (Agamben, 1998). Agamben describes bare life as "the state of living dead; a life stripped of every social protection rendering life subject to exercises of all kinds of violence and whose inclusion within the political order is limited to their exclusion from the political order" (1998, p. 71). For instance, O'Neill (2012) uses the case of Communist-era gulags and extraordinary renditions in Romania to illustrate the captivity of human beings as bare life objects in spaces with absent infrastructures. In these secret detention centers, the suspected terrorists were illegally captured, tortured, and rendered (O'Neill, 2012). The scope of the spaces for infrastructural violence expands to an entire metropolis in the case of Argentina's Los Lajitas, where deforestation, evictions, violence, and poisoning occur in secrecy within the city (Gordillo, 2019). Gordillo (2019) elaborates that the metropolis, with its geographical core and edges, is home to class polarization, racism, atmospheric disruptions, and ambient toxicity.

The metropolis also holds reactions to these human rights violations through visual and artistic expressions that show opposition to this violence. Murphy (2018) argues that visual texts induce a form of affective seeing and knowing of human rights violations to at least some extent. However, although the urban spaces are home to nonhuman animals, infrastructural violence that manifests in violating nonhuman rights is missing from the discussion. In the case of Istanbul, affective seeing throughout the visual text also involves nonhuman animals. Borrowing from the anthropological theories of infrastructural violence, I now discuss how human infrastructures act similarly and differently regarding nonhumans, focusing on street animals in Istanbul.

## Management of "Bare Life" in and Beyond Animal Shelters: Infrastructural Violence in State-Run Formal Shelters

As a metropolis, Istanbul is both the perpetrator and the victim of slow and structural forms of infrastructural violence. While certain groups are excluded by the state based on their gender, wealth, class, and status, some are excluded based on their species. Anand (2012) argues that infrastructural disconnect is used as a tool for abjecting and denying certain bodies of an entity and defines the connections between the government and the governed. With a lack of protective law and proper management policies in Istanbul, street animals are subject to misery through the infrastructural violence in and outside of state-run animal shelters. Animal abuse in distinctive forms has been a profound and somber fact of urban life, including the absence of proper law. As Ozen (2017) lists, during the Ottoman Empire in the sixteenth century, the first enactment was legislated to protect pack animals and define punishments when they were abused. Thus, until unfavorable developments in the eighteenth and nineteenth centuries, animals were protected by law to some extent.

The failed or absent law and the lack of formal infrastructures for street animals are tools of this structural violence. There are over 20 state-run animal shelters in Istanbul needing more infrastructure and staff capacity (Yigit et al., 2020). All of them are overpopulated, causing health risks for resident animals (Yigit et al., 2020). In addition to limited material infrastructures and insufficient staffing, these state-run shelters are established in the city's peripheries or have been moved from the core to the edges of Istanbul, reproducing the legacy of exile in managing animals roaming the city. For instance, in the late Ottoman Empire (late nineteenth century), street dogs of Istanbul were deported three times by the sultans in power to the deserted islands off the coast of Istanbul in the Sea of Marmara (Bayraktar & Bayraktar, 2022). This was done with secrecy to avoid scandals, as over 11,000 street dogs died in exile on this island (Alkan, 2016; Fortuny, 2014).

State-organized violence and abuse led to inevitable counter actions: with the public's will, a society for protecting animals in Istanbul was established in 1912, which was counted as the country's first formal organization to protect animals (Fortuny, 2014). It was followed by two failed attempts to enact separate laws for the protection of animals in 1912 and the 1980s (Ozen, 2017). Until 2004, all the enacted laws, codes, and regulations targeted the mistreatment and harm due to veterinary acts or related practices with either farm or laboratory animals used for research and educational purposes instead of street animals (Ozen, 2017). As mentioned above, the 2014 Animal Welfare Act, No. 5199, made torture, abuse, and the general mistreatment of all street animals a misdemeanor subject to fines but was not enforceable through the courts. Not surprisingly, the article on the Misdemeanor Law fell short of mitigating escalated abuse cases, including murder, torture, and sexual harassment of street animals (Haytap, 2009).

In 2021, the Turkish Parliament amended the Code of Animal Protection. This amendment to Turkish Criminal Law has brought significant changes in the treatment of animals. No longer classified as mere commodities, animals are now afforded greater protection. Municipalities must sterilize stray animals, and acts of violence against them, including physical and sexual abuse as outlined in the law, carry a penalty of six months to four years in prison (CNNTurk, 2021; Haytap, 2021). However, the law must be revised to guarantee animal safety in many ways. First, similar to many animal cruelty laws in the United States and supported by animal protection organizations, it is exclusionary and speciesist as it is only designed for "pets" and street cats and dogs and does not address the violations against the well-being of farm animals live under human domination (i.e., slaughter) or prohibition of dolphin parks and zoos that promote animal captivity (see Marceau, 2019). Second, although the sterilization of street animals was assigned to the local governments, the new code did not bring appropriate and clear rules compatible with the 3R principle (reduction, refinement, replacement) (English, 2021a). Third and most important, there is no central control mechanism to hold the people accountable and enforce the punishment (as problematic as punishment is from a critical animal studies perspective).

The local government's role is also important in determining animal rights implementations in the city. For instance, the leading progressive party, which identifies as relatively leftist and socially democratic to the central government, came to power in Istanbul Metropolitan Municipality (I.M.M.) in 2018 after the 15-year ruling of the populist and conservative government party. These shifts in local government led to improvements regarding urban animal rights: the mayor abolished the phaetons (horse-drawn carriages), the main mode of transportation and a tourist attraction in the Prince Islands scattered on the shores of the Istanbul mainland (Bayraktar & Bayraktar, 2022). Phaetons were replaced with electric vehicles. The phaetons were long known as a form of exploitation of nonhuman animal labor, as many horses were injured and killed over time (Bayraktar & Bayraktar, 2022). The mayor also promised to establish new and modern rehabilitation shelters for street animals and improve the infrastructural capacity of the existing ones (CHP EU Representation, 2020). Although these developments are promising, the local government's efforts fell short of protecting nonhuman animals in the city without a central control and enforcement mechanism.

Additionally, the negative public attitude toward street animals has been precipitated by several incidents in which street dogs attacked or injured the city's residents (Aljazeera, 2022). Social media campaigns were organized to deliver hate speech against street animals, and self-organized groups gathered to murder street dogs by poisoning them (Bianet, 2019; Yesil Gazete, 2022). Tension was raised between the residents of the city who wanted to protect the animals and those who did not. The anti-animal residents even attacked some who fed the street animals (English, 2021b). The discursive strategies of the politicians exacerbated the negative attitude of the public. They stigmatized street dogs instead of offering a proper solution and taking responsibility for establishing safety for both human and nonhuman animals in the city.

The long history of mismanagement of street animals in Turkey, the absence of an inclusive law and control mechanism, and anti-street animal discursive strategies resonate with the idea of state-sponsored slow and structural violence. As Farmer (2004) indicates, oppression is the main component of the structural violence exerted systematically by everyone who belongs to a certain social order. Nourished with the oppression, the lack of robust state policies gradually jeopardized street animals' lives as a mundane act in line with Nixon's (2011) definition of slow violence. Since the late nineteenth century, the mismanagement of street animals has been gradually violating the welfare of the animals.

While subjected to slow and structural violence, street animals of Istanbul represent the concept of bare life. As further described by Agamben, "bare life refers to life stripped of every social protection, rendering life subjects to exercises of all kinds of violence without having committed a crime" and "exists as the living dead caught within a zone of indistinction—a liminal space that is both lawless and yet created by law" (cited in O'Neill, 2012, p. 470). O'Neill (2012) locates the brutal management of bare life in Communist-era gulags and rendition camps. Yet, a similar connection can be made between the position of street animals in Istanbul and their management in and beyond the walls of state-run shelters. The conditions behind the walls of shelters and their remoteness from the centers of the city draw correspondence with the secret detention centers/camps in Romania used by the U.S. government in its program of rendition whereby intelligence agents illegally rendered, detained, and tortured suspected terrorists (O'Neill, 2012). Likewise, street animals are stripped of every social protection the state provides. As the concept of bare life offers, although they are not human beings, street animals and their lives in and outside the shelters are subject to violence without the culpability of committing any actual trespasses. The dimensions of infrastructural violence beyond the state-run shelters are discussed in the following section.

## *Beyond Shelters: Streets as Contested Spaces*

State-run shelters tangibly encapsulate the infrastructural violence that street animals are exposed to, yet they are not their sole representation. As O'Neill (2012) suggests, spaces that capture and maintain bare life cannot be located just anywhere, like the center of the cities under the everyday focus of the people. Yet, the camp is everywhere with the dissemination of the control produced in the physical spaces of the camp. Without a robust protection mechanism and increasing numbers of crimes against street animals, including murder, torture, and even sexual harassment, the streets of Istanbul are spaces where the violence in the shelters expands (Haytap, 2009). This is also in direct conversation with how Gordillo (2019) defines the metropolis:

> The idea and constitution of metropolis—with its cores and edges—itself can produce and reproduce infrastructural violence as decentering the structuration of motion, containment, acceleration by closely surveilled walls and fences. (p. 74)

As a dynamic, multilayered combination of multiple urbanized planetary networks and nodes, the metropolis reserves countless dimensions of human and nonhuman life in urban and non-urban spaces (Gordillo, 2019). Frequently, these dimensions escape the reach and control of the metropolis aligned with the history and political flavor stitched into the fabric of the metropolis (Gordillo, 2019).

Well-fitting to Gordillo's proposition of a metropolis, in Istanbul, street animals escape the reach and control of the municipality in terms of law, regulations, and legislation. Some of them are contained by closely surveilled walls and fences of animal shelters that are either located in the heart or at the edges of the metropolis. Yet, every corner of every street is also a potential scene for quotidian violence. Hence, if the camp is everywhere, and the municipality produces and reproduces violence with (and within) its cores and edges, Istanbul, as a metropolis, is an enormous camp for street animals. In this colossal camp, the responsibility for the welfare of street animals is often displaced to the will, consciousness, and varying capabilities of its human denizens. While representing systemic state failure, this occasionally makes the streets safe for some of the nonhuman residents of Istanbul through the goodwill efforts of citizens.

Resident-made informal infrastructures are one of the main forms that make the caring relations between humans and nonhumans in Istanbul visible. While not necessarily well-constructed, and insufficient in terms of numbers, it is possible to encounter a resident-made informal sheltering, feeding, and watering facility in nearly every corner of the city. The leftover rocks and bricks of a construction site, cardboard, newspapers, laundry baskets, plastic bottles, plastic yogurt containers, clothes, and blankets are some of the building blocks of these structures. Through these resident-made/sponsored infrastructures, street animals are provided with relatively safe spaces for sleeping, resting, feeding their babies, and can feed and drink.

However, resident-made infrastructures need to improve in establishing a healthy and durable solution for caring for all the street animals in the long run since they are individual informal attempts that run against the exclusive structures of the state. As Anand (2012) asserts, the abjection of urban infrastructures defines the relationship between the government and the governed and determines which city residents are denied which protections. In conversation with Anand's (2012) argument, through the lens of the state, the street animals are abject residents of the city subject to a lack of robust infrastructures that would result in healthy and sustainable protection for them. Their lives and welfare are precarious without access to safe water and basic material resources. Thus, the streets of Istanbul are contested spaces for managing bare life and infrastructural violence to street animals. On the other hand, those who can be cared for by the human denizens of the city become beloved parts of the city's landscape via graffiti and statues.

## Street Animals in Istanbul's Artistic Landscape

At the nexus of state-sponsored violence and affective caring of the denizens, the artistic representations of street animals of Istanbul are essential components of the urban landscape. While some of these visual works remind us of the significance of nonhuman life in Istanbul, others constitute awareness raising for state-sponsored violence against street animals. Murphy (2018) asserts that activism through visual work against human rights violations is possible. In that sense, the aesthetic process of "memory mapping" (Murphy, 2018) works to develop affective, visual maps of the relations between the bodies, lived experiences, and memories neglected in official narratives. Moreover, these visual maps induce affective witnessing and knowing of human rights violations by making temporal and spatial connections between them (Murphy, 2018).

Not only for human-rights activism, but activism through visual work against nonhuman rights violations is also possible. The trajectories of artistic activism can be followed through two specific examples from the routine urban life of Istanbul. Erected on the Asian side of Istanbul, one is known as "Companion of the Cats," a statue of the street dogs Tarcin (meaning ginger in English) and Tommy, who lost their lives in car collisions. Both animals were in a very close daily relationship with the human residents of the city. Tragically, 18-year-old Tarcin was killed by a hit-and-run driver going in the wrong direction (Hurriyet Daily News, 2016). Yet, the perpetrator was not even attempted to be found and justly held accountable. With these statues erected in the exact location of these dogs' former residency, the human neighbors can convey their gratitude to them and the shared memories, as well as draw attention to animal abuse and failures of the animal welfare law. Although not a subject of violence, Tommy has been a resident of an affluent neighborhood of Istanbul since 2006, and his statue was erected after his death.

The presence of statues is a form of visual activism against violations of nonhumans' rights. The bodies and lived experiences of street animals, as nonhuman residents of the city, are constantly neglected and violated by the state. These statues invite the viewer into affective observing and knowing of infrastructural violence addressing street animals in Istanbul. Tarcin and Tommy are still the residents of their neighborhood with their nonhuman and human companions around them. Putting Murphy's (2018) concept of memory mapping (drawing temporal and spatial connections between neglected bodies, lived experiences, and memories in the dominant narrative) in conversation with Larkin's (2011) description of infrastructures (built networks that facilitate the flow of people, goods, or ideas over time and space and generate the ambient environment of everyday life), the statues assert temporal connections with the past, present, and future residents and memories of the city as they become part of the urban environment.

In line with Larkin's (2012) definition of infrastructures as generators of ambient environment in daily life, a second example is graffiti depicting street animals. Graffiti is tied to the extremely mundane urban spaces of Istanbul;

the walls of an open-air parking lot in Istanbul, an electric box, or a front side of an ordinary apartment building. One instance of graffiti illustrates a man reading a book in a chilly atmosphere created in 2018 by an artist named Artez (No Grey Walls, 2018). When a closer look is taken, on the left side, there is a frame filled with a dog's face, and the name of the book he is reading is "Beautiful Journey with Luna the Dog." In other words, the images of street animals become visible by covering unsightly urban infrastructures like the walls of a parking lot or an electric box and by making the decorated infrastructures memorable and enjoyable through their rejuvenated presence. In Larkinian terms, they generate an ambient environment where interactions occur in daily life. With these pieces of artistic work combined, the metropolis, to some degree, can transform its violent cores and edges into spaces for visual activism.

## Conclusion: Infrastructures in Contested Spaces

This paper takes a snapshot of the different mundane forms of infrastructural violence that street animals of Istanbul are exposed to. In so doing, I problematize the familiar into becoming "strange" and open space with(in) which to challenge social norms. Drawing on anthropological literature on slow, structural, and infrastructural violence, I conclude that these concepts are applicable to explain the state's (mis)management of the street animals in Istanbul and its manifestation in the urban life of the metropolis. As the representatives of bare life, street animals are subjects of systematic and gradual exclusion and abjection through infrastructures built by the state. The failed law and state-run shelters are tools of state infrastructural violence, the violence of which disseminates beyond these structures into the streets of Istanbul. With that, the metropolis becomes an enormous space for violence, with its corners and edges in line with Gordillo's (2019) spatial argument. Yet the space is contested: While exclusion and abjection are present, there are also moments, spaces, and places of caring interactions and affective seeing (Murphy, 2018) through the informal infrastructures and artistic pieces covering the landscape of the city.

In closing, I would like to state that the manifestation of infrastructural violence is not limited to the mismanagement of street animals in Istanbul or the examples posed in this chapter. However, these examples can be reference points to extrapolate the experiences of other marginalized groups in the city. Women, the L.G.B.T.Q.I.A.+ community, refugees, ethnic minorities, and countless other marginalized "others" are subjected to distinct forms of state-sponsored violence in the cores and edges of the city. Therefore, this research should be expanded with future works applied to the other forms of infrastructural violence in the city. With that, promising avenues can be found for supporting and creating safe harbors for each other as (potential) victims of structural violence without robust infrastructures to protect each living creature.

## *References*

Agamben, G. (1998). *Homo sacer: Sovereign power and bare life*. Stanford University Press.

Aljazeera. (2022). Turkey's street dogs face off against app, and win. *Aljazeera.com*. https://www.aljazeera.com/gallery/2022/9/8/photos-turkeys-street-dogs-face-off-against-app-and-win.

Anand, N. (2012). Municipal disconnect: On abject water and its urban infrastructures. *Ethnography, 13*(4), 487–509.

Appel, H. C. (2012). Walls and white elephants: Oil extraction, responsibility, and infrastructural violence in Equatorial Guinea. *Ethnography, 13*, 439–65.

Bayraktar, D. H., & Bayraktar, O. (2022). A comparison of the local governments in terms of approaches to stray animals in Turkey. In N. Poirier, A. Nocella II, & A. Bernatchez (Eds.), *Emerging new voices in critical animal studies: Vegan studies for total liberation* (pp. 101–114). Peter Lang.

CHP EU Representation. (2022). *Animal rights activist partners with Istanbul mayor Imamoglu on app aiming to protect street animals*. https://chpbrussels.org/2020/10/29/animal-rights-activist-partners-with-istanbul-mayor-imamoglu-on-app-aiming-to-protect-street-animals/.

CNN Turk. (2021). *Hayvanlari Koruma Kanunu Maddeleri-2021 Hayvan Haklari Yasasi Kabul Edildi*. https://www.cnnturk.com/turkiye/son-dakika-hayvanlari-koruma-kanunu-maddeleri-2021-hayvan-haklari-yasasi-kabul-edildi-mi.

English, D. (2021a). *Turkey's long-awaited animal rights bill turns out to be massive disappointment*. https://www.duvarenglish.com/turkeys-long-awaited-animal-rights-bill-turns-out-to-be-a-massive-disappointment-news-58342.

English, D. (2021b). *Turkish family attacked for feeding stray dogs in residential complex*. https://www.duvarenglish.com/turkish-family-attacked-for-feeding-stray-dogs-in-residential-complex-video-58849

Farmer, P. (2004). An anthropology of structural violence. *Current Anthropology, 45*(3), 305–25. https://doi.org/10.1086/382250.

Fortuny, K. (2014). Islam, westernization, and posthumanist place: The case of the Istanbul street dog. *Interdisciplinary Studies in Literature and Environment, 21*(2), 271–297.

Gordillo, G. (2019). The metropolis: The infrastructure of the Anthropocene. In K. Hetherington (Ed.), *Infrastructures, environment and life in the Anthropocene* (pp. 66–94). Duke University Press.

HAYTAP. (2021). *Summary of Turkish animal laws and pending legislation as of 2021 April.* https://www.haytap.org/tr/chris-green-summary-of-turkish-animal-laws-pending-legislation

Hurriyet Daily News. (2016). *Statue of famous dog killed by hit-and-run driver to be built in Istanbul.* https://www.hurriyetdailynews.com/statue-of-famous-dog-killed-by-hit-and-run-driver-to-be-built-in-istanbul-99384

Larkin, B. (2013). The politics and poetics of infrastructure. *Annual Review of Anthropology, 42,*

Middle East Eye. (2020). *Hagia Sophia's beloved feline of 16 years dies after short illness.* https://www.middleeasteye.net/news/hagia-sophia-gli-cat-dies

Murphy, K. M. (2018). *Mapping memory: Visuality, affect, and embodied politics in the Americas.* Fordham University Press.

Nixon, R. (2011). *Slow violence and the environmentalism of the poor.* Harvard University Press.

No Grey Walls. (2018). *Mural Istanbul Festival 2018 Part one.* https://nogreywalls.org/mural-istanbul-festival-2018-part-one/

O'Neill, B. (2012). Of camps, gulags and extraordinary renditions: Infrastructural violence in Romania. *Ethnography, 13*(4), 466–486.

The New York Times. (2019). *A new deal for Turkey's homeless dogs.* https://www.nytimes.com/2019/10/02/opinion/turkey-stray-dogs.html

TrtWorld. (2020). *Haghia Sophia mosque's famed feline Gli passes away.* https://www.trtworld.com/turkey/hagia-sophia-mosque-s-famed-feline-gli-passes-away-41257.

Yigit, A., Aslim, G., & Hilal, C. (2020). Evaluation on shelter medicine and stray animal shelters in Turkey. *Kafkas Üniversitesi Veteriner Fakültesi Dergisi, 26*(1), 17–24.

# 7 Ida B. Wells' Historical and Contemporary Legacy, and Relevance to Critical Animal Studies

ZANE MCNEILL AND NATHAN POIRIER

Patricia Hill Collins (2008) begins *Black Feminist Thought* by discussing how Black feminist theory has a long lineage. Collins highlights Sojourner Truth as an early articulator of Black women's positionality. Many involved in contemporary social justice issues, especially anti-racism and women's liberation, may be familiar with Kimberlé Crenshaw, Angela Y. Davis, bell hooks, Audre Lorde, Tarana Burke, and Patricia Hill Collins. Fewer people know how historical figures like Truth have influenced contemporary Black feminism. Another historical figure in this tradition is Ida B. Wells, an afro-feminist and anti-lynching crusader who fought against dominant stereotypes of Black women and Black individuals in the Southern United States in the decades surrounding 1900. Although Wells has been well-studied, her legacy is somewhat underrepresented in the contemporary scene, especially in critical animal studies (CAS), given its interest in Black liberation, gender liberation, and the (de)construction of the "human/animal" dualism.

The Black freedom struggle is based on historical and inter-generational exploitation and deprivation, but white supremacists also ground their system of oppression in the *great again* past. Therefore, the work of activists like Wells remains relevant. This highlights the thoughts and actions of Ida B. Wells for a CAS audience and establishes her as an important figure in the history of social justice struggles. We are interested in Wells' anti-lynching journalism, specifically her troubling of the violent and animalizing logic of White supremacy and her tension with the White suffrage movement. We address the mechanisms by which Wells circumvents racial and gender barriers in the U.S. to challenge, subvert, and dismantle the white supremacist logic used to construct and uphold anti-Black mythologies and discourses. To do so, Wells attacks the gendered nature of white supremacy, which might be described today as manipulating the prevailing symbols of White cishetero-patriarchal masculinity. Wells transforms these symbols through a politics of shame, relying on Northern insecurities about civilization and the damaging potential of lynch law on the global stage.

This chapter analyzes her main writings to illuminate what her work offers to CAS, which has much to learn from Wells and Black radical thinkers more broadly. It is imperative to acknowledge that the authors of this paper are both White. We wrote this chapter partly to educate ourselves about intersectional Black history and activism, but also to highlight Wells' relevance to CAS struggles for racial justice, abolition, Black liberation, and Black feminism.

CAS was formed through learning about historical social justice movements of all kinds (Nocella II et al., 2014) and continually uses this history to inform present theory and activism (Nocella II & Socha, 2022). CAS owes a great debt to Black feminism, particularly the concept of intersectionality and the works of Kimberlé Crenshaw, Aph and Syl Ko, Breeze Harper, Sylvia Wynter, Bénédicte Boisseron, among others. To this day, CAS describes itself as intersectional and draws inspiration from Black feminism as reflected in, at least, its 2nd, 4th, 6th, and 9th Principles, reproduced below. As described by Best et al. (2007, pp. 4–5), CAS:

> 2. Rejects pseudo-objective academic analysis by explicitly clarifying its normative values and political commitments, such that there are no positivist illusions whatsoever that theory is disinterested or writing and research is nonpolitical. To support experiential understanding and subjectivity.

> 4. Advances a holistic understanding of the commonality of oppressions, such that speciesism, sexism, racism, ableism, statism, classism, militarism, and other hierarchical ideologies and institutions are viewed as parts of a larger, interlocking, global system of domination.

> 6. Rejects reformist, single-issue, nation-based, legislative, and strictly animal interest politics in favor of alliance politics and solidarity with other struggles against oppression and hierarchy.

> 9. Openly supports and examines controversial radical politics and strategies used in all kinds of social justice movements, such as those that involve economic sabotage from boycotts to direct action toward the goal of peace.

Principles 4 and 6 derive directly from intersectionality, that race and gender cannot be untangled from each other. This idea also extends to class, (dis)ability, sexuality, citizenship status, species, and others. As a result of this recognition, single-issue politics are insufficient, and oppression must be examined and resisted holistically (Principle 4). Principle 2 is a nod to the noticeable and admirable characteristic of Black feminist writing from experience and in an accessible style (e.g., hooks, 1984; Collins, 2008; Lorde, 2007), as many Black women, such as Ida B. Wells, did and still do. Principle 9 recognizes that desperate situations call for desperate measures, and Black people frequently—perhaps continuously—navigate hostile environments (Anderson, 2021). By examining and highlighting the tactics used by Ida B. Wells, we support and recognize that the means of resistance must come from within communities according to their own situation(s) and abilities.

## *Racial-Gender History and Context in the 19th and Early 20th Centuries*

Kimberle Crenshaw (1989) begins her foundational paper on intersectionality by discussing how race and gender are commonly made out to be separate issues. She points out that in legal settings, the term "Blacks and women" overlooks the specific experiences of *Black women*. The 1890s to the 1920s was an era of revolutionary Black female political, social, moral, and community activism, with Black women struggling with identity, femininity, colonization, and racial discrimination (Bay et al., 2015). Post-Reconstruction and early Progressive scholarly studies give attention to either racial or gendered movements without successfully connecting the two, often skimming over Black female experiences (Gillespie & McMillen, 2014; Kraditor, 1965; Wood, 2009; Dray, 2003). Some historians attempt to rectify this by reevaluating Black women's roles in this era and compiling an intellectual history of Black women (Bay et al., 2015; Waters & Conaway, 2007; Lerner, 1972) in terms of navigating multiple, overlapping oppressions.

Some academics construct new feminist narratives of this era concerned with early Black female activism (Carby, 1985) or how particular Black women, such as Ida B. Wells define their oppressions (Watkins, 2008). Similarly, studies on the Wells-Willard controversy (more on this below) say little about the larger themes of gender and race in politics. Both the Black Rights Movement, which was led mainly by men and the White suffrage movement were hard for Black women to join because they did not fit the mold of "true womanhood" at the time. In a sense, "Black women were forced to choose between African-American patriarchy and White female racism" (Waters & Conaway, 2007, p. 331). Wells' reality is one of marginalization in both Southern society and progressive movements. This positioning is not uncommon for Black women, as they are routinely made to feel excluded from both White society and (white) feminism (hooks, 1984).

To challenge both sexual and racial exploitation, Black women shifted intellectual boundaries and created space for their voices to be heard and respected (Bay et al., 2015). Double marginality created conditions ripe for a Black feminist leadership model to emerge in the nineteenth century (Waters & Conaway, 2007). White suffragists and Black rights activists worked together before the passing of the fourteenth amendment to create a narrative of universal suffrage. However, the fifteenth amendment included the word *male*, making it more difficult to fight for woman suffrage by legally gendering the right to vote (Free, 2015). Coalitions between the Black rights and White suffrage movements began to disintegrate. The suffrage movement then shifted its goals and strategies from using state elections to a federal initiative, creating the need for the support of the South. How to gain this support was known as the "Southern Question." In short, Southerners needed assurance that women's suffrage would not challenge the existing gender and racial hierarchies.

Recognizing Southerners' concerns about these hierarchies, the suffrage movement shifted their narrative away from universal suffrage and toward "true womanhood" and White supremacy. Black women are routinely excluded from the definition of authentic womanhood (hooks, 1984). One of Wells' greatest challenges is to subvert these expectations and create room in this narrative for the empowerment of Black women. She writes for a primarily Black audience and argues that it is harder for a Black woman to be seen as a true woman because Blackness is attached to a stigma of immorality, preempting early iterations of Black women's "controlling images" (Collins, 2008). Some suffragists used white supremacist arguments to further women's status. Suffragists argued that women voters deserved political power because they knew best how to protect their homes and children. Voting would only be an extension of their usual domestic, womanly duties. Leveraging the oppression of one group to gain liberation for another is something CAS is against. As the suffrage movement gained popularity in the early twentieth century, more people who did not share race consciousness joined the movement. Most early suffragists believed that the government depended on "intelligent" people voting and supported voting restrictions, such as mandatory literacy tests, that targeted Black people (Kraditor, 1965). Such policies are not only racist but also ableist and reflect eugenicist (il)logics. Southern White women went so far as to argue that they deserved the right to vote because their enfranchisement would ensure "the permanency of White supremacy" (Kraditor, 1965, p. 165).

Despite interdisciplinary studies that connect Black feminism to gender and racial politics in the South, they often fall short in analyzing how Black feminists circumvented their marginalization in both White Southern society and the White-dominated suffrage movement. This includes works on Wells and her connection to these movements.

## Ida B. Wells' Historical Legacy

Throughout history, Black women have created their own Black empowerment and afro-feminist movement that was politically oriented, engaging within and outside the Black rights and women's suffrage movements (Giddings, 1984). During the late nineteenth and early twentieth centuries, many organizations attempted to change the public's opinion of lynch law in the South. Lynch law, a form of vigilante justice, emerged in the early nineteenth century and after the Civil War, became a way to control Black men and women and strengthen White supremacy in the South. It warned Black men and dissenting Whites not to cross economic, sexual, or political boundaries created by White men (Williams et al., 2021). The most renowned anti-lynching Black feminist during this era was Ida B. Wells. Wells was a talented journalist and rhetorician who published myriad works on the horrors of lynching (Giddings, 2008; Wells-Barnett & Royster, 1997). Wells was born into slavery in July 1862 to James and Elizabeth Wells, all of whom transitioned to freedpersons when Ida was no older than three (Giddings, 2008). In 1884, 71 years before Rosa Parks' famous refusal to give up her bus seat for White passengers, Ida boarded a "colored" car on a train as a first-class passenger, before recognizing a drunken man in the car (Giddings, 2008). Fearing for her safety, she transferred to the women's car, but was forced out by the conductor because she was Black (Allen, 2021). As described by Allen (2021, p. 35):

> Ida B. refused to give up the seat that she had paid for. The conductor then attempted to physically drag her off the train until she bit his hand in protest. In response, he secured two additional men to assist him in forcing her out of the first-class section. She sued the company, enraged and humiliated, only to lose in appellate court. This incident caused Wells to lose faith in the law (Giddings, 2008). Between 1884 and 1889, Wells became more involved with journalism and became editor of the Black newspaper *Memphis Free Speech & Headlight* (Giddings, 2008). This position gave her the authority to combat White supremacy and the marginalization of black women in both the suffrage and black empowerment movements.

Wells' political anti-lynching journalism is inspired by arguably the most transformative event of her life: the 1892 lynching of her friend Tommie Moss and two other men who worked at People's Grocery, Calvin McDowell and Will Stewart (Giddings, 2008). A fight between a Black and White boy turned into a racially charged mob. Six armed White men arrived at the store and were greeted with a hail of gunfire (Giddings, 2008). The three men were arrested, and at 2:30 am on March 9th, 75 men entered the Shelby County Jail, where Moss, Stewart, and McDowell were held, dragged out of their cells, and shot a mile outside the city (Giddings, 2008).

When Wells returned to the city, she "struggled to get beyond her own paralyzing sense of disbelief in order to write an editorial about the lynching" (Giddings, 2008, p. 189). This began her incessant fight against lynching in the South. She responded with her editorial, "Eight Men Lynched," in *Free Speech* on May 21 (Wells-Barnett & Royster, 1997). Wells wrote for the White press in hopes of molding public sentiment. She recognized that she did not have the power to influence White politicians and community leaders, and, therefore, attempted to create a movement where Whites would pressure each other to act in Black interests (Wells-Barnett, 1970). Between 1892 and 1900, Wells became known as a crusader through her writings *Southern Horrors: Lynch Law in All Its Phases* and *A Red Record* and her work in the community. She was a vocal force in the post-Reconstruction and early Progressive eras, having a ripple effect on social and political justice movements that inspired activists long after her death in 1931 (Allen, 2021; Taylor, 2018; Wells-Barnett & Royster, 1997).

### Deconstructing Mythologies of the Black Rapist and the "Bestial Race"

Anthropocentrism is not simply reducible to generalized human supremacy. To animalize any race reifies the false human/animal dichotomy, and deconstructing this binary is a fundamental tenet of CAS. Wells' rhetoric in *Southern Horrors* and *The Red Record* challenges the narrative of the Black rapist that justified White Southern men's barbarism cloaked in the rhetoric of chivalry (Wells-Barnett & Royster, 1997). A talented rhetorician, she effectively uses rhetorical gymnastics to invert White conceptions of manliness, class, gender, and race. Fearing the loss of their manhood after the Civil War, White men attempted to retain their social standing by attacking Black men and women through the threats of lynching and sexual violence (Pinar, 2006). The original narrative was that White men were *manly* for lynching the Black *rapist* who endangered their White women. White men were *civilized* and had to protect their society from the *primitive*, unrepressed sexuality and violence of Black nature. The *civilized* North forgave Southern violence directed toward Black men if it was done to protect White womanhood. Wells understood "how fragile this constructed identity was, how easily it might unravel if she only inverted the link between manhood and White supremacy" (Pinar, 2006, p. 167). One of Wells' greatest successes is that she "used her activism to challenge the system or program of racialization and gendering that masked the brutal and unjustified murder of Black men and sexual exploitation of Black women, while simultaneously [re-conceptualizing] 'true womanhood' in her personal and professional life" (Watkins, 2008, p. 112).

In *Southern Horrors* and *A Red Record*, Wells juxtaposes White men raping Black girls and White women and Black men engaging in consensual relationships. "Nobody in this section of the country believes the old thread bare lie that Negro men rape White women," contends Wells, and "If Southern White men are not careful, they will over-reach themselves and public sentiment will have a reaction; a conclusion will then be reached which will be very damaging to the moral reputation of their women" (Wells-Barnett & Royster, 1997, p. 1). Wells contended that *raped* White women were actually involved in consensual sexual relationships with Black men, a concept that directly unraveled the narrative of a *chivalrous* South that protected *virtuous* women. "There are many White women in the South who would marry colored men if such an act would not place them at once beyond the pale of a society and within the clutches of the law" (Wells-Barnett & Royster, 1997, p. 53).

In some cases, white women were even "compelled by threats, if not by violence, to make the charge" of rape (Wells-Barnett & Royster, 1997, p. 57) against Black men with whom they were consensually intimate. Wells' studies further challenge the South's myth of the Black rapist, vilifying White men who are not acting to protect women, but are the "despoiler[s] of virtue" themselves, who sexually assault marginalized Black women and lynch innocent Black men (Wells-Barnett & Royster, 1997, p. 54). Wells understood that the issue of lynch law and White supremacy was one of racialized class. White men were apologists for "lynchers of the rapists of White women only [...] when the victim is a colored woman, it is different" (Wells-Barnett & Royster, 1997, p. 58).

Wells understood that lynching was used as a fear tactic to warn Black people not to challenge White supremacy economically or socially by consorting consensually with White women. White Southern men feared "Negro domination" (Wells-Barnett & Royster, 1997, p. 77). Looking for a justification to instill a new era of fear and domination, the South created the myth of the Black rapist to cloak their barbarism in courageous rhetoric. If men were avengers, not murderers, justifications could be made for their actions. If *pure* White women were assaulted, the charge of rape put the "Negro [...] beyond the pale of human sympathy" (Wells-Barnett & Royster, 1997, p. 78). White Southerners took the law into their own hands to protect the "weak and defenseless women [from the] bestial propensities of the Negro race" (Wells-Barnett & Royster, 1997, p. 62). Recognizing the power of this narrative, Wells argues that instead of being protective and chivalrous, Southern men were actually rapists and murderers who mocked the law, violently kept Black people in subordination, "cheated him out of his ballot" and had a "growing disregard for human life" (Wells-Barnett & Royster, 1997, p. 66). Wells challenged this myth by drawing upon case studies of consensual interracial sex and the phenomenon of White men raping Black women without being charged with any crime. Wells contends that White men "assume a chivalry that they do not possess. True chivalry respects all womanhood," not just White womanhood, for "virtue knows no color line" (Wells-Barnett & Royster, 1997, p. 80). This statement emphasizes that White men are a danger to women, especially Black women, and it faces and challenges the doctrine of true womanhood that only granted White women protection from physical and sexual violence.

Her argument encouraged Northerners to reevaluate their position on Southerner's use of the lynch law. Instead of seeing the South as unworldly but courageous, the North began to be embarrassed by the South as Wells continued to argue that the South illustrated the "decay of manhood" through the "submission of mob reign" (Wells-Barnett & Royster, 1997, p. 67). Using gendered language, Wells confidently turns a narrative of masculine chivalry into one of White men's hostile and uneducated urges that encourages violence against Black folks. Wells believed that Black people possessed immense social power and could influence politics by boycotting White businesses, emigrating to the North, and engaging with the press. As she writes:

The appeal to the White man's pocket has ever been more effectual than all the appeals ever made to his conscience. Nothing, absolutely nothing, is to be gained by a further sacrifice of manhood and self-respect. By the rights exercise of his power as the industrial factor of the South, the afro-American can demand and secure his rights, the punishment of lyncher, and a fair trial for accused rapists. (Wells-Barnett & Royster, 1997, p. 116)

## White Insecurities: Civilization and the Global Stage

Critical animal studies has a preoccupation with language. In CAS literature, nonhuman animals should never be referred to with objectifying terms such as *it* or *that*. Furthermore, "animals" should never be rhetorically distinguished from "humans," as this is a false distinction that emphasizes separation rather than connectedness. With the importance of language in mind, this section examines the rhetorical devices used in an important component of Wells' activism, her schism with the English suffragist Francis Willard. Wells and Willard used different discourses to push similar yet qualitatively different agendas.

Though Wells believed Black Americans could use their agency to end lynch law, she also understood the need to play on White sympathy and U.S. insecurity. She recognized 1894 as the beginning of "a pronounced awakening of the public conscience to a system of anarchy and outlaw" (Wells-Barnett & Royster, 1997, p. 75). Instead of lynching representing masculinity and control, Wells manipulated it into a symbol of American shame. "From England comes a friendly voice," writes Wells, "the current English thought deprecates the rule of mob law, and the conscience of England is shocked by the revelation made during the present crusade" (Wells-Barnett & Royster, 1997, p. 136). Recognizing that the nineteenth century U.S. was a nation dependent on the respect of other powerful countries, Wells traveled to England in 1893 and 1894 to help shame the U.S. into condemning lynch law (Wells-Barnett & Royster, 1997).

During this time (as today), the U.S. was caught up in global imperialism (Wells-Barnett & Royster, 1997). This quest depended on respect from other industrial nations, and therefore, "they did not want the nation's reputation tarnished by accounts of lynching [...]" (Wells-Barnett & Royster, 1997, p. 34). Wells contends that there was an awakened conscience in the U.S., and with an active anti-lynching campaign abroad, lynch law would be unable to "flourish in the future [...] [as it had] in the past" (Wells-Barnett & Royster, 1997, p. 135). Wells knew that the "civilized" British could get the U.S. to denounce their "barbaric" ways by playing on American fears. Wells succeeded in linking "imperialism abroad to racism at home[...]" and questioned "Whiteness and civilization [...] as a strategy designed to embarrass the U.S. and its 'civilized' people" (Wells-Barnett & Royster, 1997, pp. 34, 36). Yet, this caused controversy in the South and many papers, appalled at her attack on the Southern chivalrous narrative, angrily attempted to defame her.

Wells' trips to England created a rift between herself and Frances Willard, the President of the Women's Christian Temperance movement, who was "internationally recognized as a former abolitionist, a highly respected social reformer, and a leader of a great vision" to organize and empower women (Wells-Barnett & Royster, 1997, p. 38). Willard was a believer in incrementalism and reformism (Slagell, 2001). She aimed to raise consciousness in women who were otherwise not directly involved in the suffrage movement. She utilized the "home protection argument" to inspire conservative evangelical Christian women to "see themselves as serious participants in the political community" (Slagell, 2001, p. 2).

The Wells-Willard controversy arose during Wells' England tours when Wells claimed that Willard had done nothing to combat lynch law (Wells-Barnett & Royster, 1997). Wells argued that to gain support, Willard resorted to race-baiting. Willard's discourse was an attempt to justify suffrage for white women at the expense of Black men and women. In 1890, Wells contended that Willard called Black men "great dark-faced mobs" and compared Black people to the "locusts of Egypt" (Wells-Barnett & Royster, 1997, pp. 81, 120). Willard also argued that Black men were inherently sexual and would attack *pure* White women after drinking (Wells-Barnett & Royster, 1997). In an 1890 interview in *The Voice,* Willard "attributed the South's racial problems to one categorical culprit: the drunken Black beast rapists [...] she tapped into the cultural capital of this mythical figure, which was frequently invoked to deny the ballot to Black men following Reconstruction" (Parker, 2008, p. 56). Willard's narrative used the ideology of true womanhood, "namely, purity, piety, domesticity, and submissiveness" to garner support for women's rights by not attacking Southern racial and gendered hierarchies (Parker, 2008, p. 59). As a woman suffrage supporter, Willard believed that Black men should not be able to vote since many were illiterate (Parker, 2008). Like the stances of leading White women suffrage organizations, she argued for an educational test to curb Black political power.

Wells' rhetoric deconstructed a "well-entrenched patriarchal system [that] was able to control the behavior of African American men and women as well as White women" (Wells-Barnett & Royster, 1997, p. 33). She contended that the "charge of the rape of White women was used to justify lynching [and] other mob violence to terrorize, oppress, and control African Americans" (Wells-Barnett & Royster, 1997, p. 32). To strengthen her arguments, she decodes several racial and gender stereotypes and the connection between White masculinity and civility. Her main arguments were that "the term *rapist* more logically applied to White men than to Black men" and that Black men and women were often engaging in consensual sex (Wells-Barnett & Royster, 1997, p. 31).

On an argumentative level, Willard could not agree with Wells in any manner, lest her own ideological narrative fall apart. Wells and Willard saw gender identity and sexual desire differently: Willard viewed White women as lacking sexual desire and refused to concede to Wells' argument that White women were not morally superior and did engage in inter-racial sex (Wells-Barnett & Royster, 1997). This tension between Wells and Willard illustrates the marginal status of Black women within the male-dominated Black rights movement and the White-dominated women's movement. Wells argued that both Willard and Lady Somerset, a British philanthropist and temperance leader, "joined hands in the effort to crush an insignificant colored woman who had neither money nor influence nor following—nothing but the power of the truth with which to fight her battles" (Wells-Barnett, 1970, p. 178). Wells also created an image of herself that was non-threatening. She expressed that she was not searching for power, celebrity, or money but rather was motivated by a passion for protecting her people. This proved successful and made Willard seem very out of touch.

Wells and Willard opposed White men's suffrage and through contrasting narratives, each redefined white womanhood to reflect their opposing views on social change (Parker, 2008). Their differences came from having different ideas about how race and sexuality shape identities. Parker contends that "Wells exposed this tension in Willard's public persona between her professed moral superiority and her refusal to condemn deadly aspects of Southern race relations" (Parker, 2008, p. 59).

## Ida Wells' Contemporary Legacy

Although very much a product of her time, Wells still bears contemporary relevance. Many themes from the above analysis echo in today's racial and gender struggles, particularly in Black women's movements (see Alabi et al., 2021). For instance, Demita Frazier says the Combahee River collective are "daughters" of Ida B. Wells (Taylor, 2018) and Shonta' E. Allen (2021) draws inspiration directly from Wells by deriving (at least) four lessons from Wells' activism for contemporary Black feminist sociologists.

Perhaps the clearest contemporary lineage of Wells is the situation Black women still face in social justice struggles, particularly in the feminist movement (hooks, 1984). In interviews with Barbara and Beverly Smith and Demita Frazier, the three primary authors of the Combahee River Collective Statement, all point out how, in their early organizing, feminist collectives consistently overlooked or downplayed Black women's concerns (Taylor, 2018). Barbara, Beverly, and Demita frequently mention how carving out a space for themselves was critical to getting Black feminism's standpoint "out there." This is what the CRC meant by coining the term *identity politics*. hooks (1984) explicitly states that she wrote her book *Feminist Theory: From Margin to Center* in response to such marginalization. Additionally, serious and often defensive debates about the proper use and meaning of the term *intersectionality* to theorize Black women's positionality continue (Nash, 2019).

Black women have always held a precarious place in U.S. society. hooks (1981) dedicated *Ain't I a Woman* to showing that the continued devaluation of Black womanhood has remained in place since slavery. Black women's survival represents resistance after centuries of sexual and physical violence (Lerner, 1972; hooks, 1981). This is still a current sentiment and reality for people of color, especially for Black women: "It is a fugitive praxis of daring to exist, a double refusal that the site of Black and woman engages by neither leaving nor complying. Living in the face of imposed death, sanctioned death, beatified death, is itself liberatory" (Bey, 2019, p. 119). Thus, Black women continually challenge(d) and circumvent(ed) the boundaries placed upon them by confronting and redefining womanhood.

Not to mention the more direct contemporary connections between Black struggle and slavery. Michelle Alexander (2012) reminds us that the contemporary Black condition in the United States still bears too close a resemblance to the Jim Crow era and retains direct connections to slavery. Saidiya Hartman (2007) traces a Black feminist genealogy of the afterlife and aftereffects of transatlantic slavery. This is similar to Christina Sharpe's (2016) notion of *the wake* to illustrate how contemporary Black life exists in the shadow of slavery. Samudzi and Anderson (2018) argue that anti-Blackness has been foundational to racial violence in US history stretching back to European colonialism and manifests today in Black people not being "true"—read: not recognized and identify as—citizens of the U.S.

Lynching also has a profound and persistent legacy in the U.S. Williams et al. (2021) found that places where lynching and other forms of racialized violence happened in the past, have higher rates of poverty and less money invested in social infrastructure today. This history and pattern sustain extreme economic and political inequity (Williams et al., 2021). Not to mention that lynching only became a federal crime in 2022, and ongoing police brutality could be considered a contemporary form of lynching. The federal criminalization of lynching is at least a century and a half too late. Additionally, the institution of prisons is also a problem for CAS, as it believes in penal abolition and is anarchist, so it is against punishment and for transformative justice (Nocella II et al., 2019). Criminalizing lynching, while (at least implicitly or partially) acknowledging the wrongness and violence of this act, does not address the root causes of racism and leaves its underlying ideology and social structures intact.

In terms of Wells' tactics, she exploited U.S. society's sense of being *civilized* and a *civilization*. Alex Zamalin (2022) makes explicit the implicit racism in civility discourse, using Wells (among others) as an example. Likewise, Vergès (2021) warns against "civilizing feminism" which insidiously seeks to privilege notions of White feminism at the expense of feminisms of color. Wells also did not seek celebrity but remained focused on Black liberation. Echoing yet not referencing Wells, avoiding celebrity status and celebrity worship is something Anderson (2021) strongly argues against in the ongoing quest for Black liberation.

Wells foreshadows some of today's most prominent radical Black scholar-activists by deconstructing the animalization of Black people (primarily Black men) (Ko & Ko, 2017; Boisseron, 2018; Jackson, 2020). As discussed above, the Southern reign of violence under lynch law relied on the propagation of the myth of the "Black rapist" and the concurrent animalization of Black men. In *Southern Horrors*, Wells details how the white press maliciously characterized Black men in the South who had been lynched as "bestial" (Wells-Barnett & Royster, 1997, p. 72). The human/animal dualism has often been weaponized against racialized others to reify their lower position in the hierarchical ordering of society (Kim, 2015, p. 17). The animalization of Black men in the South was essential to establishing Black body dominance and repression. As Claire Jean Kim posits, "Race has been articulated in part as a *metric of animality*, as a classification system that orders human bodies according to how animal they are—and how animal they are not[...]" (2015, p. 18).

The white press was actively and consciously engaging in the animalization of Black men in the South when publishing statements such as "no man can leave his family at night without the dread that some roving Negro ruffian is watching and waiting for this opportunity" (Wells-Barnett & Royster, 1997, p. 72). This image of Black men roving the night to "devilish[ly]" and "bruta[ly]" gratify "his bestial desires" abhorrently rationalized the political repression of Black men in the South (p. 72). The media's current portrayals of Lebron James and Barack Obama as monkeys or apes are similar to those from the past.

Benedicte Boisseron (2018) explores how the animalization of Black people renders them "fungible and disposable" (p. xv). Southern whites used the Otherization and animalization of Black men as an excuse to repress and control Black communities violently. This Otherization relied heavily on the human/animal hierarchy, as Syl Ko (Ko & Ko, 2017) explains: "The racial hierarchy tracks not just a color descent but also a species descent," she asserts. "At the top of the hierarchy sits the white male human and at the bottom sits the shady and necessarily opposite figure of 'the animal'" (p. 66). As demonstrated, Wells was a primary figure in interrogating the "Black rapist" and "bestial race" discourses that dehumanized and animalized Black men especially. Wells described an early "controlling image" for Black men that functioned concurrently with the Aunt Jemima image of Black women (Collins, 2008). She turned this discourse on its head and instead showed how harsh white society is by exposing and reflecting it. Black people are not any more *animal* than white people. They were (and are) *animalized* in an attempt to affirm an erroneous and feeble white supremacy.

Also recognizing the white privilege present in even some of the most critical veins of animal studies, M. Shadee Malaklou (2021) uses the horror/suspense films by Jordan Peele, *Get Out* and *Us*, to illustrate how notions of Blackness and animality are intertwined. She reinvigorates the maxim that no group can be liberated until Black women are liberated. Malaklou argues that the notion of animality is already raced and that notions of race are always and already animalized. In so doing, it is clear that animality and race are not just linked or intersect but always exist simultaneously. Wells' deft deconstruction of this binary over a century ago helped create a historical lineage of Black and eco-feminists from which CAS draws inspiration.

## Conclusion

By focusing on Ida Wells, the major point of this chapter is to highlight the historical and foundational influence the Black feminist body of work plays for CAS. For CAS, all the themes discussed above in Wells' life and work resonate with the goal of total liberation—that struggles for nonhuman liberation are inextricably linked. CAS asserts that Black liberation is animal liberation and vice versa. This is of further importance to CAS (and beyond) because scholars of color, particularly women of color, have been and continue to be left out of not only CAS history but also present-day CAS activism. It is important to realize that contemporary activism has evolved from earlier struggles, sometimes mimicking tactics and other times abandoning them, but always learning from past efforts. CAS must do likewise, and Ida B. Wells is one such guiding light.

## Acknowledgment

We would like to thank William Horne for thoughtfully providing suggestions for an early draft of this chapter.

## References

Alabi, K., Greenlee, C. R., & Zinzi, J. A. (2021). *The echoing Ida collection*. Feminist Press at CUNY.

Alexander, M. (2012). *The new Jim Crow: Mass incarceration in the age of colorblindness*. New Press.

Allen, S. E. (2021). The Black feminist roots of scholar-activism: Lessons from Ida B. Wells-Barnett. In Z. Luna & W. Pirtle (Eds.), *Black feminist sociology: Perspectives and praxis* (pp. 32–44). Routledge.

Anderson, W. C. (2021). *The nation on no map: Black anarchism and abolition*. AK Press.

Bay, M., Griffin, F. J., Royster, M. S., & Savage, B. D. (2015). *Toward an intellectual history of Black women*. The University of North Carolina Press.

Best, S., Nocella II, A. J., Kahn, R., Gigliotti, C., & Kemmerer, L. (2007). The ten principles of critical animal studies. *Journal for Critical Animal Studies*, 5(1), 4–5.

Bey, M. (2019). *Them good rules: Fugitive essays on radical Black feminism*. University of Arizona Press.

Boisseron, B. (2018). *Afro-dog: Blackness and the animal question*. Columbia University Press.

Carby, H. V. (1985). On the threshold of Woman's Era: Lynching, empire, and sexuality in Black feminist theory. *Critical Inquiry 12*(1), 262–277.

Collins, P. H. (2008). *Black feminist thought: Knowledge, consciousness, and the politics of empowerment* (2nd ed.). Routledge.

Crenshaw, K. (1989). Demarginalizing the intersection of race and sex: A Black Feminist critique of antidiscrimination doctrine, feminist theory and antiracist politics. *University of Chicago Legal Forum, 1*, 139–167.

Dray, P. (2003). *At the hands of persons unknown: The lynching of black America*. Modern Library.

Free, L. E. (2015). *Suffrage reconstructed: Gender race, and voting rights in the Civil War era*. Cornell University Press.

Giddings, P. (1984). *When and where I enter: The impact of Black women on race and sex in America*. W. Morrow.

Giddings, P. (2008). *Ida, a sword among lions: Ida B. Wells and the campaign against lynching*. Amistad.

Gillespie, M., & McMillen, S. (Eds.). (2014). *North Carolina women: Their lives and times—volume 1*. University of Georgia Press.

Hartman, S. (2007). *Lose your mother: A journey along the Atlantic slave route*. Farrar, Strauss, and Giroux.

hooks, b. (1981). *Ain't I a woman? Black women and feminism.* South End Press.

hooks, b. (1984). *Feminist theory: From margin to center.* South End Press.

Jackson, Z. I. (2020). *Becoming human: Matter and meaning in an antiblack world.* NYU Press.

Ko, A., & Ko, S. (2017). *Aphro-ism: Essays on pop culture, feminist, and black veganism from two sisters.* Lantern.

Kraditor, A. S. (1965). *The ideas of the woman suffrage movement, 1890–1920.* Columbia University Press.

Lerner, G. (1972). *Black women in white America: A documenting history.* Pantheon Books.

Lorde, A. (2007). *Sister outsider: Essays and speeches.* Crossing Press.

Malakou, M. S. (2021). Surviving the ends of man: The animal and/as black gaze in Jordan Peele's *Get Out* and *Us. Journal for Critical Animal Studies, 18*(2), 70–99.

Nash, J. (2019). *Black feminism reimagined: After intersectionality.* Duke University Press.

Nocella II, A. J., Seis, M., & Shantz, J. (2019). *Contemporary anarchist criminology: Against authoritarianism and punishment.* Peter Lang.

Nocella II, A. J., & Socha, K. (2022). *Radical animal studies: Beyond respectability politics, opportunism, and cooptation.* Peter Lang.

Nocella II, A. J., Sorenson, J., Socha, K., & Matsuoka, A. (2014). *Defining critical animal studies: An intersectional social justice approach for liberation.* Peter Lang.Parker, M. (2008). Desiring citizenship: A rhetorical analysis of the Wells/Willard controversy. *Women's Studies in Communication, 31*(1), 56–78.

Pinar, W. F. (2006). The emergence of Ida B. Wells. *Curriculum & Teaching Dialogue 8*(½), 153–170. Academic Search Complete, EBSCOhost. Accessed October 17, 2016.

Samudzi, Z., & Anderson, W. C. (2018). *As black as resistance: Finding the conditions for liberation.* AK Press.

Sharpe, C. (2016). *In the wake: On blackness and being.* Duke University Press.

Slagell, A. (2001). The rhetorical structure of Frances E. Willard's campaign for woman suffrage, 1876–1896. *Rhetoric & Public Affairs, 4*(1), 1–23.

Taylor, K.-Y. (2018). *How we get free: Black feminist and the Combahee River Collective.* Haymarket Books.

Vergès, F. (2021). *A decolonial feminism.* Pluto Press.

Waters, K., & Conaway, C. B. (2007). *Black women's intellectual traditions: Speaking their minds.* University of Vermont Press.

Watkins, R. N. (2008). The Southern roots of Ida B. Wells-Barnett's revolutionary activism. *Southern Quarterly, 45*(3), 108–126. Academic Search Complete, EBSCOhost. Accessed October 8, 2016.

Wells-Barnett, I. B. (1970). *Crusade for Justice: The Autobiography of Ida B. Wells.* University of Chicago Press.

Wells-Barnett, I. B., & Royster, J. J. (1997). *Southern horrors and other writings: The antilynching campaign of Ida B. Wells, 1892–1900.* Bedford Books.

Williams, J. A., Logan, T. D., & Hardy, B. L. (2021). The persistence of historical racial violence and political suppression: Implications for contemporary regional inequality. *The ANNALS of the American Academy of Political and Social Science, 694*(1), 92–107.

Wood, A. L. (2009). *Lynching and spectacle: Witnessing racial violence in America, 1890–1940*. University of North Caroline Press.

Zamalin, A. (2022). *Against civility: The hidden in our obsession with civility*. Beacon Press.

# 8 Listening to and Learning with African Anarchism, Black Anarchism, and Anarcho-Blackness

NATHAN POIRIER & SIMON SPRINGER

This chapter highlights the importance of studying African and Black anarchism and the fundamental philosophies behind the scholar-activists who support these modes of thought. Given this chapter's subject matter, its authors wish to declare our identities for transparency. Nate is a straight, white, middle-class cisgender person who, at the time of writing, is a doctoral candidate at a leading research university in the United States. Simon is straight, white, male, and a recent migrant to Australia, where he works as a university professor and in a middle management position as a Head of a Department. None of these facets, nor all of them together, grant us any authority to offer universal thoughts on African and Black anarchisms. There cannot be a single authority on such a topic, and otherwise, our positionalities situate us as outsiders to this philosophy and practice with much to learn. We follow Marquis Bey (2022, footnote 8, p. 230) in signaling our identities to situate ourselves, but also note that this "outsiderness" does not intrinsically preclude us from being able to understand conditions and social locations that are not our own. Nor do they function as excuses for *not* doing so. This chapter, then, aims to summarize, think about, and learn from African anarchism, Black anarchism, and anarcho-blackness to become better anarchists and advocates for global social justice. This analysis is for people interested in anarchism, anti-authoritarianism, or total liberation from an African or Black perspective. We direct readers to the primary sources cited herein for further details, in the authors' own words, borne of their individual and sometimes shared experiences. We also note that in recent handbooks on anarchism, such as Levy and Adams (2019) or Chartier and Schoelandt (2021), neither gives space to African or Black anarchism. This chapter is as much an attempt to learn from these traditions as it is to open a dialogue about the importance of foregrounding other-than-white anarchisms.

The authors' interest in the topic stems from our belief that all oppression is fundamentally linked and mutually reinforcing. Anarchism's universal dictum of "no gods, no masters" and inherent skepticism towards authority resonate with our feeling that all oppression is equally wrong and must be resisted holistically. We were both initially influenced by classical anarchists from Europe and North America. Reading outside this familiar setting became necessary after realizing that this ethnocentric profile of authors is contrary to the fundamental tenets of anarchism itself. Therefore, this chapter focuses on four anarchist texts from African and Black authors originally published between 1979 and 2021. The texts are *African Anarchism: The History of a Movement* by Sam Mbah and I.E. Igariwey (1997/2014), *Anarchism and the Black Revolution* by Lorenzo Kom'boa Ervin (1979/2022), *The Nation on No Map: Black Anarchism and Abolition* by William C. Anderson (2021), and *Anarcho-Blackness: Notes Towards a Black Anarchism* by Marquis Bey (2020). This chapter uses the 2014 edition of *African Anarchism* and the 2022 Pluto Press edition of *Anarchism and the Black Revolution* because they are slightly more up-to-date versions than their original editions. Each text will be briefly summarized individually and then brought together for discussion along with additional texts on African and Black anarchism to help inform commentary and provide additional context and dimensionality.

A particular point bears acknowledgment before proceeding. Of the authors centered in this chapter, most are described or describe themselves (either in the description or biographies for the books under consideration) with masculine pronouns. Bey is known to favor they/them pronouns but also includes "or any" on their website, accompanied by a note that directly gets at Bey's general disdain for gender markers and ultimate indifference to pronouns (Bey, 2021a). Therefore, the main authors studied in this chapter identify as and "appear" male. This will necessarily diminish the overall representativeness of the authors, their works, and this chapter. Perhaps the best-known Black woman anarchist is Lucy Parsons, although she subordinated gender issues to class issues (see a large collection of her writings in Ahrens, 2003). We are aware there are Black women anarchists and African/Black anarchists of all genders. But the aforementioned texts were chosen because they are book length treatises of fairly recent (re/)publication(s) that focus on and use the term "anarchism" explicitly.

Lastly, just as this book was going to production, this chapter's authors became aware of *Black Anarchism and the Black Radical Tradition*

(Bagby-Williams & Suekama, 2022) published in late 2022. It was too late to integrate this text, so suffice it to mention that this short work compliments this chapter. Bagby-Williams & Suekama cover similar ground but do so with a different approach, highlighting different points and provide some critique, a feature this chapter intentionally lacks.

## An Overview of the Main Texts

### African Anarchism—*Sam Mbah and I.E. Igariwey*

Mbah and Igariwey open their book on the history and basic principles of European anarchism, and a couple of middle chapters are devoted to the rise and failure of African socialism. As our chapter is concerned specifically with African anarchism, our overview focuses on the remaining chapters of *African Anarchism* that deal with this directly. The central point of Mbah and Igariwey is that traditional, pre-colonial African societies (which they deem "communalist") were based "to a greater or lesser extent" on anarchist elements (p. 26). African communalism was centered around local collectives that worked to produce for and support each other. Surpluses were shared via barter with those who had deficits, and the entire community took part in ceremonies and dealt with transgressors. Nevertheless, "despite the marked equality and egalitarianism generally associated with African communalism," the authors caution, "communalism was not an anarchist utopia" (p. 32). There existed a caste system in which women were often given less social status than men. However, this was not uniform throughout pre-colonized Africa, where there were several matrifocal communities led by women leaders. Indeed, the authors open their chapter on African anarchism by discussing the immense diversity of African peoples and practices that have always existed. Even so, traditional African societies were similar in their degree of decentralization, diffused concentration of authority, and general leaderlessness (p. 37).

Mbah and Igariwey argue that European capitalism and subsequent colonization of the continent displaced Africa's traditional social and cultural organization, if only unevenly, "haphazard[ly] and incomplete[ly]" by western modes of production and governance, and continue to this day (p. 43). Colonialists instituted western means of education, law, military, and ethnic and class consciousness. The western education system in Africa seeks to educate a privileged few, resulting in massive illiteracy and inequality, which prevents the spread of ideas, especially radical ones. The authors recognize the law as a social construction that can be and often is arbitrarily applied, where protections can be withdrawn at any time (see also Jackson in BRAF,

2016). The military acts as the violent wing of the state to suppress radical consciousness raising, and the elite pit ethnicities and classes against each other to undermine solidarity and unified resistance. Nevertheless, Mbah and Igariwey see hope in this darkness. Although slow and difficult, they see an "undeniable" overall trend towards individual and collective freedom: "Given the endemic and irresolvable crises of both capitalism and state socialism, humanity's next step must almost inevitably be toward greater individual freedom and greater social equality—that is, toward anarchism...." (p. 95). In fact, despite capitalism, colonialism, and state control, Mbah and Igariwey see great potential for anarchism to emerge (p. 100): "The relevance of anarchism to human society has nowhere been more obvious than it is in Africa. ... anarchism is really the only liberating concept capable of turning 'the dark continent' in a truly forward-looking direction."

As a point of note, Mbah and Igariwey structure their discussion of African colonialism to essentially suggest that all significant social problems in Africa arose after Europeans arrived. In some ways, this is undeniably true. The introduction of capitalism and a certain view of the human, values, and ethics by Europeans (not just white Europeans) destroyed the continent and pre-colonial societies. But pre-colonial Africa was not utopian. Not only was there fairly widespread gender inequality (which Mbah and Igariwey acknowledge) but also intracontinental slavery (although through various slave narratives at least, it is known that African slavery was qualitatively more "tolerable" and less brutal than U.S. slavery). Thus, we must avoid placing blame and instead focus on understanding the history, theory, and practice of African and Black anarchism.

## Anarchism and the Black Revolution—Lorenzo Kom'boa Ervin

As Ervin explains in the introduction to the fourth edition of his book, *Anarchism and the Black Revolution* is a classic in the radical Black tradition. Ervin's Black anarchism is the ideas of European anarchism applied to the Black condition (see also Umoja, 2019). It critiques previous Black rights and liberation struggles and western anarchism from a Black anarchist perspective. His take is that western anarchists do not take the concerns of Black people across the globe seriously, and that most Black struggles were and are not anarchist. Something readers will likely notice is Ervin's support of violence. Before anyone dismisses Ervin and/or Black anarchism in a knee-jerk reaction to this, Ervin's "support" is nuanced, conditional, and seen as a regrettable, last resort. Yet, Ervin also views violence as a necessary part of Black revolution. This is because, as he repeatedly points out, those invested in the current capitalist-colonialist world order will not relinquish power without using all conceivable violence themselves. So, those waging a (Black) revolution must also be knowledgeable about and willing to use so-called violence as self-defense to secure their right to an autonomous life. Furthermore, Ervin distances himself and Black anarchism from western anarchists' "propaganda by the deed," which often refers to violent attacks on heads of state or other elites with the intent to kill. Nor does Ervin support acts of terrorism or militarism. Ervin envisions arming the masses to defend themselves from violent outsiders who will try to crush their anarchist uprisings and autonomous existences.

Ervin keeps one critical eye on the state and anyone fashioned as a leader, while keeping another on the people. This represents a turning away from the state and authorities and towards communities: "As long as Black people believe that some moral or political authority of the white government has legitimacy in their lives, ... then they cannot effectively fight back. They must free their minds of the ideas of American patriotism and begin to see themselves as a new people" (p. 127). Ervin envisions this happening through a series of nested federations beginning with local communities and extending outwards to encapsulate the entire globe eventually. He acknowledges that a Black revolution will take time and happen gradually, and that between now and Black liberation, a time of "survival programs" is necessary, "meaning surviving under this system pending a social revolution" (p. 131). This time of survival is where Ervin sees violence as necessary.

Ervin also continually refers to additional non-Black people of color, including the (white) poor and working class, and their struggles. This, he explains, could be done through building alliances and recognition of a common, yet specifically unique, subjugation to capitalist-colonialist conditions. Ervin emphasizes that liberation will only happen with the vast majority of oppressed people in every nation rising together in solidarity. He offers numerous lists and demands for this purpose but realizes that each community must work within the constraints of its local circumstances. His suggestions generally cluster around two principles. One is that the oppressed have the numbers and ability to overthrow the ruling class through economic warfare, meaning boycotts, labor, and rent strikes, and withholding taxes (see pp. US100–107). His other focus is on building Black life forms, such as transformative justice, self-sufficiency in food production, and community control of business, housing, and schools (see pp. 123–124 and 132–134).

## *The Nation on No Map*—*William C. Anderson*

To a good extent, *The Nation on No Map*, extends the Black anarchism of Ervin. The book rests on how Black people have never been and were never meant to be citizens of the US, and, therefore, they also never will be. The US would not exist but for the brutal and ongoing enslavement of Black people, requiring this to function. Anderson argues that since Black people and citizenship (of anywhere, really, but mainly speaking from and about a US context) are mutually exclusive, there is nothing to be gained by engaging the state in any of its apparatuses. Rather, the state should be completely abandoned without compromise. All other attempts are futile. This is the essence of anarchism but grounded in the US Black experience. Like Ervin, Anderson discusses Black capitalism and the adverse effects of idolizing Black "leaders" or celebrities. Anderson says such idolatry plays into and maintains white supremacy by glorifying the logic of oppression and hierarchy that reinscribes subservience and capitulates to the white power structure:

> The people occupying these high positions in white society are safety valves to quell Black uprising and complaints. We are all supposed to be happy because "one of us" made it. However, what does any of this matter if *where* they're making it is a place that needs to be completely torn down? (p. 61).

This is the radicalism of (Black) anarchy. Always studying history, Anderson notes that there is no evidence that elites, the state, capitalism, or leaders will ever lead to Black liberation or even create the conditions where liberation becomes possible as "Wealth cannot exist without poverty" (p. 51). Black anarchism is not about overturning white supremacy for Black supremacy but eradicating the notion of supremacy. Black liberation is not *only* Black liberation, but liberation of all the oppressed.

There is a limited discussion of violence as self-defense. Mostly for Anderson, Black anarchism/liberation/autonomy is rooted in solidarity, mutual aid, and free sharing. But an awareness of the necessity of violence to sustain peaceful coexistence is ever present, if lamentable. He says the Black community is not welcome anywhere (hence the book's title). More distressing than Anderson's discussion of self-defense is his discussion of the yearning –one might even say lusting—for a civil war by white supremacists. They are just aching to wreak a wholesale onslaught on those unwilling to explicitly and directly uphold a fascist state in the US. Under these circumstances, it is unsurprising that Anderson would advocate knowledge of weapons and a willingness to use them to defend life. He calls the lack of willingness to unite in accepting this fact and preparedness in this area "a recipe for a massacre" (p. 124). He eschews incremental changes and advocates finding ways to resist capitalism in our everyday lives.

## *Anarcho-Blackness—Marquis Bey*

Bey theorizes connections between Blackness and anarchism, questioning the term "Black anarchism" or the application of "anarchism" or "anarchist" to any particular radical. Bey removes the "ism" and focuses instead on the "anarcho" and "blackness." Black anarchism, or anarcho-Blackness, cannot just be a meeting of these two critical spheres, but something that pushes anarchism outside its European containment. In Bey's terms, a meeting with Blackness, particularly of a queer and trans feminist kind, "anarchizes" anarchism. This echoes Hannibul Balagoon Shakur who says, "Anarchism like anything else finds a radical new meaning when it meets blackness." Thus, Bey's formulation is almost a re-theroization of anarchism itself which does not need to take the name anarchism, or any other name for that matter. Bey is more concerned with actions and how those actions are orientated within and towards freedom, abolition, and on behalf of the marginalized. This is not to say anarchism per se is ignored. Bey acknowledges that anarcho-Blackness is "indebted" to anarchism but that its spirit is diminished if not thoroughly infused with Black trans feminism.

Bey argues from the beginning that anarcho-blackness has a strong current of radical black feminism running through it. She spends a lot of the book talking about this point. Bey asserts that Blackness, queerness, transness, and gender nonnormativity embody anarchic elements in thwarting authorized and prescribed ways of existing. Marquis also is clear that an anarchist revolution is not an endpoint. Instead, there is always more—more work to do and, especially, more possibilities. "It is misguided to presume that an anarchic world, …is the 'end' of anarchist pursuits" (p. 23). An anarchic world is always unfolding and indeterminable, and it plans for this: "Fugitive planning plans for what it cannot plan for by refusing to plan for it" (p. 26). This openness continues into Bey's suggestions for praxis that involve a radical and unconditional inclusivity towards (care for) others, "a lesson learned in the Black Radical Tradition, Black feminisms, and trans activism" (p. 28). Admittedly, this sort of openness creates vulnerability and risks betrayal, but also "leaves the door open" to those needing help. Forfeiting the potential to help others is unacceptable. The book ends with a call for autonomy in an "anarcho-Blackness manifesto":

> We want you to demand better by planting a garden and calling out white supremacist patriarchal cisheteropatriarchy; demand better by asking comrades

and accomplices "You good?" and punching Nazis; demand better by opening the door for the many-and-non-gendered kinfolk who you've just met for the first time and literally stealing from universities and jails and corporations. Do what you can, do all you can, where you're at right now and wherever else you might end up (p. 107)

## Touchstones, Departures, and Lessons: Towards Greater Solidarity for Total Liberation

Just as the European-named and -theorized tradition of "anarchism" may have influenced anti-authoritarian struggles around the world, so too have Black people moved around the world, bringing revolutionary ideas with them. This sort of anarchism as mutual aid dates to time immemorial. European theorists simply gave a name to the patterns of mutual aid that could be witnessed all across the globe. There are similarities and differences between African and Black anarchism. We interpret African anarchism as anarchism by African people applied to an African context specifically, as this is how Mbah and Igariwey seem to apply it. And we think about Black anarchism as anarchism by and applied to Black people outside of Africa as this seems to be the context of all the Black anarchist sources we've read. So to us, the distinction is merely geographical but important. African and Black anarchism, although distinct in many ways (as Ervin notes, many US Black radicals feel no connection to Africa whatsoever), also contain much overlap. The global Black diaspora has its origins in Africa, and many Black anarchists see their oppression as a direct extension of "the invasion of Africa to capture slaves" (Balagoon, in Black Rose Anarchist Federation, 2016, p. 76). *Black Anarchism: A Reader* (Black Rose Anarchist Federation, 2016), referred to hereafter as BRAF, is a preeminent source that brings many works of Black anarchism together where many comment on the link between contemporary (at their time of writing) Black struggle and European colonization of Africa. This sense of continuity is born of slavery and carries through to mass incarceration (Umoja, 2019; Williams, 2015), as made explicit by Pedro Ribeiro: "when the slavery of the children of Africa was carried out by chain and whip instead of uniforms and patrol cars...." (BRAF, 2016, p. 91). Indeed, Kuwasi Balagoon, Lorenzo Kom'boa Ervin, and Ashanti Alson became anarchists while in prison. And then, of course, the thirteenth amendment of the US Constitution directly connects and extends slavery through incarceration (Jackson in BRAF, 2016). This link leads to African and Black anarchist support for "third world" and colonized peoples (Ervin, 2022; Balagoon in BRAF, 2016).

*African Anarchism* is more about trying to recreate pre-colonial societies in Africa to achieve anarchy (again). Such a mode of living predates any encounter with European thought about anarchism. In contrast, Bey's anarcho-Blackness emphasizes the openness and imaginative possibilities of the future to create *new* conditions for liberation, what Bey sees as central to anarchism and queer/transness. All African and Black anarchisms we examined are resolutely against reforms which are perceieved as loosening the handcuffs but not removing them. Black anarchism is about turning one's back on reforms and all legal and state means to instead create conditions in the here and now that foster one's liberation. It is creative and productive. Black anarchism can be thought of (although not entirely) as a reaction to white anarchism (an adaptation of its ideas to Black people), and anarcho-Blackness as somewhat of a reaction to Black anarchism. Yet, Black anarchism and anarcho-Blackness support community autonomy with community control over social discipline (deemed transformative justice), schooling, food production, housing, health care, and more.

As mentioned, the Black anarchism of Anderson and Ervin are similar. Anderson wrote the foreword to the 2022 edition of *Anarchism and the Black Revolution*, while Ervin wrote the afterword to *The Nation on No Map*. Both authors strongly advocate for self-defense. It is also clear that neither likes the idea of "violence" nor wants to see or use it. The emphasis is on peaceful solutions. It seems obvious that Ervin, Anderson, people in their communities and in others, would be perfectly content with peacefully creating their own autonomous lives and living centers, and leaving it at that. As Ervin says, "We would all choose to be pacifists if that were possible" (p. 63). It may seem ironic, but it is this insistence on peace that necessitates the use of "violence" for self-defense, for the capitalist white-supremacist system will not allow marginalized peoples and communities to live under their own wills. As Francoise Verges states, "if the state wants to crush a movement, it will use all the means and resources at its disposal to both repress and to divide the oppressed" (2021, p. 8). Ervin and Anderson use the murder of Black Panther Fred Hampton as an example. If revolutionaries become successful, their lives become direct targets of the state. For Kuwasi Balagoon, "the state's escalation of the war against Black people" is what convinced him that "I would have to go underground and literally fight" (in BRAF, 2016, p. 76). Greg Jackson (in BRAF, 2016, pp. 100–111) provides historical precedents of state use of, support for, or indifference to violence against Black communities and individuals to keep them from acting autonomously, *and* the "violence" it took to enforce the rights of Black citizens to vote after the Civil War which was a right supposedly constitutionally guaranteed.

Samudzi and Anderson (2018) note how "countless other Black leaders" including Martin Luther King, Jr., Malcolm X, W.E.B. Du Bois, Fannie

Lou Hammer, Ida B. Wells, explicitly noted the importance of self-defense (what the state would term "violence") to defend against white supremacy (p. 61). White supremacist, cisheteropatriarchal capitalism structurally cannot promote or even foster conditions for care because that would necessitate dismantling the entire oppressive system. Violence is implicitly supported by Bey, too, entering only at the very end as if to express, "Oh yea, that will be there too." Again, Bey focuses on peace and, in particular, on love, "a multifaceted love, caressing some while slapping the shit out of others.... asking comrades and accomplices 'You good?' and punching Nazis" (p. 107). We can see that this is not mindless, selfish, wanton, authoritarian violence but the protection of vulnerable people. It is self-defense. As Bey (2021, p. 4) says, "Anderson, and black anarchism and abolition, are about life and conditions for living, very much so." This discussion of "violence" could be a whole other discussion in its own right. We only wish to add that the so-called "violence" of Ervin, Anderson, Balagoon, and others is not necessarily "violence" as commonly defined. The state attempts to define what constitutes "violence" (thereby refusing to acknowledge its own monopoly of violence as violence), which should be rejected.

It is also of note that Bey's anarcho-Blackness is suffused with gender, particularly nonnormative genders. This is somewhat lacking in this chapter's three other main texts and many other sources on African or Black anarchism, although the gender question is far from ignored. Ervin and Anderson (2021; Samudzi & Anderson, 2018) continually mention the need for solidarity with additional oppressed groups, such as women, multiple times throughout their texts, but none give gender the centrality Bey does. Bey's anarcho-Blackness is nothing without a radical sense of gender abolition. Similarly, Mbah and Irariwey make scant mention of African women's conditions, either past or present. They note that women were often subservient to men even in pre-colonial African societies that they see as either anarchic or containing anarchic elements. Importantly, they note this was not always the case, and sometimes it was the other way around. But in general, Mbah and Igariwey, Ervin, and Anderson's African and Black anarchism focus on race over gender.

In Paul Sharkey's translation of *Black Anarchism: A Reader,* we learn that Dimingo Passos, the "Brazilian Bakunin" "put his all into the fight to emancipate men and women" but he does not explain what emancipating women entailed. Ashanti Alson tried to introduce anti-sexism to the Black Panther Party but was met with hostility (Alston, 2004). Umoja (2019, p. 34) raises our attention to Balagoon's bisexuality and that in the Revolutionary Armed Task Force, to which Balagoon belonged, "Differences over ideology and sexual orientation were tolerated and subordinated" to the greater goals of anarchic rebellion. In other words, while sexuality or queerness never became a particular issue in a primarily heteronormative Black Liberation Movement, Balagoon was not internally persecuted for his sexuality. Part of Balagoon's legacy stems from this aspect of his identity, used by some in the Black Liberation Movement and queer groups to challenge homophobia and patriarchy within society and radical Black spaces (Umoja, 2019).

Anderson derives his insight from being a janitor and cleaning up messes. In other words, directly witnessing the shit that is white supremacy. In this manner, Anderson would seem to align with Pedro Ribeiro (in BRAF, 2016, p. 93), a Black Brazilian anarchist who says, "The fact is, we know oppression. We live it, we experience it. ... We do not conceptualize it. We do not sit down and intellectualize about pain because ... we lost the need to understand pain philosophically when we learned it physically." Bey (2021b) respects this but wonders "a bit selfishly, if there are other avenues of discovery and struggle, radicalisation and radicality" (p. 2). Not to denigrate lived knowledge, nor remove itself from it, Bey proposes that an educational vantage point can shine a complementary light on becoming radical. Bey (2021b) also points out how Anderson seems to view abolition as a means to revolution, or one might say contained within revolution. In contrast, Bey suggests that "abolition is not the revolution itself—it is *more*" (p. 3). This difference Bey surmises is only one of semantics, as "I aim only to offer the same, or a similar, goal with different language," (p. 3).

So, what can be learned? Much! Much more is realized than is currently realized or listed here. Nevertheless, by way of conclusion—that is also a beginning—here are some initial lessons we have learned by listening to African anarchism, Black anarchism, and anarcho-Blackness:

1. Strict pacifism won't cut it. Obtaining knowledge of weapons and self-defense is unfortunate and difficult to accept but unavoidable. In the US, the far-right is aching for a civil war (Freedman, 2021), including police saying they cannot wait for a race war so they can kill Black people (MSNBC, 2020) and even encouraging white supremacists to join the Russia-Ukraine war to obtain combat experience (Miller-Idress, 2022). In less than two weeks in the spring of 2022 in the US, 10 Black people in Buffalo, NY, and 19 Latinx children in Texas were killed by mass shootings. For those who wish to stand with the oppressed, "The question is not about being pro-violence or pro-non-violence, but about refusing the bourgeois condemnation of

the violence of the oppressed and favoring a multiplicity of tactics and thus the flexibility and autonomy of struggle" (Verges, 2022, p. 106).

2. African and Black anarchism have always existed. As Mbah and Igariwey note, pre-colonialist African societies contained many anarchic elements, and some could be said to be anarchist. Similarly, due to colonization and slavery in Africa, the Black diaspora has always created its own anarchic survival modes. Both are ongoing, living, and breathing processes with the potential for ongoing cross-pollination between these two trajectories of anarchist praxis.

3. White anarchists must seek out and learn from African and Black anarchisms to learn about these communities' circumstances and visions for obtaining freedom in ways that support them. African and Black history must be learned by those outside these regions, ethnicities, and communities, especially regarding radical underground resistance, to understand tactics and historical circumstances. Such knowledge can lead to understanding a place and community that is not one's own and to more effective strategizing, organizing, tactics, and coalition building. Yet, white people will always remain secondary in Black anarchism. As Ashanti Alston (in BRAF, 2016, p. 74) says, "WHITE ANARCHISTS, DEAL WITH BEING THE BEST ANTI-RACIST ALLIES YOU CAN. WE NEED YOU BUT WE WILL DO THIS SHIT WITHOUT YOU" (emphasis original).

4. Some people and communities that practice anarchism or have anarchist elements might not call it that. Similarly, some people might call their politics "anarchist," while others might not. Both situations are okay! In fact, it would be damaging for outsiders to label others' politics, and if done by whites, it reinforces colonialism. As Ashanti Alston says, those "outside of our [African/Black] experience need to respect that they aint got no monopoly on revolutionary thinking and dam[n] sure aint got none on revolutionary practice" (BRAF, 2016, p. 73).

5. Anarchism, in whatever form and under whatever name, must be the backdrop for liberatory praxis. Anything less allows for and creates a ruling class and those who are ruled. This is unacceptable as it is just a recasting of the present situation. Frustration with the lack of a revolutionary potential has been a primary impetus for Black anarchists (see Alston [BRAF, 2016]; Balagoon [BRAF, 2016]; Umoja, 2019; Ervin, 2022; Anderson & Samudzi, 2017.)

6. Black anarchism(s) are part of an overall liberation movement involving people of color, economically exploited peoples, (dis)abled, women, queer and trans folks, children, indigenous peoples, and the Earth

(see especially Ervin, 2022, p. 86). While unique in various ways, there is a realization that people and groups share certain features of oppression. This can even extend to those who can oppress and are oppressed by oppressive systems. The point is not to dominate the dominators but to eliminate all domination.

7. It is up to us as white radicals (although "radicals" should be superfluous) to engage with African and Black anarchisms, communities, and individuals. We must support and join Black, Indigenous, and people of color as they struggle for liberation. As Greg Jackson says, "the choice facing whites is to adapt themselves to, and make meaningful contributions to, the mass uprising and revolution of non-white workers and poor people or to join the various forces of reaction from the right of center politicians to far-right militias/nazis/Klan extremists." Bringing about revolution will entail giving up much of what some of us already have, but we all stand to gain so much more in return.

## Acknowledgment

We thank Marquis Bey for providing helpful comments on an earlier draft of this chapter.

## References

Ahrens, G. (Ed.). (2003). *Lucy Parsons: Freedom, equality & solidarity – writings and speeches, 1878–1937.* Charles H. Kerr.

Alston, A. (2004). Black anarchism. *Anarchist Panther* (Spring), 6.

Anderson, W. C. (2021). *The nation on no map: Black anarchism and abolition.* AK Press.

Anderson, W. C., & Samudzi, Z. (2017). The Anarchism of Blackness. *ROAR Magazine, 5.*

Bagby-Williams, A., & Suekama, N. Z. (2022). *Black anarchism and the black radical tradition: Moving beyond racial capitalism.* Daraja Press.

Bey, M. (2020). *Anarcho-blackness: Notes toward a black anarchism.* AK Press.

Bey, M. (2021a). https://www.marquisbey.com.

Bey, M. (2021b). [Review of the book *The nation on no map*, by W. C. Anderson]. *Antipode*, 1–4. https://antipodeonline.org/2021/11/19/the-nation-on-no-map/

Bey, M. (2022). *Black trans feminism.* Duke University Press.

Black Rose Federation. (2016). *Black anarchism: A reader.* Black Rose Anarchist Federation. http://blackrosefed.org/black-anarchism-a-reader/

Chartier, G., & van Schoelandt, C. (2021). *The Routledge handbook of anarchy and anarchist thought.* Routledge.

Ervin, E. K. (2022[1979]). *Anarchism and the black revolution.* Pluto Press.

Freedman, D. H. (2021, December 20). Millions of angry, armed Americans stand ready to seize power if Trump loses in 2024. *Newsweek.* https://www.newsweek.com/2021/12/31/millions-angry-armed-americans-stand-ready-seize-power-if-trump-loses-2024-1660953.html

Levy, C., & Adams, M. S. (Eds.). (2019). *The Palgrave handbook of anarchism.* Palgrave Macmillan.

Mbah, S., & Igariwey, I. E. (2014[1997]). *African anarchism: The history of a movement.* Bolo'bolo Books.

Miller-Idress, C. (2022). *Fighting Russia in Ukraine sadly appeals to racist, far-right extremists.* MSNBC. https://www.msnbc.com/opinion/msnbc-opinion/fighting-russia-ukraine-sadly-appeals-far-right-extremists-n1290901.

MSNBC. (2020). NC police officers' racist rant caught on tape: 'I Can't Wait' for race war | all in | MSNBC. *YouTube.* https://www.youtube.com/watch?v=0HveFM0Npz0.

Samudzi, Z., & Anderson, W. C. (2018). *As black as resistance: Finding the conditions for liberation.* AK Press.

Umoja, A. (2019). Maroon: Kuwasi Balagoon and the evolution of revolutionary new Afrikan anarchism. In M. Meyer & K. Kersplebedeb (Eds.), *Soldier's story: Revolutionary writings by a new Afrikan anarchist* (pp. 13–45). AK Press.

Verges, F. (2021). *A decolonial feminism.* Pluto Press.

Verges, F. (2022). *A feminist theory of violence.* Pluto Press.

Williams, D. M. (2015). Black Panther radical factionalization and the development of black anarchism. *Journal of Black Studies 46*(7), 678–703.

# 9 Vegan Mutual Aid: Anarchist Solidarity in Times of Crisis

WILL BOISSEAU

> ONLY THE PEOPLE CAN SAVE THE PEOPLE.
> —Brighton Mutual Aid Vegan Foodbank, 10 April 2020

This chapter explores how anarchists, including vegan anarchists, use "mutual aid" to show solidarity in times of crisis. Mutual aid is an increasingly important topic for activists (Spade, 2020), but vegan mutual aid is often missing from this discussion. The chapter begins by defining the anarchist organization theory of mutual aid, popularized by Peter Kropotkin (1996) in his work *Mutual Aid: A Factor of Evolution* (first published in 1902). The term "vegan mutual aid" is used in this chapter to describe initiatives that take an anti-speciesist and total liberation approach to mutual aid, which could include providing vegan meals or caring for both humans and other animals. Other examples of vegan mutual aid might encompass campaigns that support workers in the animal industrial complex, particularly helping workers leave that industry to find new employment, and campaigns against the huge government subsidies in Europe and America that fund the meat and dairy industries (Schleifer & Fischer, 2022). The chapter focuses on using vegan mutual aid during times of crisis, including during the COVID-19 pandemic. The chapter argues that vegan mutual aid provides an organizational framework that will be used with increasing frequency and importance by anarchists as we move into a period of worsening crises of late capitalism— from imperialist wars and climate breakdown to rising poverty and inequality. While statists and capitalists understand crises and disasters as "episodic events that represent a rupture," anarchists recognize that "capitalism is an ongoing disaster" (Firth, 2022, p. 9).

The theme of crisis is an important one for anarchists. Indeed, the sixth Anarchist Studies Network conference, held in 2020 when many comrades were still in lockdown, was themed around "anarchy in crisis" and included panels on climate breakdown, imperialism, global pandemics, war, and revolutions (Anarchist Studies Network, 2020). The chapter ends by discussing examples of vegan mutual aid from ongoing crises worldwide and exploring the lessons for building vegan anarchist solidarity movements. This global dimension is important because colonized and indigenous people have engaged in campaigns linking the oppression of humans and other species (Schleifer & Fischer, 2022). Black, Brown, and Indigenous People of Color (B.B.I.P.O.C.) have been at the forefront of grounding vegan mutual aid in total liberation, which campaigns for human, animal, and environmental liberation simultaneously.

## *What Is Mutual Aid?*

The year 2020 was unprecedented. In the U.K., the coronavirus pandemic has caused the deaths (up to July 2022) of over 198,000 people (UK Health Security Agency, 2022). During this time, the conservative government used the pandemic as a shield to further privatize the National Health Service (N.H.S.) and transfer wealth and power to corporate interests. For anarchists, one unexpected result of the pandemic was that the theory and practice of mutual aid, previously an obscure term primarily used by activists and anarchist academics, went mainstream. Along with words like furlough, social distancing, and super-spreaders, "mutual aid" became a term that defined 2020. The COVID-19 Mutual Aid U.K. Network defines a mutual aid group in the following way, "A mutual aid group is a volunteer-led initiative where groups of people in a particular area join together to support one another, meeting vital community needs without the help of official bodies. They do so in a way that prioritises those who are most vulnerable or otherwise unable to access help through regular channels" (Covid Mutual Aid).

The Network explains the importance of working autonomously, encouraging local mutual aid groups to work independently and avoid working with the police, local councils and authorities, political parties, and government departments (including the Home Office, which controls immigration enforcement), as doing so could prevent vulnerable people from accessing support from the group. Without mentioning the word "anarchist," it is clear from the Network's description that these mutual aid groups are anarchistic in practice:

It is, by definition, a horizontal mode of organising, in which all individuals are equally powerful. There are no "leaders" or unelected "steering committees" in mutual aid projects; there is only a group of people who work together as equals… it's about people coming together, in a spirit of solidarity, to support and look out for one another (Covid Mutual Aid).

Mutual aid is often characterized by spontaneity (Morales, 2021). Activist Christopher Morales explains that "this spontaneous emergence of mutual support has resulted from self-organization to supply what the state could not provide" (2021). During the COVID-19 pandemic, examples of mutual aid included helping people who are homeless by providing accommodation, helping the elderly or other groups who were unable to leave their homes during the pandemic, and providing shelter, support, and safe spaces for victims of domestic violence (Morales, 2021). Mutual aid can be labelled "disaster anarchy" because in times of crisis, such as natural disasters, mutual aid groups emerge to help local communities. Anarchist academic Rhiannon Firth (2022) gives the following examples:

The self-managed autonomous brigades in Mexico after the 2017 earthquakes, a grassroots village solidarity network in Indonesia after the 2004 tsunamis, anarchist responses to Typhoon Yolanda in the Philippines in 2013, and self-management and direct action against the militarisation of disaster zones after earthquakes in Italy in 2012 and 2009 (p. 5).

Naomi Klein (2017, 2007) discusses the shock doctrine, or disaster capitalism, in which the ruling class uses "the public's disorientation following a collective shock […] to push through radical pro-corporate measures." Klein (2017) says that governments will declare a time of "extraordinary politics" after a crisis in capitalism, which is often caused on purpose by the ruling class. During this time, when the public is disoriented or scared, governments can pass legislation that benefits corporations without the usual level of democratic accountability. Examples of this are Chile after the 1973 coup d'état or Russia after the fall of the Soviet Union.

This helps explain how the conservative government in the U.K. was able to distribute £3.5 billion worth of public money in COVID-19-related contracts to companies that had links with their party, to award thousands of these contracts with no tender process, and to hand N.H.S. functions to private companies that wished to destroy the N.H.S. (Rayner, 2021). The ruling class uses disasters as a way to transfer wealth and power further from the hands of the people to the hands of the rich. Mutual aid is the "shock doctrine" of the working class. It is an attempt to use a collective shock or crisis to raise awareness, put power and responsibility in the hands of the people, and set up structures that do not depend on capital or the state.

## Anarchism and Mutual Aid

Firth explains that mutual aid groups "tend not to self-define or follow a single ideology as they value diversity and hybridity" (2022, p. 11). On the face of it, it is understandable that mutual aid groups that operated during the COVID-19 pandemic did not use the term "anarchist." Firstly, key activists might not have been ideologically anarchist, they simply recognized that at a time of crisis when the government was too incompetent and uncaring to help people in dire situations, communities, neighborhoods, and networks had to help each other. Secondly, anarchist activists might have felt that avoiding the A-word would help build larger networks across diverse communities, bringing in people not traditionally involved in activist circles. Aiden and Sam (2021), who were active with mutual aid groups in Glasgow (Scotland) and Brighton (on the south coast of England), explain that mutual aid groups "don't have a specifically anarchist position or a clearly defined critique of the capitalist system." This reflects the broad range of people who participated in mutual aid groups, and "another factor is the urgency of the crisis, which meant that groups needed to be set up quickly without having a lot of political discussions beforehand" (Aiden & Sam, 2021). That said, anarchists can take great pride in the effectiveness and spread of mutual aid groups during the pandemic.

Peter Kropotkin's *Mutual Aid*, published in 1902, has had a long-lasting impact on the imagination and political development of anarchists. Kropotkin's (1996) essential belief was that in the natural world, "we already find the feature which will also be distinctive of human societies—that is, work in common" (p. 45). Kropotkin's writings have given anarchists ideas for organizations based on mutual support, solidarity, and equality. Kropotkin believed societies thrived on solidarity and support, not competition and social Darwinism. As two anarchist academics, Thomas Swann and Ruth Kinna (2020), explain:

> As an ethical idea, mutual aid describes the efforts people make to help others without seeking reward. It thrives in local, voluntary organisation. The Lifeboat Association, initiated in the U.K. by William Hillary to support the foundation of a national institution to save victims of shipwrecks, was an example of the ethical self-organising that Kropotkin had in mind.

In the case of the COVID-19 pandemic, mutual aid efforts included local networks that collected and delivered food and other essential items to people who couldn't leave their homes and communities, pooling resources to help those who needed help (Swann & Kinna, 2020). These efforts to help each other are like the Black Panthers' community groups, whose goal was "survival until the revolution." However, the Black Panthers framed their initiatives within a Maoist concept of "serving the people" rather than the anarchist concept of mutual aid (Lachowicz & Donaghey, 2021, p. 430).

Over 4,300 mutual aid groups have formed in the U.K. since the start of the COVID-19 pandemic (Power & Benton, 2021). Groups have formed in every part of the country and are typically organized around local communities and neighborhoods. Most of the 2,062 groups listed on www.mutual-aid.co.uk/ cover specific neighborhoods, boroughs, or postcodes. Other groups have been formed around churches, political parties, community groups, and football (soccer) teams. The Dons Local Action Group, a mutual aid network in South West London based around the local football team, was formed in March 2020 with the aim of "collecting and delivering food to vulnerable and self-isolating residents" (Dons Local Action Group). The group expanded from delivering food to supporting children who did not have computer access, supplying essential furniture and white goods to residents, supporting refugees, tidying local areas, and growing food for the community in local allotments.

Many of these mutual aid groups sprang up when the need arose in local communities and disbanded when the immediate urgent need for them receded. However, 40 percent of the groups formed in the first months of 2020 still exist two years later, helping communities with the rising cost of living crisis as millions of people in the U.K. fear falling into fuel poverty (Hall, 2022). *Guardian* journalist Rachel Hall explains that these groups have "moved on to help people in other ways, for instance, through community kitchens, food banks, and skills exchanges" (Hall, 2022). Such avenues are ideal for vegan activists who want to provide healthy and nutritious vegan meals to their local community.

There is a slight contradiction between the anarchist roots of mutual aid and the direction that some groups have taken since the pandemic; this is partly because of the "adoption of mutual aid by non-anarchist Leftists" which "has involved reinterpreting (or misinterpreting) the concept within a statist framework" (Lachowicz & Donaghey, 2021, p. 430). In some parts of the U.K., mutual aid groups spontaneously formed to help people in need and became part of the local government's official emergency response (Hall, 2022). Some groups welcomed this and were happy to see their role formalized within local government structures. Other groups recognized that this contradicted the anarchistic principles on which the mutual aid groups were founded. In Brighton, the council attempted to form a mutual aid network "from above," but without the spontaneity and support of local activists, this was not successful (Aidan & Sam, 2021). Ann Power and Ellie Benton (2021), two researchers from the London School of Economics, argue that local authorities have a duty to support mutual aid groups, in particular by helping them secure sources of funding and by helping the groups become "sustainable" in the long term. Power and Benton (2021) view the informal nature of mutual aid groups negatively, and believe that formalizing the groups, including bringing in safeguarding policies and systems to manage and fund them, would help sustain them long-term. In this way, mutual aid groups would act like local governments or bigger charities.

Power and Benton (2021) recognize that there will be a balance so as not to undermine the existing way that mutual aid groups operate. The community empowerment organization We're Right Here is calling on the government to introduce a "Community Power Act," which would provide mutual aid groups with a sustainable funding model and would allow councils and local people to have a greater say over local services and public spaces (Hall, 2022). Anarchists will be shocked to hear mutual aid groups discussed this way because if the groups are not horizontal, voluntary, decentralized, and autonomous, the group structure loses its connection to anarchism. Aiden and Sam (2021), two activists from Glasgow and Brighton, explain the problems of governments attempting to co-opt mutual aid groups:

> Here a good example is the "big society" slogan used by the Conservative party in the 2010 election, which reflected their belief that austerity and cuts to the already threadbare social safety net could be offset by local voluntary provision. Far from challenging the capitalist system and the state, mutual aid is here welcomed as a way to prop up disintegrating state support.

States have not just sought to remove the radicalism of mutual aid groups through formalization and incorporation. When deemed necessary, states have used spies and agent provocateurs to disrupt mutual aid efforts, as was the case with the Common Ground Collective, which operated in New Orleans after Hurricane Katrina in 2005 (Williams & Crow, 2014).

Mutual aid groups should stay separate from state and local governments for practical and philosophical reasons. One of the reasons mutual aid groups can immediately help those in need is their spontaneity and connection to local communities. In contrast, if group structures are formalized, there is a danger that they will be bogged down in local government bureaucracy and lose their efficiency.

## Vegan Mutual Aid

Vegan mutual aid refers to approaches that consider both humans and other animals as part of the communities that are being supported. Rebecca Maness (2021), a People for the Ethical Treatment of Animals (PETA) activist, explains that the goal of mutual aid organizing is to create a community based on equality and compassion. To achieve that, animals should also be taken into consideration. Additionally, vegan food is often less expensive, healthier, and better for the environment.

The most obvious example is giving vegan food to people who need it. Other examples include caring for human and nonhuman animals, helping people with companion animals, protecting local wildlife, and keeping parks and natural areas clean. The most obvious example of vegan mutual aid groups operating under the Food Not Bombs banner is that Food Not Bombs groups do not simply aim to share free vegan food with protesters and the hungry. They also practice prefigurative ways of "working together using consensus and implementing their visions independent of government or corporate control" (McHenry, 2012, p. 12). Vegan mutual aid also provides anarchists with the opportunity to suggest sustainable, non-hierarchical alternatives to the existing system. For instance, Food Not Bombs activists believe that the skills they develop in collecting and sharing food can be used for a range of projects that serve the community, from growing food to providing fresh water and even providing shelter, healthcare, education, and entertainment (McHenry, 2012, p. 12). In this way, Food Not Bombs activism helps participants build an anarchistic community.

Other examples include community refrigerators that stock vegan items. Community fridges are spaces where people can donate food items to other members of the community who may not be able to afford the items. Some community fridges only ask for meat and dairy-free items to ensure healthy vegan food is distributed to those who need it (Maness, 2021). Most mutual aid groups that distribute food include vegan options for those who request them. Specific groups also supply vegan food, such as the Mutual Aid Vegan Foodbank in Brighton, which aims "to provide vegan food and toiletries to anyone in need of help with basic supplies" (Cowley Club). The group explains that, "Part of our mission is also promoting alternative choices that don't involve using animal products. For this reason the food bank is vegan, but any donations that are not suitable for us will be passed on to other food banks in the area" (Cowley Club).

The Brighton Mutual Aid Vegan Foodbank highlights its flexibility in ensuring that non-vegan products are distributed to those in need by other food banks. This is typical of the response from vegans, who always prioritize the most urgent needs. For instance, during the mutual aid efforts following Hurricane Sandy in 2012, Rainbow Rapid Relief "deviated from their vegetarian principles to accommodate local tastes, for example, by offering hamburgers and pork-roll sandwiches in New Jersey" (Firth, 2022, p. 110).

## Vegan Mutual Aid and the COVID-19 Pandemic

We are in the middle of a series of crises made worse by the animal-industrial complex caused by capitalism. Vegan anarchists are right to think that, as the animal-industrial complex is partly responsible for our state of crisis, vegan anarchists can be part of the solution. The most obvious example is the global warming crisis facing the planet. Food production is responsible for a third of all planet-heating gases emitted by human activity, with 60 percent of this coming from the meat industry (Milman, 2021). Vegan groups such as the Vegan Society U.K. have promoted veganism because "the International Panel on Climate Change has explicitly highlighted that a vegan diet has the highest G.H.G. (greenhouse gas) mitigation potential" (Vegan Society). The coronavirus also has its roots in the animal-industrial complex. The UN and the European Food Safety Authority believe coronavirus originated from industrial agriculture and "wet" markets. Other scientists have pointed out that many previous pandemics, such as the 1918 Spanish flu and Ebola, were caused by human interaction with (and abuse of) other animals (Askew, 2021). This allows vegans to engage in mutual aid and community while also explaining that the meat industry is the cause of the crisis we now face.

Vegan food banks are the best example of how vegans helped each other in the wake of the COVID-19 pandemic. Examples include Made in Hackney, which opened in 2012 in the east end of London as the U.K.'s first fully vegan cookery school and responded to the pandemic by providing emergency vegan meals for households needing food support (Made in Hackney). At the peak of the COVID-19 pandemic, Made in Hackney provided 500 meals each day to households in need across Hackney and hopes to continue doing so for as long as there is still a need (Made in Hackney). Others include the Vegan North East Foodbank, which is a community-led organization that makes vegan food parcels for those in need (Vegan Food Bank NE), and the Bath Vegan Foodbank, which was created to help the people of Bath provide food to their families and purchase essential items (Bath Vegan Foodbank).

These vegan food banks are all locally operated and volunteer-run, with a similar structure and ethos to mutual aid groups nationwide. They typically don't mention anarchism in their public-facing material. However, the Brighton Vegan Mutual Aid group, linked to the radical social center the Cowley Club, is the most clearly leftist. These groups all have certain key features in common, most notably a desire to help their local communities, whether the recipients of mutual aid are vegans or not. In January 2021, during a "school meals crisis" caused by the Conservative government's willingness to let children go hungry during school holidays, the Vegan Food Bank North East explained, "Honestly, I don't give a shit if you're vegan, if your kid is struggling we will feed them—but it will all be vegan food" (Vegan Food Bank NE). This fits with the approach of vegan activists, who have decided to "forgo top-down, universalizing judgments" and instead promote "contextual moral veganism," which takes into account "contextual exigencies" that may affect a person's food choices (Gruen, 2014, p. 130). Despite not being explicitly anarchist, these vegan food banks have an anarchist structure in that they are anti-hierarchical, community-led, and critical of government support. The vegan food banks have no formal leader, and decisions are made within the group by consensus.

Vegan food banks are reacting directly to the failure of the state to protect and support ordinary people. The Vegan Food Bank North East explained that "if the government can't provide adequate packed lunches, then screw it, we will" (Vegan Food Bank NE). The group aimed to support schoolchildren and families who had been neglected by the state by providing packed lunches during school holidays (ibid). The Brighton Mutual Aid Vegan Foodbank explains that "It is a damning testimony to how this government continues to fail people so badly, that initiatives like ours are needed more and more" (Facebook post, 2022), and the group's ethos is that "We need to help keep it going because no one else will. The state certainly won't" (Mutual Aid Vegan Foodbank). For the Brighton Mutual Aid Vegan Foodbank, this was not simply the failing of government in times of acute crisis but represented the wider failings of the capitalist state in which the rich are getting richer during the pandemic, whilst the working class is getting poorer because of the cost of living crisis, spiralling inflation, and reduced welfare provisions (Mutual Aid Vegan Foodbank). These groups are operating on vegan anarchist lines to directly support local communities in times of crisis. It is a model that vegan anarchists across the world are mirroring.

## Vegan Mutual Aid Around the World

In times of worsening crisis around the world, vegan activists are engaging in community mutual aid projects to support humans and other animals. For instance, after the August 2020 explosion in Beirut, Lebanese Vegans formed a mutual aid group to distribute vegan food and drinks to people in need and arrange vet care for injured animals (Vegans Against World Hunger). Another project, supported by the U.K. activist group Vegans Against World Hunger, is the Uganda Food Parcel Project. This project, run by activists in Uganda, gives vegan food directly to those who need it in the Mubende district of Uganda (Vegans Against World Hunger).

Another example of a vegan mutual aid group operating in a crisis is the Plant the Land—Gaza project. Plant the Land is a vegan food justice project co-founded by Anas Arafat, a lawyer and aid activist based in Gaza, and Laura Schleifer, a Jewish American critical animal studies scholar activist, whose work is included in this collection. Gazan volunteers are in charge of organizing and running Plant the Land. It is completely run by Palestinians, which is important for an anarchist group because anarchists believe that the group that is being oppressed is the best one to fight against it. The Plant the Land Team does many things to help each other, such as giving out vegan food, planting food forests on public land, giving seeds and planting tools to Gazan farmers, and providing medicine. Food forests and community gardens are important forms of aid because they offer a long-term solution that will provide freely available food to communities.

Vegans and anarchists can find inspiration from these projects as, around the world, we move to a time of permanent crisis, when the emergencies caused by late capitalism—poverty, inequality, war, pandemics, global warming—become permanent, and people around the world realize that all we have is each other.

## Conclusion

In times of crisis, anarchists have worked together to support humans, other animals, and the planet. This has been a source of inspiration and anarchists should take great pride in mutual aid efforts that have emerged in times of crisis, including during the COVID-19 pandemic. Just as capitalists have used times of crisis to redistribute wealth and power to the ruling class, anarchists have used times of crisis to build grassroots, non-hierarchical, spontaneous initiatives that are willing and capable of providing mutual support when states are not willing or able to do so.

Capitalism, including the animal-industrial complex and carnal ways of perceiving the world, has led to our current state of permanent crisis, especially the rise of zoonotic diseases and global warming. Vegan anarchists will provide a solution that challenges the hierarchical view of the world. Vegan mutual aid groups were often formed in the U.K. to provide short-term support to local communities during the COVID-19 pandemic; these groups continue to this day because activists recognize the need to help communities during the ongoing disasters caused by the energy, poverty, and health funding crises. Crises are no longer one-time events that happen after a disaster. Instead, they are a permanent part of capitalism. Vegan mutual aid will be a permanent feature of our collective resistance to this crisis.

## *References*

Aidan & Sam. (2021). Experiences of mutual aid organising in Glasgow and Brighton. *Anarchist Studies Blog.* https://anarchiststudies.noblogs.org/article-expe riences-of-mutual-aid-organising-in-glasgow-and-brighton/

Anarchist Studies Network. (2020). *ASN6: Anarchist Studies Network Conference 2020* https://anarchiststudiesnetwork.org/2020/08/11/asn6/

Askew, K. (2021). Scientists warn factory farming raises future pandemic risk: 'COVID-19 could be a dress rehearsal.' *Food Navigator.* https://www.foodnavigator.com/Article/2021/02/02/Scientists-warn-factory-farming-raises-future-pandemic-risk-COVID-19-could-be-a-dress-rehearsal

Bath Vegan Foodbank. (n.d.). Home [Facebook page]. *Facebook.* https://www.facebook.com/BathVeganFoodBank

Covid Mutual Aid. (n.d.). *Frequently asked questions.* https://covidmutualaid.org/faq/

Cowley Club. (n.d.). *Vegan foodbank.* https://cowley.club/vegan-food-bank

Dons Local Action Group. (n.d.). *Our story.* https://donslocalaction.org/our-story/

Firth, R. (2022). *Disaster anarchy: Mutual aid and radical action.* Verso.

Gruen, L. (2014). Facing death and practicing grief. In C. J. Adams & L. Gruen (Eds.), *Ecofeminism: Feminist intersections with other animals & the earth* (pp. 161–178). Bloomsbury.Hall, R. (2022). Four in 10 pandemic-era mutual aid groups still active, UK data suggests. *The Guardian.* https://www.theguardian.com/business/2022/jun/13/four-in-10-pandemic-era-mutual-aid-groups-still-active-uk-data-suggests

Klein, N. (2007). *The shock doctrine.* Penguin.

Klein, N. (2017). Naomi Klein: How power profits from disaster. *The Guardian.* https://www.theguardian.com/us-news/2017/jul/06/naomi-klein-how-power-profits-from-disaster

Kropotkin, P. (1996). *Mutual aid: A factor of evolution.* Black Rose Books.

Lachowicz, K., & Donaghey, J. (2021). Mutual aid versus volunteerism: Autonomous PPE production in the COVID-19 pandemic crisis. *Capital & Class, 46*(3), 427–447.

Made in Hackney. (n.d.). *About*. https://madeinhackney.org/about

Maness, R. (2021). These vegan community fridges are fighting food insecurity. *PETA*. https://www.peta.org/living/food/vegan-community-fridges-mutual-aid

McHenry, K. (2012). *Hungry for peace: How you can help end poverty and war with food not bombs*. See Sharp Press.

Milman, O. (2021). Meat accounts for nearly 60% of all greenhouse gases from food production, study finds. *The Guardian*. https://www.theguardian.com/environment/2021/sep/13/meat-greenhouses-gases-foodproduction-study

Morales, C. (2021). Mutual aid in the COVID-19 crisis—A short-lived exception? *Anarchist Studies Blog*. https://anarchiststudies.noblogs.org/article-mutual-aid-in-the-covid-19-crisis-a-short-lived-exception/

Mutual Aid. (n.d.). https://www.mutual-aid.co.uk/

Power, A., & Benton, E. (2021). Where next for Britain's 4,300 mutual aid groups? *LSE Blog*. https://blogs.lse.ac.uk/covid19/2021/05/06/where-next-for-britains-4300-mutual-aid groups/

Rayner, A. (2021). Crony COVID-19 contracts hit £3.5bn of taxpayers' money. *Labour*. https://labour.org.uk/press/crony-covid-contracts-hit-3-5bn-of-taxpayers-money/

Schleifer, L., & Fischer, D. (2022). Animal liberation is climate justice: Struggles and strategies from below. *New Politics, 18*(4). https://newpol.org/issue_post/animal-liberation-is-climate-justice/

Spade, D. (2020). *Mutual Aid: Building solidarity during this crisis (and the next)*. Verso.

Swann, T., & Kinna, R. (2020*)*. This anarchist thinker helps explain why we feel so driven to help each other through the coronavirus crisis. *The Conversation*. https://theconversation.com/this-anarchist-thinker-helps-explain-why-we-feel-so-driven-to-help-hackne-other-through-the-coronavirus-crisis-134494

UK Health Security Agency. (2022). *Deaths in the United Kingdom*. https://coronavirus.data.gov.uk/details/deaths

Vegan Food Bank NE. (n.d.). Home [Facebook page]. *Facebook*. https://www.facebook.com/veganfoodbankNE/

Vegan Society. (n.d.). *Climate emergency*. https://www.vegansociety.com/takeaction/campaigns/climate-emergency

Vegans Against World Hunger. (n.d.). *Projects*. https://www.vegansgainstworldhunger.org

Williams, K., & Crow, S. (2014). *Witness to betrayal/profiles of provocateurs*. Emergency Hearts Publishing.

Worthing Vegan Foodbank. (n.d.). https://veganfoodbank.wixsite.com/worthing

## 10 Create Meat Though the World May Perish: A Vegan Critique of In Vitro Meat and Clean Milk

Nathan Poirier

"All these things I will give You if You will fall down and worship me."
—Matthew 4:9

In March 2017 I had the opportunity to have a personal phone conversation with Carol Adams about in vitro meat (IVM). I was writing a master's thesis on the topic, and she was conducting research for her book on the cultural history of the burger (Adams, 2018) and was going to dedicate the last chapter to IVM. IVM is an approach to making meat derived from innovations in tissue engineering with the goal of solving problems associated with animal agriculture. It does so by creating animal flesh in laboratories, using biopsied animal cells, nearly dispensing with the need to slaughter animals for meat. After chatting with Adams for a little while about what IVM was, how it was made, etc., she asked me what I thought about it. I replied that I was deeply concerned about the wider associations of meat that IVM is likely to retain. Adams replied: "*Who cares*!?" She seemed almost offended that I would have such reservations. Perhaps she has since altered her outlook, but she made me feel too intimidated to try to talk to her again.

Having read Adams and been positively influenced by her work which is well known for connecting oppressions, I was struck by this reply. I politely replied that, being meat, IVM would probably retain its sexist symbolism of hegemonic masculinity, among other things. Her reply was that she was focused on the potential positive impacts for nonhuman animals. I didn't pursue this further because Adams made me feel like it was inappropriate for me as a graduate student to question her. For some reason she was not worried about what trade-offs or side effects, might result from technology being used to solve social problems. Adams has also brushed off critiques of her theory on the sexual politics of meat as applied to plant-based meat products (Adams, 2016). Simonsen (2015) and Poirier and Russell (2019) discuss specific ways the sexual politics of meat apply directly to IVM. I wonder if Adams cares more about upholding her own theory that built her career, to the point of overlooking contradictory evidence, than to think critically about IVM. This encounter shows just how tempting IVM can be, even for vegans. Such instances are a major impetus for this essay.

From the literature in support of IVM, it is understandable how it could be viewed as in line with vegan positions. Indeed, many vegans and animal advocates have voiced support for IVM. Numerous authors have referred to IVM as vegan (see Poirier, 2018b) or, to current/former vegans who have eaten IVM, as "post vegan" (Poirier, 2021). Kleeman (2020) calls IVM "vegan" because it is a movement largely led by vegans. Others have argued that ve(getari)ans should eat IVM (Hopkins & Dacey, 2008; Schafer & Savulescu, 2014) or animal-free dairy (Milburn, 2018). Proponents of IVM promise or expound aspirations to largely—if not completely—replace animal agriculture, mitigate climate change, use far fewer natural resources such as land area, and to make healthier food products (Shapiro, 2018). All of these are vegan aspirations. Thus, it is understandable why those who identify as vegan might support cellular animal products. Some may think it makes sense (even moral sense) to accept IVM. Theoretically, IVM could be a giant leap towards a vegan world, where the want of animal products is eschewed in favor of an ethical virtue of a nonviolent relationship with non/human nature. While I recognize that IVM could essentially eliminate animal farming and environmental destruction associated with meat—fundamental vegan goals—ultimately, I argue that a vegan viewpoint must look far beyond what might happen to farmed animals, as highlighted in my exchange with Adams.

Because IVM is to be synthesized completely apart from animal bodies in a laboratory, yet made out of basic biological constituents, it has been debated as to whether or not it is "real" meat. However, the initial harvesting of cells comes directly from an animal. The end product is indeed an amalgamation of animal cells and animal muscle tissue just as traditional meat is. Because of this, I see IVM as meat and as an animal product. This seems straightforward. Vegans do not eat or support the eating of meat or the use of animal products.

In a section titled "In vitro meat, as continuity and contrast," Erik Jönsson highlights some examples of how IVM discourse presents IVM as different from traditional meat by possessing enormous transformative power, while simultaneously being meat and "nothing more, nothing less" (Jönsson, 2016, p. 734). This is how vegans could make a point for IVM. Because IVM requires minimal if any behavioral change, it may provide the path of least resistance with the greatest gain. For this reason, it may be viewed as practical or pragmatic. By seeming to decouple meat and slaughter, the previous incompatibility of meat and animal liberation appear to work together. Many meat eaters share a common view with vegans that there are inherent problems with industrial animal agriculture, which may lead to agreement on IVM. If IVM can live up to its promissory potential of the substantial reduction in the number of farms, slaughterhouses or factories, it might also induce a ripple effect extending outward toward the reduction of other animal products and byproducts: milk, eggs, internal organs, blood, hair, skin, feathers, bones, etc., or significantly displace animal experimentation (Alexander, 2011). It should be kept in mind, though, that animal-free replacements already exist. All told, the positive impacts of IVM could go a long way toward achieving the goals of vegans and animal liberationists.

The remainder of this essay proceeds by first laying out how belief in IVM is like that of any technological fix and similar to religious faith. Particularly, I argue that faith in technology and faith in religious entities are connected in that like religious faith, all evidence points to there being no reason for such faith in technology. Then I discuss Josh Milburn's "vegan" support of IVM and "clean milk," and how his reasoning comes across as crass. I then go on to address activist implications and matters of indigeneity. Indigenous perspectives or concerns, and the matter of colonialism have been almost completely overlooked by the IVM industry.

## Technological and Religious Faith: Belief When All Evidence Points to the Contrary

First and foremost, while it promises much, there is yet no concrete demonstration of IVM's ability to deliver. Hopeful speculation is surely attractive, but there is a chasm between theory and reality, and what actually results when we cross the divide is (or should be) held in higher ethical regard. The lack of a material existence of IVM—in terms of both products and facilities—requires uncritical faith at this point.

Promissory rhetoric is part of the production cycle of technological innovation. Hype, in the form of grandiose promises at the outset, serves as an initial booster of interest and a lucrative form of publicity (Chiles, 2013). At early stages of IVM, proponents are free to make claims without fear of rebuttal, for there is little evidence available to refute most claims. Stakeholders could potentially secure a foothold from which the technology may begin to be actualized. This is how vegans could view IVM as part of the solution; a shiny new idea that can help vegans more quickly achieve their goals. But besides not being value-neutral and open to corruption, the claims of IVM proponents border on what might be called delusions of grandeur. As Erik Jönsson (2016, p. 743) remarks: "[I]n striving to provide a platform for [IVM], the promissory discourse comes not only to repeat earlier hopes for biotechnology and biocapital but also to stretch these to cover everybody and everything, everywhere." Such an omnipotent and benevolent presence suggests resemblance to a religious entity.

Indeed, "savior" and "salvation" are popular words of choice that indicate this phenomenon. Jönsson (2016) and Galusky (2017) use "salvation" and "savior" to describe how some people view technological fixes, including the perceived benefit of IVM. Similarly, Chiles (2013) utilizes "savior" to summarize the framing of IVM and chooses "agnostic" to label a non-committal stance of some on the issue (p. 520). Miller (2012) describes the brimming optimism over IVM as "miraculous," a word that invokes divine intervention. Galusky (2017, p. 242) describes the technological world as "a world made in our own [human] image," a reference to the biblical proclamation that humanity was made in God's image. Indeed, extracting cells from an animal resembles plucking a rib from Adam for the creation of Eve.

Schaefer and Savulescu (2014) argue that vegetarians should support IVM because it would have the same effect as vegetarianism in terms of lessening animal suffering and environmental harm. They claim that even if IVM is not quite as revolutionary as promised, that it may appeal to meat "agnostics," those "who would like to be vegetarians for ethical reasons, but just love the taste of meat too much to convert" (Schaefer & Savulescu, 2014, p. 189). Besides the religious rhetoric, we encounter the support of IVM presented as a "you've got nothing to lose" scenario; it either fulfills its promises or, if it falls short, at least causes no harm. This argument as akin to Pascal's wager for the belief in the Christian god, where, if correct, believers could gain eternal bliss after death, but there is no harm done if the wager is lost.

Huesemann and Huesemann (2011) draw four parallels between acceptance of technology and religious belief: "the promise of salvation, the means of controlling and maintaining systems of mass acceptance, the reliance on the wisdom and authority of 'experts' and the ignorance of believers" (p. 152). All four apply to the promotion of IVM. Promissory discourse illustrates the "promise of salvation." Many academic papers, and to a large extent the popular media, are in favor of IVM. Together they create a near one-sided presentation of the issues surrounding the technology. This acts as a means of manufacturing consent (e.g., hype cycles).

To the point of experts and public ignorance, historian Richard Hofstadter (1965) traces a history of the expert in United States society, noting that the need for and influence of experts increases at times when the "problems of the state" become too "various and complex" for elected officials to handle on their own (p. 201). In these circumstances, a deferment of power from elected government officials to authorized experts—in order to sustain democracy—is required to guide people through crises. This encapsulates the current situation of the range and depth of global environmental problems. Precisely to sustain the attachment to meat consumption, experts are needed to develop IVM. The highly technological nature of IVM and the significant critiques strategically ignored by proponents (such as Adams above and Milburn below) ensure that the public will remain largely ignorant of the more subtle nuances, distracted by shimmering promises. This in turn fosters a reliance on the opinions of experts.

Thus, IVM discourse rings with religious overtones. Primarily this consists of asking the public to have faith in an "industry" and technological meat products that for all intents and purposes do not exist and may never exist. There is hardly reason to put faith in such a system when almost all evidence points towards the contrary.

## *The Case of "Clean Milk"*

Here I comment on "clean milk" (CM), a more-or-less dairy analog of IVM, and in particular, respond to Milburn's (2018) "vegan" promotion of cowless dairy consumption. Milburn argues that eliminating the dairy industry is *right* (p. 271) and cautions that CM should not support conventional dairy (p. 274). One leading approach to CM production does not need cows except for using cow DNA to identify casein and whey producing genes (2018, pp. 265, 269). These genes are then

> artificially created, after which they are added to yeast. This yeast [...] is then added to a mix of water and plant-based sugars. The yeast then ferments the sugars, creating whey and casein proteins. The yeast is then filtered from the resulting mixture [....]. Plant-based fats, sugars, and nutrients are then added to the water-and-proteins mixture, and the result is something that, physically, closely approximates milk from a cow. (p. 265)

Taking a "non-ideal" approach starting with the injustice of milk production and thinking of a way to circumnavigate it, Milburn (2018), who identifies as vegan, argues there is little to no reason vegans should oppose CM, arguing that a CM dairy industry will create humane jobs, not just eliminate inhumane jobs (p. 267). So far, CM sounds like it falls in line with veganism. Thus he concludes that "the prospect [of CM] is one that animal activists should both welcome and embrace" (p. 262).

Additionally, Milburn offers "an explicit decoupling of the ethics of clean milk from the ethics of clean meat; it is, I hold, plausible to support one but not the other" (p. 263). "It is my view that all who have concerns about the dairy industry [...] have reason to offer full support to the development of clean milk" (p. 264). It is clear the production mechanisms for CM and IVM are distinctly different, but both do involve creating animal material in vitro (as opposed to in vivo) to create an animal product. Because of this, I argue that if there is a reason for vegans to reject CM, then there is an even stronger reason to reject IVM.

While Milburn is resolute that CM should not support the contemporary dairy industry, he brushes off the influence of capitalism as not "particular to clean milk" (p. 269). Why this would be the case is difficult to fathom. Everything is subject to becoming part of capitalism. The popular vegan movement has become largely co-opted by capitalism (Giraud, 2021) and the main thrust of the alternative protein space (plant-based, fermented, and in vitro meat) is thoroughly capitalist (Poirier, 2021). Closer to Milburn's argument, plant-based milks are significantly caught up in capitalism and all of its unethical trappings (Howard, 2021, Ch. 8), including benefiting traditional dairy via acquisitions (Howard et al., 2021). There is no reason to think (one might say "have faith" that) capitalism will not exert a negative influence on CM.

Perhaps the biggest problem with CM is that it functions as a distraction from other actions and issues that could be addressed in the here and now. People could consume plant-based milks that already exist in a variety of forms (although, as mentioned, they too are subject to the destructive ways of capitalism). CM is highly technical and an intervention on nature. Resources are better spent elsewhere. Milburn realizes that some may still consider CM to constitute exploitation or be unjust based on the use of bovine DNA at some point to identify the relevant genes for milk production. This is something vegans should deeply consider (and not brush off as Milburn does with CM and capitalism or with IVM below), since veganism rests on abstaining from exploiting others unless it is necessary.

Although my responses to Milburn may not be many, I think they are foundational. I acknowledge that Milburn is using a non-ideal approach, but just because one starts with a non-ideal situation does not mean that in thinking about how to navigate present circumstances we cannot also promote and prefigure an ideal situation, even if it is never—and maybe never can be—reached. At best, CM is one possible alternative to conventional dairy but many other alternatives exist. CM might be "helpful" in disrupting the dairy industry, but if the cost is expensive development of technology—which always has unintended consequences, uses resources, and is entangled with capitalism—then CM should be avoided. Otherwise, things may happen but change toward total liberation will not occur because of trade-offs incurred.

It is not surprising Milburn holds this position. Milburn presented at the 2021 conference *In Vitro Meat: Ethics and Culture* with the title "Having Our Cow and Eating Her Too" on the ethics of the "pig-in-the-backyard" model. This model envisions one or two so-called "donor" animals who are kept captive in people's backyards or a community lot "as pets and a cell donor" simultaneously (van der Weele & Driessen, 2013, p. 656) to periodically source cells from to keep up IVM production. Within this context, Milburn raised the idea of thinking about donor animals as workers. At the end of the presentation, an attendee asked Milburn the following question:

> [...] you mention the right for a choice in one's own work – at first glance it does not seem possible for animals to choose their participation in whether their cells are used and I wonder if you could say more about this.

Although paraphrased, Milburn's reply was that, ultimately, we must violate the rights of animals to make IVM simply *because we want to.*

I find this absurd, dangerous even. Here we have an animal ethicist and "vegan" actively promoting ethics up to a point: when human desires conflict with that of nonhumans, humans are automatically favored. Therefore, this discussion of CM only adds to the argument that IVM can—and does—ultimately put human interests before those of nonhuman animals to fulfill (unnecessary) desires. The mentality of "we want this, so we're going to take it" is like that of colonialism. Millburn simply reiterates this in a different context. Adams, too, in the vignette at the beginning of this chapter, was seemingly dismissing a further entrenching of what she has built a career critiquing as being harmful for nonhuman animals, humans, and the environment—the sexual politics of meat. Frankly, both positions seem unacceptable and decidedly nonvegan.

## Some Forward-Looking Thoughts on the General Landscape and Discourse of IVM and CM

This article has been largely "negative" in the sense that I argue vegans should *not* support IVM or CM. So, what should activists *do* on more political and collective levels? It seems clear that there should be a variety of actions. This includes personal lifestyle practice and promotion of wholefoods, local, organic veganism, and the praxis of prefiguration. But history shows that peaceful resistance, when it directly threatens the establishment, will be repressed violently. Thus, radical, direct actions should especially be widely supported, encouraged, and engaged in. Vegans should follow the model of the A.L.F., E.L.F., Sea Shepherd and other similar activist organizations and commit clandestine, underground, decentralized acts of property destruction, blockades, occupations, rescues, and other actions aimed at tearing down systems of violence (Best & Nocella, 2004; Nocella II et al., 2019). The world is in multiple crises and all beings are threatened. There is not time to sit back and hope technology (IVM) might fix social problems. We cannot just wait and hope that incremental improvements will overcome major global crises, or that those with a stake in creating and sustaining oppressions will stop doing so. There should be continued and renewed emphasis on extralegal means of veganism, activism, and mutual aid.

The second "positive" point is that I would like to see the general IVM space engage with the topic of decolonization. To date, the literature on IVM has not wrestled with what a cellular agriculture industry might mean within the context of ongoing colonialism. At least in the US, the (metaphorical and geographical) IVM space is dominated by settler descendants who occupy stolen land. The only formal written piece I know of on IVM and indigeneity is by Margaret Robinson (2016) who argues that, despite possessing numerous reservations, IVM may potentially be helpful to the Mi'kmaq people of southeastern Canada where their relationship with moose could be preserved through eating IVM moose meat without hunting, suffering, or killing. In an updated presentation, Robinson (2022) highlighted the thoughts on IVM by a couple other indigenous people, Atlanta Grant and Tabitha Robin Martens.

As Robinson summarizes from Grant:

> Atlanta Grant considers what impact cultured salmon might have on Indigenous nations of the west coast, for whom the fish plays a significant cultural role. Grant worries that sushi grade salmon produced in a lab could further separate Indigenous Peoples from their sacred animals and further undermine Indigenous food sovereignty, in the name of addressing climate change, which indigenous people did not actually cause.

And from Martens:

> Cree scholar Tabitha Robin Martens, an assistant professor at the University of British Columbia, views cultured meat as violence. "Moose, salmon, deer are kin, not just food," Robins explains. "For Indigenous Peoples, the healthiest food we can eat is food that contains the most relationships," she wrote. "Because moose is in contact with sun, wind, stars, soil, plants, etc., it is full of good relationships. Cellular 'food' is devoid of good relationships."

Robinson's point is that indigenous views on IVM are varied. To be clear, I am not saying that it is (solely, at least) the responsibility of indigenous people to raise these issues. Instead, my point is that the IVM "industry" is not raising these issues at all and doesn't appear to be concerned with them. But it is precisely the question of how IVM may or may not align with decolonization, indigenous interests, and settler-indigenous relations that IVM proponents should be asking.

In addition to what Robinson (2016) sees as a potential benefit of IVM, one other significant possibility, although this is almost entirely theoretical and unlikely, could be that IVM production could nearly completely do away with land for animal agriculture and crops to feed those animals. This land covers most of Earth's habitable land surface. If all that land could be freed up, perhaps it could be given back to the indigenous peoples from whom it was taken. Of course, there would be nuance here in terms of talking to the indigenous peoples whose present territories may or may not coincide with their traditional territories, and this would have to happen at a local level, varying by location, all over the globe. Not to mention it seems probable that such land would be simply repurposed for settler extractive initiatives. Nevertheless, this would be a major step towards decolonization and Land Back initiatives. It is telling that no one in the IVM space is suggesting it.

## Conclusion

The opening quote of this chapter is of Satan tempting Jesus to worship him. When Jesus refuses, this symbolizes Paradise regained, lost after the Fall. Temptation is also present in IVM as it is currently being pursued, tempting vegans to comply with animal exploitation while gaining IVM. Plenty of vegans and activists will and do support IVM and CM. They are admittedly attractive propositions. But this support comes from a position of perceived necessity, pragmatics, or uncritical ignorance. In other words, essentially fatalism regarding vegan activism. Uncritical acceptance of IVM represents succumbing to temptation and a bargain with technology to the detriment of the vegan movement and nonhuman animal autonomy, a human-contrived techno-fix that may also conflict with movements such as decolonization.

Given potential benefits, it is understandable why some vegans might choose to *critically* accept IVM. But one can differentiate between an uncritical acceptance and a critical one based on a broad consideration of issues at play, as well as distinguish between "acceptance" and "support," the latter of which implies a much stronger affirmation while the former is closer to toleration. I *support* the benefits of IVM and CM in and of themselves, independently of the animal products they (re)create. Only under certain necessary conditions could I (critically) *accept* them (see especially Poirier, 2018a, 2018b, p. 22). And only under additional sufficiency conditions could I *support* IVM or CM, perhaps one example being Robinson (2016). We need to think critically about this issue and make sure that it not only helps nonhuman animals but that it does not impede other social justice movements. And as far as I can tell, voices of marginalized groups are not being invited into the conversation by the cellular animal product "industry" to a meaningful extent.

The uncritical support of Adams and Millburn reflect an incompatibility with veganism and total liberation. Within a total liberationist framework, IVM is a double admission of failure. Explicitly it is an admission of the failure of animal agriculture. Implicitly it denotes a failure of humans to act ethically amidst staring down multiple crises. For currently farmed animals, IVM may represent an improvement. But for "the animal"—what it is to be (a nonhuman) animal—IVM represents the ultimate in oppression: nonexistence. IVM discourse does not allow for humans and (formerly) farmed animals to coexist, free of exploitation, attempting to erase them from the picture. Perhaps what IVM ultimately discloses is that "[c]ruelty-free meat may simply be another element of the fantasy that humanity will ever be able to dwell with and among other species equitably" (Simonsen, 2015, pp. 20–21). IVM creates meat while the world perishes.

## References

Adams, C. J. (2016). Ethical spectacles and seitan-making: Beyond the sexual politics of meat—A response to Sinclair. In B. Donaldson & C. Carter (Eds.), *The future of meat without animals* (pp. 249–256). Rowman & Littlefield.

Adams. C. J. (2018). *Burger.* Bloomsbury.

Alexander, R. (2011). In vitro meat: A vehicle for the ethical rescaling of the factory farming industry and in vivo testing or an intractable enterprise? *Intersect, 4*(1), 42–47.

Best, S., & Nocella, A. (Eds.). (2004). *Terrorists or freedom fighters? Reflections on animal liberation*. Lantern Books.

Chiles, R. M. (2013). If they come, we will build it: In vitro meat and the discursive struggle over future agro food expectations. *Agriculture and Human Values, 30*(4), 511–523. Galusky, W. (2017). Technology, responsibility, and meat. In D. M. Kaplan (Ed.), *Philosophy, technology, and the environment* (pp. 229–246). Massachusetts Institute of Technology.

Giraud, E. H. (2021). *Veganism: Politics, practice, and theory*. Bloomsbury Publishing.

Hofstadter, R. (1965). *Anti-intellectualism in American life*. Vintage.

Hopkins, P. D., & Dacey, A. (2008). Vegetarian meat: Could technology save animals and satisfy meat eaters? *Journal of Agricultural and Environmental Ethics, 21*, 579–596.

Howard, P. H. (2021). *Concentration and power in the food system: Who controls what we eat?* Bloomsbury Publishing.

Howard, P. H., Ajena, F., Yamaoka, M., & Clarke, A. (2021). "Protein" industry convergence and its implications for resilient and equitable food systems. *Frontiers in Sustainable Food Systems, 5*, 684181.

Huesemann, M., & Huesemann, J. (2011). *Techno-fix: Why technology won't save us or the environment*. New Society Publishers.

Jönsson, E. (2016). Benevolent technotopias and hitherto unimaginable meats: Tracing the promises of in vitro meat. *Social Studies of Science, 46*(5), 725–748.

Kleeman, J. (2020). *Sex robots and vegan meat: Adventures at the frontier of birth, food, sex, and death*. Pegasus Books.

Milburn, J. (2018). Death-free dairy? The ethics of clean milk. *Journal of Agricultural and Environmental Ethics, 31*(2), 261–279.

Miller, J. (2012). In vitro meat: Power, authenticity and vegetarianism. *Journal for Critical Animal Studies, 10*(4), 41–63.

Nocella II, A. J., Parson, S., George, A. E., & Eccles, S. (Eds.). (2019). *A historical scholarly collection of writings on the earth liberation front*. Peter Lang.

Poirier, N. (2018a). Technical difficulties: Toward a critical, reflexive stance on in vitro meat. *Animalia: An Anthrozoology Journal, 3*(2), 1–18.

Poirier, N. (2018b). The continued devaluation of vegetarianism in light of in vitro meat. *Journal for Critical Animal Studies, 15*(5), 3–27.

Poirier, N. (2021). Alternative animal products: Protection rhetoric or protection racket? *Journal for Critical Animal Studies, 18*(3), 27–54.

Poirier, N., & Russell, J. (2019). Does in vitro meat constitute animal liberation? *Journal of Animal Ethics, 9*(2), 199–211.

Robinson, M. (2016). Is the moose still my brother if we don''t eat him? In J. Castricano & R. R. Simonsen (Eds.), *Critical perspectives on veganism* (pp. 261–283). Macmillan.

Robinson, M. (2022). *Lab-grown mooseburgers? An L'nuwey view on food technology*. Earthsave Canada. September 19, 2022. https://www.youtube.com/watch?v=SnM2SX6i8dc

Schaefer, G. O., & Savulescu, J. (2014). The ethics of in vitro meat. *Journal of Applied Philosophy, 31*(2), 188–202.

Shapiro, P. (2018). *Clean meat: How growing meat without animals will revolutionize dinner and the world*. Simon and Schuster.

Simonsen, R. R. (2015). Eating for the future: Veganism and the challenge of in vitro meat. In P. Stapleton and A. Byers (Eds.), *Biopolitics and utopia: An interdisciplinary reader* (pp. 167–191). Palgrave Macmillan.

Van der Weele, C., & Driessen, C. (2013). Emerging profiles for cultured meat; Ethics through and as design. *Animals, 3*(3), 647–662.

# 11 The Others Called 'Humans' Amidst the Many: Anthroponomy and the Planetary Problem

JEREMY BENDIK-KEYMER

*The writing of this note took place on land in violation of the Treaty of Greenville. I thank the editors of this volume. Nathan roped me into it during coffee at a vegan donut shop in East Lansing, Michigan, and Sarah helped with good editing. I also thank my co-participants, my family, who supported my work, and my human and other animal neighbors in Shaker Heights, Ohio. To the predator of other animals, I apologize.*

## Total Liberation

This volume reaches out heartily in the spirit of "total liberation." At its core is a moral commitment to resist and dismantle institutions, practices, and mindsets of domination. One necessary component of this goal is to disestablish norms of domination, for norms structure the operation of institutions, the order of practices, and the logic of mindsets. Even further, to dismantle norms, it is necessary to delegitimize them. Otherwise, they will remain authoritative for people even when removed from institutions, practices, or overt mindsets. Without delegitimization, norms persist as a cultural unconscious. Hence, one goal of this collection is to delegitimize the norms of domination.

Norms of dominance can persist in inherited common sense, aspects of practice, or institutional rules of play, despite what people are aware of daily. Using powerful ideas to dispel domination, thoughtful people can illuminate the residual normative domination at work, make connections between things that were not perceived as linked, and draw needed inferences. Critique exposes norms that, upon reflection, should be delegitimized by resurfacing them from their sunk institutional, practical, or commonsense contexts.

My contribution to the project of total liberation is to discuss a powerful idea that advances non-domination across the human species and with respect to other species too. Prior to this occasion, I had not focused on the relationship between "anthroponomy" and animal liberation. The purpose of this note is to do so initially, reflecting on the potential of anthroponomy to help with the critique of the domination of animals by humans in a "planetary age" (Chakrabarty, 2021). The basic motivation behind my discussions is that since our condition today demands that we consistently coordinate anti-domination on planetary scales, some such thing as anthroponomy is needed to delegitimize norms of domination in a planetary age. By contrast, if our efforts are un-anthroponomous, they will not resist domination consistently around the planet and so will fail to be sufficiently critical as well as fail to be total in their liberation. In other words, given the planetary condition in which we all exist as a matter of our biophysical reality, it strikes me that anyone committed to total liberation will need to develop their own idea of (something at least like) what I call "anthroponomy" (Bendik-Keymer, 2020a). This is all the more so since the only way to have an idea of anthroponomy is to have one that makes sense to *you*, i.e., your idea of it (cf. Gibson, 2020). All this is the overt rationale for this note as a critical intervention into contemporary norms.

But there is also more going on here, namely, an in-house debate among environmentalists who rail against anthropocentrism. In addition to the planetary problem to which anthroponomy responds, I am interested in noting the sense of humanity implied within the rough idea of anthroponomy. This narrower interest is because it changes how we view speciesism and the old view of environmentalism, "anthropocentrism." They involve some norms that should be unsettled, but not for the reasons most environmentalists give. Rather, their use displays social alienation internalized within environmental thought. And I want to get at that through anthroponomy too.

Moreover, my overt rationale and my in-house debate are bound up in the recent history of the globe following European colonialism that has structured and driven the planetary condition in which we find ourselves, with the "we" including other animals too. But this same history, by way of its dominant ideologies, has perpetrated a view of the human that remains alienated from its social and ecological dimensions (see the discussion of Wynter's Man 1 and 2 in Parker, 2021; Mignolo & Walsh, 2019). And this view of the human has ended up as a kind of conceptual misanthropy in environmental thought in how it understands our sense of humanity (Bendik-Keymer, 2006). To put these things together—our planetary problem and social alienation—is part of the critique of coloniality. In a more nuanced way, that is what is up here.

## *The Planetary Problem*

Let me begin with the planetary problem to which anthroponomy responds. Consider the aggregate effect of humankind on the geology and biology of the planet since our emergence as a species. Other hominid extinctions, such as Neanderthals, occurred around 40,000 years ago, as did mega-fauna and monocultures around the same time. There is also the deforestation of the Mediterranean some 2,000 years ago. And the beginning of the reshuffling—and extinction—of forms of life around Earth beginning during the age of global exploration, European colonization, and genocide some 500 years ago. That is where things get going globally.

Each of these massive effects at varying scales is contested by incomplete historical records and competing interpretations, although the reality of humankind expanding over time is inevitable. After thinking about it, what is debatable but interesting and clear is that European colonialism started a socially constructed view of the globe as a narcissistic object of conquest. Think of the creation of the first globes as maps of conquest and empire. By the nineteenth century, this same intention to master the globe passed through industrial capitalism into the metaphysically rationalized belief that everything on Earth should be put to work, especially what was not an Anglo-European "white" and "male," upper-class human being (Daggett, 2019; Latour, 2017; Ferdinand, 2022). The long unwinding of the history of European colonialism has given us global problems preceding planetary ones (Chakrabarty, 2021).

Nonhuman animals have figured heavily in this industrial energetics. They have been metabolized through factory farming and the machinery of modern science, the staging of which emerged with agribusiness, land clearing, and massive amounts of poorly processable waste involving numerous toxicants (Liboiron, 2021). Factory farming is just one way this global narcissism shows itself. It controls the glorious striving of other beings by making them objects that can be taken, squeezed, twisted, and used up in economies of production, distribution, and waste connected worldwide (see Nussbaum, 2023).

There has been a complex movement of domination downwards and outwards in this modern history. What I call "vertical privilege" and "horizontal subjugation" has structured many changes. The Europeans were on top and everything else on the bottom, especially in racist metaphysics. Meanwhile, the

Earth beyond Europe was to be conquered and nature subdued (Ferdinand, 2022). Non-European human animals were to be dominated, enslaved, converted, or killed. And nonhuman animals were to be put to use, eradicated, or tolerated under human appreciation and use conditions. A scale of natural beings (Nussbaum, 2023) and of human beings (Ferdinand, 2022) served as rationalizations for domination based on the purported value of some human beings over all other beings and all human beings over all other animals. Staged by the "theological" idea of the globe (Latour, 2017), territorialized by the imperial framework of nationalism and internationalism, resourced by industrial extraction, and driven by the economy of capitalism, the class stratification of the Earth has intensified between humans and between human beings and all other beings to this day.

Horrifying as this is, these things preceded the global awareness of even more unsettling planetary problems like global warming and the risk of the sixth mass extinction since life began on Earth (Kolbert, 2014). Therein has arisen recently in modern societies the realization of a profound and far-reaching moral and political problem: although humankind has become a geological agent (Chakrabarty, 2021), we have not yet become responsible for our unintentional agential effects as a collective, that is, as humankind. There still seems to be a great deal of intentional and unintentional denial of this situation. Social processes for which people are responsible continue to transform the planet with unintended aggregate effects. Humankind has not yet organized collectively to become morally responsible for them and their structural injustice and wantonness (Bendik-Keymer, 2016; cf. Young, 2010 on structural injustice, and Bendik-Keymer, 2012 on structural wantonness), which include major injustices to animals, both human and otherwise (Nussbaum, 2023; Gardiner, 2011).

There is a planetary problem that, while as deep as prehistory in some respects, is primarily structured by the half-millennium-long age of European colonialism that is slowly unwinding, carrying with it its inertia of vertical privilege and horizontal subjugation to this day, largely in the form of continued inequalities of advantage and disadvantage (Táíwò, 2022) involving continued domination. And this history points to a dangerous future that could be even worse and more destructive than what has come before it in modernity. How should we think critically about this complex planetary problem? What can be said about its basis about animal liberation? There is a need here for a radical and planetary idea to shatter the vertical privilege and horizontal subjugation of modern history's hold on our institutions, practices, and minds while building a world forward for climate justice, protection of the order of life, and collective responsibility for justice (Táíwò, 2022) involving animals of all kinds (Nussbaum, 2023).

## *The Idea of Anthroponomy*

Within the historical context just sketched, the idea of anthroponomy is morally urgent, and its rationale straightforward. Anthroponomy is the species-level idea of autonomy, the collective of humankind becoming responsible for itself. Here, autonomy does not mean independence—that is a liberal idea. It means, instead, living a life that makes sense to you. This "to you" is the same general explanation as Aristotle articulated when he realized that all animals strive because the world matters to them (Nussbaum, 2023). Initially, it is our human version of it. When we are autonomous, we are not enclosed solipsistically but connect with our world as making good enough sense to us, even being trustworthy.

Like autonomy, anthroponomy is born of the moral idea that imposing a life that doesn't make sense on someone, dominating them, is simply unacceptable. (Imposing a life is different than, in some cases, being a temporary and justified imposition on another's behavior, for instance, when they must be confronted for their domination of others.) Because of this, anthroponomy must be open to those who are subjugated or erased. Anthroponomy reaches out. This point will become important later when discussing animals other than humans.

Genealogically, anthroponomy comes from the Enlightenment. But during the Enlightenment, anthroponomy was not theorized, only hinted at as an aside when thinking about the history of the human species (Bendik-Keymer, 2020a). Before the planetary age, anthroponomy was an inchoate idea emerging from within the Enlightenment's critique of tyrannical authority and social inequality, its invention of autonomy (Schneewind, 1998). Anthroponomy was, we might say, no more than a potential, a dream fragment, even an unconscious. But the planetary problem changed all that.

Given its history, one way to understand anthroponomy is as a turning back against the European imperialism that harnessed and co-opted the Enlightenment. With its prioritization of self-determination and the autonomy of people to make sense of the world in their own ways, anthroponomy was destined against the racist, patriarchal, and Anglo-European abuses of the Enlightenment anchored in epistemic injustice and domination. Anthroponomy un-self-consciously located a skeletal juncture inside modernity that can, to this day, speed the long unwinding of European imperialism and the massively violent, abusive inertia of the "colonial matrix of power (CMP)" (Mignolo, 2021). This matrix includes speciesism, too.

Today, anthroponomy is an idea of non-domination on a species level, now a planetary scale (Chakrabarty, 2021). Anthroponomy has become something to address the planetary problem sketched thus far. A moral-political concept rooted in the conceptual unconscious of the Enlightenment against its colonial evil has thus come into its own due to the problem of our planetary situation addressing both a colonial past and an unstable planetary future. Because of the central role of autonomy in anthroponomy, should humankind become collectively responsible in this century for its aggregate effects on Earth, that collective responsibility will have to become horizontally accountable to others and vertically collapse into moral equality. Anthroponomy becomes planetary thinking for human agents that is anti-colonial and—as I explain—relationally autonomous, and anti-narcissistic. Thus, anthroponomy reaches back into pre-history while remaining resolutely oppositional to the last five-hundred-year constellation of geopolitical control that has been the long unwinding of European colonialism. It does this by reaching into a constructive future for a better world here on Earth.

### *Anthroponomy Is a Connector*

As you might imagine, anthroponomy supports total liberation. It does this in a non-arbitrary, non-libertarian way. Anthroponomy is relationally autonomous rather than indulgent in license. This is because the core of anthroponomy is autonomy between people, and this is within and between many practices of collective life such that they can sync up with each other to reach collective responsibility for ourselves as humankind (Bendik-Keymer, 2020a). But do these practices of collective life include multi-species communities?

One thing to keep in mind is that anthroponomy needs to be found between communities and within them. It can conveniently appear in the social organization of institutions and in practices used to approach how institutions interact. Anthroponomy is about laws and the way they are made, but it goes beyond the European idea that law is something that is separate from social institutions (Bendik-Keymer, 2020b). Its inner core of autonomy makes anthroponomy such that it coheres well with the sensibility of much Indigenous law, that is, as a *morality* (Pasternak, 2017). Anthroponomy is autonomous, from the inside out, and since it is grounded in relational freedom, it exceeds narrow universes of morality. It can help us approach the notion of a pluriverse of moralities, norms, and meanings (Escobar, 2020)—or as I prefer to say, worlds of such meanings (Bendik-Keymer, 2020a, 2021b).

For conceptual reasons, the notion of a pluriverse strikes me as internally contradictory: to assert the pluriverse is to assert a universe; so, I speak instead of "many worlds" in dialectical relationship to *the* world. Anthroponomy is a connector through its spirit of self-determination.

Unsurprisingly, then, anthroponomy is an idea of govern*ance* not govern*ment* (Bendik-Keymer, 2021b). Against the European imperial specter of a world government projected by the CMP, anthroponomy is anarchist in that it grounds all authority relations in governance between equals. The way to articulate this, following both Kyle Whyte (2018) and Søren Kierkegaard (1964) is that it is the moral relation—the free relation—that governs, and this occurs through the "moral nexus" of accountability, not license (Wallace, 2019). In relational autonomy, governance emerges *between us* in accountability to each other's freedom, against all domination. These relations govern the emerging relationship—and hence continuing social life. Such governance is inherently processual, emergent, and fluid—the lasting result of relationships between moral equals. Along these lines, anthroponomy is an idea of species-level self-governance, governing ourselves rather than an "Earth system governance" (Biermann, 2014). Anthroponomy flourishes amidst Earth's animals by leaving them free when we own our own shit.

## *A Pro-Social Core*

How should we understand relations of non-domination with beings who are not autonomous in a sense typically understood in philosophy (e.g., Wallace, 2019)? Isn't anthroponomy focused just on the "autonomous," i.e., those who can form articulable intentions, offer justifications for their actions, and be held accountable in some such process? The other animals do not engage in human accountability practices on the model of some normatively explicit discourse scene (Vogel, 2015)! And any of us who do not happen to be able to engage in such discourse scenes would also be excluded from anthroponomy. Anthroponomy would then be both speciesist and ableist.

But the core idea of responsibility inside anthroponomy is that we should approach each other—*each* other, that is, each *other*—in the spirit of meeting another as they are, according to their inner principle of freedom. This moral orientation is odd to the core. I say "odd" as queers say *queer*. "Odd" can be a violent term in ableist cultures. But we should re-appropriate it as ontologically positive. The odd is the "elemental," i.e., the primal difference that shapes everything (Parker, 2021). Similarly, being queer is being normal as being queer discloses the ontological swerve that is human freedom (Ahmed, 2006). Suppose I am disposed to some version of anthroponomy and bothered by the reality of domination on Earth. The question, then, is: How should I relate to others? Should I demand that they be like me? That would be narcissistic. I should relate to them in a spirit of respect. They have a life of their own and an inner principle of freedom. This moral orientation then grounds how I extend the core of my freedom to others who, perhaps, are differently capable to be free in their own way (Parker, 2021). The moral issue becomes how our freedoms (plural) interact with the main concern being domination. My autonomy becomes a power that gives me the capability to extend respect to others who are differently capable and to be vigilant.

The question of anthroponomy is *how to be free as a differently capable person in relation to many differently capable beings*, including the vastly more abled other animals (e.g., those who can lift many more times their body weight than a "fit" human being can, those who can go through entire metamorphoses in their lifecycle, etc.; Schmidtz, 1998). Neo-Aristotelian philosopher Martha C. Nussbaum thinks that questions like these depend on recognizing wondrous striving in the entire realm of animals (Nussbaum, 2023). All animals strive in different ways. A person seeking autonomy and committed to non-domination should begin by witnessing wondrous striving throughout Animalia on the pain of a profoundly unimaginative inconsistency, a soul-blankness, in themselves. Our "normative," "rational" autonomy is just one form of positive freedom—a human form—while there are many forms of animal freedom.

In this way, both our sense of humanity and our autonomy are odder than many think, constitutively open to respect for the positive freedom of many kinds of animals, including the variabilities in striving among many different histories of human animals, some of whom get unjustly coded as "disabled" (Bendik-Keymer, 2021a). We're not freedom-lovers if we can't use our imaginations enough to perceive an *other* outside of our own likeness. We're not freedom-lovers if we're narcissists.

## Rooted in Our Humanity

Here is where social alienation comes in. Anthroponomy opposes speciesism. This means it also challenges the old saw of environmentalism, namely, "anthropocentrism." This is a term thrown loosely around in debates concerning the more than human world. The term is equivocal, having dozens of meanings (Mylius, 2018). Usually, what is objectionable is "normative"—as opposed, say, to "descriptive"—anthropocentrism (Mylius, 2018), the idea that humans matter more than other kinds of beings. (Even saying that human beings matter more than other kinds of beings is vague because we need to know in what contexts, with what values, and why.) Normative anthropocentrism is often described as objectionable because it creates the practical conditions for using or abusing other kinds of beings or favoring human beings in trade-offs leading to the widespread abuse of other kinds of beings, for instance, in factory farming. But if we think about the sense of humanity (e.g., being humane, having common humanity) implied since its rise in human rights culture (Hunt, 2008; Zeldin, 1998), must being centered in our humanity really imply such selfishness?

This is where alienation appears. When we think that the morally objectionable abuse of other kinds of beings is somehow rationalized by being centered on our humanity, the notion of "human being" in play must be alienated. Do you think it is random that the first psalm in the Hebrew Bible figures the good person as a tree or that the Hindu gods are multi-species? In many wisdom traditions, wise or "sapient" human beings—Homo sapiens who live up to the name—are not thought*less* with the more than human world. They are capable of feeling it with sympathetic imagination and of having some modesty, even humility, in how they approach it, learning up from its strange and wondrous meaning. Implicit in the sense of humanity is a counternarrative that is multi-traditional, fragmentary, and of ancient, recorded human history: being thoughtful and considerate of other forms of life can be part of what it means to be maturely human (Bendik-Keymer, 2006). We notice the traces of some such sense of humanity in the extra "e" added to "human," we talk about being humane, for instance, with other animals.

How could environmentalism and even animal liberation have missed that? Marx's critical theory provides us with one answer. The Marxist tradition has a long and deep analysis of how we might view being human as involving being abusive or selfish. From Marx's *1844 Manuscripts* and their analysis of alienated labor to Lukács' work on reification, one Marxist tradition has looked at how political economies and their supporting cultures paint a view of being human that is in some sense anti-social, atomized, or in other ways vicious, i.e., characterized by behaviors and mentalities that are corrosive of love, compassion, trust, and respect (Vogel, 1996). Humans, on the other hand, have deep social and associative needs when they are supported in their development (Nussbaum, 2000). Moreover, they are capable of "sympathetic imagination" with other animals (Nussbaum, 2006). The Marxist tradition grappling with alienation does not put the problem of our wantonness at the doorstep of "humanity" as much Anthropocene discourse does. Instead, it shows the wanton social processes (e.g., alienating capitalism or the CMP) as the moral and political source of such conceptual misanthropy as to think that being centered in humanity is selfish.

When we encounter people saying that to be centered in humanity is to be selfish, there's an illusion at play. To be centered in humanity is to be centered on the qualities that make us human, which are also deeply other regarding. They are relational. You can't understand human beings properly without perceiving these qualities. It would be like viewing a person and perceiving a mechanical, unempathetic (non-AI) robot instead. "Anthropocentrism" is a misnomer. Anthropocentrism as environmentalists use it is alienated from the sense of humanity.

In place of "anthropocentrism," we should discuss social alienation instead. That keeps in view societies' thoughtlessness with other forms of life and the cyclical abuse of each other without giving up on our humanity. But if we want to stop the internalized social alienation and conceptual misanthropy that comes from shaming "anthropocentrism," we need to cultivate what it means to be human when we are warmly, healthily, and securely thoughtful. Being human in such supportive conditions involves reaching out into the world and connecting rather than closing in and dominating. Truly social humans see into the depths of others. They don't objectify them.

Suppose you perceive the word "anthroponomy" and have a reaction to call it "anthropocentric," thereby dismissing it. Here is a response: that challenge would then incorporate alienation into animal liberation, pitting us against other species. And this would be to get us—our potential and our striving—profoundly wrong. It would denature us by making us anti-social rather than pro-social. It would double down on social alienation based on profound conceptual and moral confusion. Instead of bandying about anthropocentrism as some problem, would not it make more sense to call out the CMP instead—or at least locate the pervasive social alienation from our true capabilities of being humane that wires modern life with its cycles of negative anxiety, competition, inconsiderateness, and abuse? Talking about "anthropocentrism" seems to be just another way of normalizing capitalist and colonial alienation.

## Anti-Narcissism and Non-Domination Extends to All Animals

We now have some more heart, some more warmth, and some more capaciousness with which to understand how anthroponomy is a planetary philosophy of non-domination. Anthroponomy is woven from an anti-narcissistic way of being, and this anti-narcissism opens up a profound orientation toward animals everywhere (cf. Nussbaum, 2023). We can imagine how this goes by remembering that anthroponomy's species-level autonomy (Bendik-Keymer, 2016) requires that we work out autonomy between ourselves. This demands that whatever we take to be autonomous must be found in a relationship in which we are free together. Otherwise, our autonomy would be conflated with some fantasy of independence that cannot make sense of a social being such as the human animal. Once we accept that anthroponomy depends on freedom in relating, we must think about working out freedom between ourselves.

Anthroponomy demands that we are accountable to others who have lives of their own and seek to live a life that makes sense to them. As such, anthroponomy depends on the moral capability to consider the other *as other*. This is essentially and resolutely non-narcissistic, and so anthroponomy is anti-narcissistic in its orientation. This moral outlook, even more than relational autonomy, underscores how anthroponomy is a philosophy of non-domination, for arbitrary control of others is problematic from the standpoint of anthroponomy. The way we affect others must be justifiable in terms of *their* autonomy. That is, it must be acceptable to them. The only forms of legitimate control are those that interfere with the arbitrary control of others, i.e., that block narcissism.

How relational autonomy and anti-narcissism support animal liberation then becomes straightforward. If we are to be consistent with our commitment to autonomy, we must approach all animals in light of their own way of making sense of their lives. We must recognize their own striving (Nussbaum, 2023). It is hardly relationally autonomous and non-narcissistic of us—the humans who think about things like autonomy—to ignore the spirit of autonomy within all animal striving.

Accordingly, anthroponomous people, practices, and institutions ought to take heart in the sow freed from gestation crates on a farm in Iowa (Nussbaum, 2023) to take just one example of pervasive animal abuse. Those crates are a cruel and dehumanizing injustice on sows, making it impossible for them to live a life that makes sense to them. The deformation of the sow shows the dehumanization of people directly in that our pro-social core gets undermined by industrial narcissism. In demanding the overthrow of factory farming, anthroponomy ties together our collective responsibility for a world that can make sense to humankind with the protection of the capabilities of animals such that they can live their lives freely. Anything else from us would not be pro-social, and that would be dehumanizing. It is worth repeating this dialectical point a few times over to let it sink in. Dominating other animals dehumanizes us, undermining our social core. We must evolve beyond those farms!

In sum, to be anthroponomous is to work out freedom between all humans and, more broadly, protect all animal striving from our abuses. Protecting animal striving includes respecting human freedom since we strive by and through our freedom. Anthroponomy starts with the self-recognition of autonomy, proceeds to the moral nexus of accountability between people as autonomous beings (Wallace, 2019), and extends analogically to other forms of striving (Bendik-Keymer, 2006). That this might seem utopian for those of us raised in the CMP—or even worse, a mere fantasy—results from how profound the alienation from our own humanity can become. Yet the idea that respecting animal striving is part of our humanity is not a foreign idea to many aboriginal or Indigenous cultures. The long unwinding of European imperialism has sorely impacted us; just not as much as it has wreaked industrial havoc on other animals.

## *A Perspective-Switch by Surpassing Alienation*

Beyond alienation, the sense of humanity's deep social thoughtfulness becomes an ongoing orientation filling and exceeding any one of our lives and any one of our communities. Humanity is a virtue with an ever-remainder of unresolved interactions and still-to-be-worked-out relationships. Informed by the virtues of humanity, we cannot accept the domination of human beings or other animals. If we are ever going to use other animals, the question becomes how to respect their inner striving in the spirit of respect and reciprocity. Moreover, if we do not even know what that means, we should recognize in that incomprehension our own alienation from our humanity and get to work on the various dimensions of the institutions, practices, and mindsets that tell us that there is no other universe in which human beings can co-exist with the other animals in a spirit of reciprocity and respect (Escobar, 2020; Mignolo, 2021; Pasternak, 2017; Liboiron, 2021; Winter 2022).

The point to emphasize above all can be found in the title of this note: "the others called 'human' amidst the many." This saying relativizes being human to being just one species among many. Even more importantly, in its imaginative form, it shows our capacity for sympathetic imagination, our sociality, such that we can imagine other animals looking *at* us in *their* midst. What is then implicit may be the most heartfelt and core assumption of my argument so far: the moral capabilities needed for anthroponomy support strong forms of relating by which we, the humans, have good reason to fashion our lives so that we keep in mind how they affect the many beings within whose midst we are so damn lucky, and without doubt thanks to them, to live. Here, by being centered in our own humanity in a truly autonomous way, we are best able to relate to the many beings for or to whom humans have historically been dangerous others. Anthroponomy here implies the condition for profound respect for other animals, not the converse.

This conclusion obviously challenges some animal liberationists, namely, those committed to overcoming the normative distinction between humans and other animals (Singer, 2009). Anthroponomy, by being relationally autonomous, goes dialectically in reverse of that alienating pursuit of similarity or identity (Bendik-Keymer, 2006; cf. Diamond, 1991). It rests on our moral responsibility, not on ontological conformism. The animals make us possible, but they are almost always not looking out for us. Instead, *we* have a responsibility to mind ourselves when it comes to *them*. We must look out for them because we can be destructive (Bendik-Keymer, 2012). Anthroponomy comes in here by centering the non-alienated moral capability of our getting truly outside ourselves to appreciate the good of another. That much rests on the critique of narcissism, not an axiological version of it.

In this light, we could then mention "anarcho-anthroponomy." The anarchism implicit in anthroponomy would be brought out such that anthroponomy's non-dominating, reciprocal qualities come to the fore. Here, in particular, the critique of alienation and alienation's narcissism is key. When we are alienated—running around in cycles of isolation, selfishness, and abuse—we are thoughtless and inconsiderate. We go so far as to say that being centered in our own humanity is selfish or dominating. We may even reify our social alienation into human essence (Vogel, 1996). But when we work hard and critically against the alienating systems turning us into our own worst enemy, we come to understand that the way forward is not to lose our humanity but to regain it in a vast, organized, swarm, an ongoing assembly (Hartman, 2019): the collective responsibility for how we affect things called *anthroponomy*. Then the anarchic spirit inside anthroponomy comes to free ourselves from internalized domination so as to free the world around us into moral accountability and governance "by the relationship" (Bendik-Keymer, 2021b). Then we undo our own abusive tendencies so that we can nurture reciprocity with other animals.

A thought experiment should become a cast of mind for institutions, practices, and people committed to anthroponomy. It is to comprehend us, the humans, as just one among many, namely, the many other animals on Earth. Then, from their perspective, we are the ones called "human" amidst the many of them, the other animals. As truly being committed to non-narcissism and reciprocity in the relationship, we then imagine ourselves from their perspective as the often dangerous and dominant outliers in the multiform plenum of the current order of life on Earth. From their perspective, we are to be guarded against, are worthy of wariness, and deserve blame and reproach, for we fail to live up to our humanity and abandon our moral capabilities when it comes to the social processes that cycle us around in seemingly inexorable, wanton abuse of each other and the more than human world.

You might say that "anarcho-anthroponomy" implies some such perspective-switch on being human on Earth, whereby we ascertain our effects on others from an imaginative extension of their perspective. How else can we become responsible for our effects on Earth if we do not take up the effort to "see" the world from the other animals' points of view? But then to resist alienation from our own humanity and to come to terms with our planetary agential effects depends on thinking *outside* ourselves in others, coming to accountability for ourselves given our effects on them. That is so far from being normatively anthropocentric in the conventionally pejorative sense among many environmentalists that the term has been pulverized into nonsense. To many of my fellow environmentalists, I then plead, "Stop trying to get outside your own humanity! Please come to terms with it instead."

### *Mass Extinction Event Horizon*

Should we care about how we affect animals everywhere on Earth, some version of the species scale concept of anarcho-anthroponomy becomes a reference point. We are in the planetary age (Chakrabarty, 2021) where the impacts animals face proceed on planetary scales, foremost through global warming, ocean acidification, industrial forms of pollution, and through the patterns of "planetary urbanization" that comprise factory farming, industrial fishing, laboratory work, and massive land use practices and habitat destruction (Brenner, 2019). The event horizon for the planetary scale is the mass extinction event, purportedly the Sixth Extinction since life began (Kolbert, 2014; Gorke, 2013). The only way to think consistently about the risk of the Sixth Extinction is on planetary scales, with humankind as a kind of collective with agential effects (Latour, 2017).

When we reflect on paleontology's and Earth system science's findings, we find that human social processes, particularly those of modernity and its CMP, have begun to drive the current order of life to extinction, leading us to a precipice where the rules of life themselves will be forced to reorganize (Bendik-Keymer & Haufe, 2017). Such a process exceeds the entire existence of homo sapiens by millions of years, a vast unknown for us human beings whose species has existed less than 200,000 years, has used technology for only 100,000 some years, and whose recorded history is only 10,000 years old. The 10,000,000 years it takes for the Earth even partly to recover from a mass extinction event reduces being human to a mere passing moment. Yet we are playing dice with this moment and risking the annihilation of our epochal bio-geological framework.

Planetary problems create planetary concepts (Chakrabarty, 2021). As the Sixth Extinction looms, not becoming collectively responsible for our species' effect on Earth is to court auto-destruction, since the Sixth Extinction stands a good chance of rendering humans extinct (Bendik-Keymer & Haufe, 2017). Not to become anthroponomous as we seek collective responsibility is to court domination, since a collective that is not anthroponomous will involve the suppression of disagreement, difference, and plurality. But most importantly for the sake of all animals within whose midst we live, not to become deeply pro-social in our practices, institutions, and sense of self is to risk their annihilation and our dehumanization. Anarcho-anthroponomy counters all these atrocities. Non-dominating, sympathetically imaginative, and non-narcissistic, such planetary perspective coherently addresses the sense of moral urgency that people concerned with the fate of other animals currently have. It also upholds self-determination, moral equality, and non-domination post-colonially. These things are all bound up.

Let's rail against factory farming and laboratory cruelty, stand opposed to wanton land use practices and global warming, and be appalled at the decimation of the oceans through fishing, acidification, plastics, and toxicants of various kinds. Let's then support the coherent politics of coordinating humankind as a collective of responsibility. If we maintain vertical privilege and horizontal subjugation in some part of that attempt, we reproduce the dynamics of alienation currently fracturing relationally autonomous collectivity. Anarcho-anthroponomy speaks to the moral and political need to complete the long unwinding of European imperialism in the same motion by which it addresses the deeper, dawning realization that humankind must become responsible for itself before the worst of humankind's processes destroy the multiform, plenitude of wondrous beings deserving our respect. The fate of the current order of life, *Animalia* and all, including humans (that odd animal who can be so destructive when given over to social histories of domination) flickers at this mass extinction event horizon.

## References

Ahmed, S. (2006). *Queer phenomenology: Orientations, objects, others.* Duke University Press.

Bendik-Keymer, J. (2006). *The ecological life: Discovering citizenship and a sense of humanity.* Rowman & Littlefield.

Bendik-Keymer, J. (2012). The sixth mass extinction is caused by US. In A. Thompson & J. Bendik-Keymer (Eds.), *Ethical adaptation to climate change: Human virtues of the future* (pp. 263–280). MIT Press.

Bendik-Keymer, J. (2016). 'Goodness itself must change'—Anthroponomy in an age of socially-caused, planetary, environmental change. *Ethics and Bioethics (in Central Europe)*, 6(3–4), 187–202.

Bendik-Keymer, J. (2020a). *Involving anthroponomy in the anthropocene: On decoloniality*. Routledge.

Bendik-Keymer, J. (2020b). Facing mass extinction, it is prudent to decolonise lands & laws: A philosophical essay on respecting jurisdiction. *Griffiths Law Review*, 29(4), 561–584.

Bendik-Keymer, J. (2021a). The other species capability & the power of wonder. *Journal of Human Development and Capabilities, 22*(1), 154–179.

Bendik-Keymer, J. (2021b). Unacceptable agency: Part I of *The problem of an unloving world. Environmental Philosophy, 18*(2), 319–344.

Bendik-Keymer, J., & Haufe, C. (2017). Anthropogenic mass extinction: The science, the ethics, & the civics. In S. Gardiner & A. Thompson (Eds.), *The Oxford handbook for environmental ethics* (pp. 427–437). Oxford University Press.

Biermann, F. (2014). *Earth system governance: World politics in the Anthropocene.* MIT Press.

Brenner, N. (2019). *New urban spaces: Urban theory and the scale question.* University Press.

Chakrabarty, D. (2021). *The climate of history in a planetary age.* University of Chicago Press.

Daggett, C. N. (2019). *The birth of energy: Fossil fuels, thermodynamics, and the politics of work.* Duke University Press.

Diamond, C. (1991). The importance of being human. In D. Cockburn (Ed.), *Human beings* (pp. 35–62). Cambridge University Press.

Escobar, A. (2020). *Pluriversal politics: The real and the possible.* Duke University Press.

Ferdinand, M. (2022). *Decolonial ecology: Thinking from the Caribbean world.* Trans. A. P. Smith. Polity Press.

Gardiner, S. M. (2011). *A perfect moral storm: The ethical tragedy of climate change.* Oxford University Press.

Gibson, J. D. (2020). On the farm. In J. Bendik-Keymer, *Involving anthroponomy in the Anthropocene: On decoloniality* (pp. 157–172). Routledge.

Gorke, M. (2013). *The death of our planet's species: A challenge to ecology and ethics.* Trans. Patricia Nevers. Island Press.

Hartman, S. (2019). *Wayward lives, beautiful experiments: Intimate histories of riotous Black girls, troublesome women and queer radicals.* W.W. Norton.

Hunt, L. (2008). *Inventing human rights: A history.* W.W. Norton.

Kierkegaard, S. (1964). *Works of love.* Trans. Howard and Edna Hong. Harper Torchbooks

Kolbert, E. (2014). *The sixth extinction: An unnatural history.* Henry Holt.

Latour, B. (2017). *Facing Gaia: Eight lectures on the new climatic regime.* Trans. Catherine Porter. Polity Press.

Liboiron, M. (2021). *Pollution is colonialism.* Duke University Press.

Mignolo, W. (2021). *The politics of decolonial investigations.* Duke University Press.

Mignolo, W., & Walsh, C. E. (2019). *On decoloniality: Concepts, analytics, praxis.* Duke University Press.

Mylius, B. (2018). Three types of anthropocentrism. *Environmental Philosophy, 15*(2), 159–194.

Nussbaum, M. C. (2000). *Women and human development: The capabilities approach.* Cambridge University Press.

Nussbaum, M. C. (2006). *Frontiers of justice: Disability, nationality, species membership.* The Belknap Press.

Nussbaum, M. C. (2023). *Justice for animals: Our collective responsibility.* Simon & Schuster.

Parker, E. (2021). *Elemental difference and the climate of the body.* Oxford University Press.

Pasternak, S. (2017). *Grounded authority: The Algonquins of barriere lake against the state.* University of Minnesota Press.

Schmidtz, D. (1998). Are all species equal? *Journal of Applied Philosophy, 15*(1), 57–67.

Schneewind, J. B. (1998). *The invention of autonomy: A history of modern moral philosophy.* Cambridge University Press.

Singer, P. (2009). *Animal liberation: The definitive classic of the animal movement.* Harper Collins.

Táíwò, O. O. (2022). *Reconsidering reparations.* Oxford University Press.

Vogel, S. (1996). *Against nature: The concept of nature in critical theory.* SUNY Press.

Vogel, S. (2015). *Thinking like a mall: Environmental philosophy after the end of nature.* MIT Press.

Wallace, R. J. (2019). *The moral nexus.* Princeton University Press.

Whyte, K. P. (2018). Settler colonialism, ecology, and environmental injustice. *Environment and Society: Advances in Research, 9*(1), 125–144.

Winter, C. J. (2022). *Subjects of intergenerational justice: Indigenous philosophy, the environment and relationships.* Routledge.

Young, I. M. (2010). *Responsibility for justice.* Oxford University Press.

Zeldin, T. (1998). *An intimate history of humanity.* Vintage.

# 12 Post-Scarcity Veganarchism

LAURA SCHLEIFER

In this brave new millennium rife with ecological collapse, social unrest, and plague, a monster is stirring. At times and places, this creature has haunted humanity throughout its existence, known to Ancient Greeks as Limos, the Norse as Nuckelavee, and Judeo-Christians as apocalyptic horsemen. Yet, for a while, it seemed the monster had been conquered, and a false version constructed to use as a tool of manipulation and control. Now, the real monster awakens, and reveals itself as the terrifying specter of material scarcity.

To the industrialized Capitalist (colonizer) world, such threats have long seemed remote. Growing reports of regional conflicts over water and other life-sustaining resources (Youness, 2015) have barely scraped the edges of consciousness. For many, the idea of water, food, air, mineral, and other shortages has seemed so inconceivable that psychologically reifying such a scenario may ironically require science fiction. Under Capitalism, the only recognized scarcity has been time and money, ironic considering that money is a construct with no innate value, and the biggest waste of time is the perennial chasing of this inherently worthless abstraction.

Thus, while inequality has reached levels not seen since the Gilded Age (DeSilver, 2013), until now access barriers, not actual resource shortages, have caused scarcity. Within this paradigm, both the cause of and solution to every problem is framed monetarily. Even regarding Global South famine, seemingly the most straightforward resource scarcity example, these tragedies have been political and economic (de Waal, 2018), with the typical "solution" of more funding serving to further impoverish recipients through debt peonage. In the globalized mass production and distribution era, the issue has not been insufficient materials, but rather materials not reaching those who need them, whether that's due to non-profit industrial complex overhead expenses, donor nation austerity cuts and restrictions on aid distribution, bureaucratic negligence, or local governments/military forces redirecting aid into their own pockets or blocking it from reaching their enemies. (Hasell, 2018) Additionally, a major cause of famine is populations deliberately being starved to weaken, punish or coerce them. Indeed, any argument that famine is caused by true resource scarcity has been typically framed in neo-eugenicist and racist terms, rooted in the neo-Malthusian idea that the problem is not unequal power and resource access, but rather "too many mouths to feed"/ overpopulation/over-breeding, with the neo-colonialist insinuation that poor and marginalized people lack the "self-control" to stop procreating. (Hasell, 2018).

Until now, the idea that famine and other resource scarcity is caused by political and economic forces, not actual material scarcity, has generally been true. While genuine scarcity may at times exist locally, globally we have lived on a planet of continuous abundance. Thus, any such crisis has been a situation where humans with the means refuse to mitigate the crisis, or even orchestrate it.

However, while our planet still provides overall abundance, real global scarcity is alarmingly approaching, regardless of one's location. As of this writing, shortages have been occurring due to climate change, production and distribution breakdowns triggered by system design flaws buckling under ecological collapse, and Covid shutdowns, including a supply chain bottle-neck caused by a wave of mail-order consumerism (Goodman & Chockshi, 2021) from restless, anxious, depressed populations suddenly forced to spend time alone with themselves. As our world becomes increasingly impacted by forces beyond individual, or even systemic, human control, these factors will likely intensify.

The proposed solutions to impending scarcity are those typically prof-fered by people who profit from, and seek to protect, the Capitalist status quo: increase productivity and economic growth (Malinovskaya & Sheiner, 2016), seek technological quick fixes to enable business to continue as usual (Kenton & Stapleton, 2022), and shift blame onto individuals (Park, 2022). These may entail foisting coercive birth control measures on the world's poorer (colonized) regions and pressuring consumers to buy newer, "greener" products in the wealthier (colonizer) nations (Kepner & Cole, 2013), all while simultaneously intensifying the real factors driving the crisis (Grant, 2011). Taking this route will guarantee we'll drive our brand new green electric cars right off the climate cliff.

This chapter suggests a more radical idea: creating a world that treats both manufactured and real scarcity at the root by combining a mass transition to veganism with anarchist forms of social organization—a.k.a, veganarchism (Dominick, 1995).

## Combining Veganism with Anarchism Can Transform Scarcity into Abundance

It is inarguable that our planet possesses finite resources, and that human activity—specifically, industrialized Capitalism, globalized through colonialism and imperialism—is threatening all species, including humans, with annihilation. As ongoing ecological collapse continues, increasingly the word "vegan" is appearing in mainstream conversations as part of a potential solution. Usually presented as a diet, everyone from the United Nations (Porre & Nemecek, 2018) to the U.N.'s own International Governmental Panel on Climate Change (I.P.C.C.) (Schiermeier, 2019) has highlighted dietary veganism as the best way to individually resist climate change. With the spotlight shining ever brighter on veganism as a possible solution, if ever a "superfood" existed, vegan food must be it.

Indeed, veganism can certainly play a pivotal role in resisting the ecological crisis and its attendant scarcity. As overall ecosystem collapsing increases at alarming rates, so do instances of true scarcity. While Western farmers have had to sell or kill "their" cows earlier than usual due to water scarcity, Madagascar is experiencing modern history's first purely climate-induced famine (Baker, 2021). Drought-caused water, food, and fertile land access conflicts have driven twenty-first century wars, starting in Sudan, the "world's first climate-driven war," and continuing with Syria, Yemen, Ethiopia, Libya, and the Arab Spring uprisings. Meanwhile, Central America's Dry Corridor's ongoing drought-induced crop failures have led to 7.1 million people experiencing hunger, and an influx of Latin American refugees facing the brutal US border (Reliefweb, 2022).

The combination of climate change, Covid—itself caused by animal exploitation, and potentially linked to climate change (see Beyer et al., 2021)—and war in Ukraine have caused a global food crisis. Currently, 828 million people are experiencing hunger, with 345 million facing starvation, up from the pre-pandemic 135 million. In Africa, almost 40 million Somalis, Ethiopians, and Kenyans face unprecedented famine resulting from five plus years of drought, plus resource-scarcity driven conflicts in Ethiopia and Kenya (Halakhe, 2022). The World Food Program has bluntly stated food will soon become unavailable even to those who can afford it. By 2025, the entire Global South, a population of 3.5 billion people, will experience drought and famine and by 2040, the world may run out of freshwater altogether (The World Counts, 2023).

Considering this situation, expecting veganism to meaningfully address this crisis may seem far-fetched, even delusional. Yet, strong evidence indicates a mass transition to veganism could significantly impede the ecological collapse. A 2022 Stanford University report that claimed 68 percent of all $CO_2$ emissions could be erased through eradicating animal agribusiness because doing so would not just remove methane emissions, but also halt deforestation and free up land for reforestation with carbon-capturing, oxygen-producing trees (Eisen & Brown, 2022.) Elsewhere, a U.N. report revealed that "livestock" farming takes up nearly 30 percent of earth's surface, which is 83 percent of farmland overall, and that, "a vegan diet is probably the single biggest way to reduce your impact on planet Earth, not just greenhouse gases, but global acidification, eutrophication, land use and water use. It is far bigger than cutting down on your flights or buying an electric car" (Poore & Nemecek, 2018). Ending animal agriculture could greatly reduce water usage and contamination, air pollution, soil erosion, ocean depletion, plastics, "dead zones," acidification, antibiotic resistance, zoonotic diseases, and, due to 41 percent of grains feeding farmed animals rather than humans, global hunger. (Schleifer & Fischer, 2022). Since animal agriculture is arguably the leading industry causing these issues, eliminating it would make regenerating the planet, meeting true human needs, and restoring ecosystems, habitats, water and food sources for other species possible.

Yet, simply eating plants instead of animals won't address the core pathology driving scarcity: the hierarchical control of resources and insatiable *wanting* fueling Capitalism's engine. As long as this remains unaddressed, veganism as a practice of avoiding animal products will remain just another market-based "solution." Indeed, the same U.N. report warning of animal agriculture's planet-destroying impact proposes other "solutions" like, "improving herd efficiency through better breeding, manure and pasture management, livestock feed, and precision-feeding techniques" (Poore & Nemecek, 2018).

Additionally, although globally shifting to veganism would free-up food currently fed to "livestock," that food wouldn't be made available to those in need. Under Capitalism, "excess" food is destroyed to keep prices high (Cook, 2020). In an ongoing situation where less grains were required for food, landowners would simply monetize another way, perhaps by using more crops for biofuels or other non-food items. Artificial scarcity would also continue because denying populations resource access creates a perennially desperate underclass easily exploited for their labor. Those in power also use resource shortages as a bait-and-switch to reward populations for obedience with food aid, and punish defiance with starvation, scaring others into submission by making an example of one (Dominick, 1995). When Gaza is deliberately starved for resisting colonialism, it sends a message to oppressed people everywhere: resistance=starvation.

Thus, transitioning into a post-scarcity reality would involve not just dietary veganism, but ethical veganism, which strives to end human domination over other animals, and anarchism, which strives to end all domination within human society, in order to counteract material scarcity and dismantle the scarcity construct itself—and the Capitalist, consumerist mindframe underlying the irrational fear, greed, selfishness, narcissistic rage, and other psycho-pathologies leading us to real global scarcity for the first time in human history. Since veganism combined with anarchism would strive to end all forms of oppression, this would necessarily require a Total Liberationist movement to end Capitalism, imperialism, colonialism, statism, incarceration, patriarchy, ethno-religious supremacy, and other hierarchical forms of social organization, and to abolish the notion of private *or* public "ownership" of other humans, animals, or land/nature.

Ironically, what often prevents this from happening is the scarcity mentality itself. Both vegans and non-vegans often share the viewpoint that human and nonhuman animal liberation exist in a zero-sum game where one must be prioritized over the other. Fearing that nonhuman animals will be "de-centered from their own movement," many vegans promote single-issue veganism "for the animals" that opposes including human and ecological issues in its approach. (Casamitjana, 2022). Meanwhile, human rights activists take a humanist approach that dismisses striving for nonhuman animal liberation as frivolous considering human oppression/suffering culturally imperialist (Kim, 2015), or even potentially reinforcing ontological associations between marginalized people and animality used to rationalize subjugating human groups, which marginalized communities are working to distance themselves from (Kymlicka, 2019). While these seem like opposing perspectives, they share two aspects: competition for resources and a one-dimensional perspective that sees a problem through a narrow lens that obscures how each issue relates to others. At their core, both perspectives are rooted in a fear-based scarcity mindset.

That fear is understandable, especially among oppressed humans fighting for full recognition of their own humanity. Yet, it may be unfounded. Ongoing research reveals that when nonhuman personhood recognition increases, empathy for marginalized humans also increases. This is because dehumanizing certain humans by comparing them to "animals," and rationalizing their mistreatment on that basis, only works if one considers "animals" lesser-than humans.

Eliminating this dichotomy neutralizes the effects of that weapon of oppression (Hodson, 2012).

If increasing respect for nonhuman animals can also positively impact our perceptions of other humans, it holds profound implications for how animal liberation might aid in transitioning society from a scarcity to abundance paradigm. It's well-known that real or perceived economic/resource scarcity incites racist and fascist ideologies (Krosch & Amodio, 2014), and that such ideologies are rooted in conceptions of otherization via animalization. Under the liberal paradigm, a divide is drawn between "civilized humans" who are "granted" legal rights because they have been sufficiently "civilized" (i.e., conditioned out of their animality) enough by the system to handle a degree of freedom, and the excluded and policed "animalized others," what Italian philosopher Giorgio Agamben called "Bios" and "Zoe". Fascism, on the other hand, rests upon the perception of all humans as "animals" existing in a perennial state of the "law of the jungle." Two ideological foundations of this self-perception are the Hobbesian view of humanity's "state of nature," in which humanity's default mode is a "war of all against all," and Social Darwinian concepts of humans existing in an eternal "dog-eat-dog" competition for "survival of the fittest." Both ideologies depict humans as inherently savage, dominance-seeking, aggressive, and lacking impulse control because they are "animals."

Thus, if resources are scarce, control is needed from above to restrain the "humanimals" from fighting over scarce resources and to secure resources for the dominant group—whether that be a "civilized" human, a "genetically superior" human (the Social Darwinian/eugenicist/ Nazi "ubermensch"), or someone claiming to act on behalf of/be appointed by a deity. This is why so many willingly submit to control from above; they lack faith in themselves, and in their fellow humaninals, to behave without it. Ergo, our perception of animals—and of ourselves as animals—lies at the root of why we accept hierarchical resource control and its attendant scarcity. Eradicating scarcity requires transforming both our treatment and perception of other animals, and of ourselves as animals. Combining veganism with anarchism holds the key.

The term "mutual aid" has gained mainstream recognition during the Covid-era (see Boisseau, chapter 9 of this, but many remain unaware of its animal origins. *Mutual Aid A Factor in Evolution* was anarcho-communist founder Peter Kropotkin's (2017) response to rising Social Darwinist ideologies in his time. Kropotkin argued that animal nature, including human nature, was in fact innately cooperative, conscientious, and caring, and that it was these pro-social traits that drove evolution. Thus, a social system based on cooperation, solidarity, reciprocity, fairness, egalitarianism, and mutual aid would not contradict our animal nature, nor result from some racial/cultural/religious "civilizing influence" or "natural superiority," but align with our nature as animals. Over the last century, science has confirmed Kropotkin's assertion that animals behave pro-socially on both the intra-species and inter-species levels. Studies have consistently shown that nonhuman animals are willing to help fellow animals out, even at a personal cost to themselves (Bartal et al., 2011; Okasha, 2013).

Of course, it makes sense that other species don't exist in a chronic "war of all against all" in which individuals or species attempt to hoard or over-consume resources. If they did, they'd be driving the ecological collapse, not us. Instead, it is human alienation from our animal nature, not our animal nature itself, which has led us to hoarding, over-consumption, competition, and endless war against each other, other species, and nature—causing scarcity for humans and nonhumans alike.

## *Veganarchism: The Road to Abundance for All*

As a "pragmatic utopianist" concept, post-scarcity veganarchism is inspired by twentieth century anarchist philosopher and social ecology founder Murray Bookchin's *Post-Scarcity Anarchism* (1971). Bookchin posited that in a "post-industrial" society, where sufficient goods had been produced and technology was sufficiently advanced to liberate humanity from menial labor if democratically-controlled and shared, implementing an anarchist system capable of providing for everyone's needs might be possible. Post-scarcity veganarchism considers that idea in light of the current reality, where manufactured scarcity is inducing real scarcity, countering that with a vision of a liberated multi-species community that creates abundance for all. Described by Bookchin (1971) as the democratic dimension of anarchism, communalism is a form of self-governance in which a network of communities self-organize to make and enact decisions on both the inter and intra-community level through local and regional neighborhood/civic/popular assemblies. In a communalist system, there is no representative government; democracy is direct, with all area residents gathering to propose, discuss, and collectively decide on all aspects of public life, from creating and enforcing laws to organizing the production and distribution of goods and services. Every individual can propose and argue in favor of policies to be voted on. There is no property in the sense of owned land or nature; communities operate on a library economy model where all goods are collectively shared and borrowed. Commodity production is based on a non-hierarchical co-op model, collectively owned and organized, and profits shared. Public services, from food provision and housing to education, healthcare, self-defense, ecological restoration, cultural production, are organized and run by the community, and provided unconditionally to all those living within it.

Forms of communalism have been practiced worldwide since time immemorial. Today, new forms are emerging in response to economic, ecological and social crises. Directly inspired by Bookchin's idea of a revolutionary communalism, the Kurdish region of Northeastern Syria, Rojava, has created and implemented their own variation of communalism called Democratic Confederalism. Currently, an ethnically diverse population of 4 million lives within this system, in which villages form communes which link together into larger regional assemblies. Each community elects one easily recallable woman and man to represent their commune. These delegates have no individual decision-making power—they simply execute decisions made by the community through a back-and-forth discussion between the communes and regional assemblies until consensus is reached. Additionally, there are no career politicians; every community member takes turns serving in these roles. Power, knowledge, and professionalism are decentralized in all areas of life, with all community residents receiving equal training in self-defense, healthcare, and food production. Those serving in specialized roles answer to, and are easily recallable by, the community. From the workplace to politics to schools, every aspect of society is non-hierarchical and directly democratic (Ocalan, 2013). While the Kurds are the biggest population living within such a system, similar movements have been rising worldwide, including the Transition Towns, Right to the City, Global Ecovillage Network, Mississipi's Cooperation Jackson, Mexico's neo-Zapatistas, and Sri Lanka's Sarvodaya Shramadana Movement (Fischer, 2022).

The road to building such a mass movement to challenge and overtake Capitalism is beyond the scope of this chapter (see Fischer, 2022; Ocalan, 2013). However, a veganarchist society that combines communalism with ending domination not only among humans but over other species could end both material and psychological scarcity. Removing hierarchical control of resources would both alleviate competition and massively reduce ecological consumption and destruction, since production would be reduced to meet human and nonhuman needs rather than produce profits or otherwise satisfy individual greed. By decreasing production, another scarce resource within the current paradigm, free time, would expand, allowing for mass participation in ecological restoration, communal care, self-governance, and other forms of individual and collective life improvement. Scarcity of specialization would also end, as universal access to education and community-wide training in basic life skills would train people in mutual aid (Bailey, 2022).

Communalism would also resolve problems caused by psychological scarcity. With no competition for scarce resources and no hierarchy within human society, the source of most conflicts would end. Empowering individuals through participatory democracy and communalism would also meet the two basic human needs pinpointed by Frankfurt School psychoanalyst Erich Fromm (1941): freedom and belonging. With liberation from wage-labor and other systemic oppressions, real political empowerment and access to participation in meaningful work that makes a real-world positive impact, many of the current society's most troubled members would finally have positive outlets to channel their energies into, such as the former gang members whose leadership experience and abilities made them enthusiastic community organizers in the 1970's Nuyorican Movement in N.Y.C.'s Lower East Side (Chodorkoff, 2014).

In that light, we might consider how communalism could address scarcity-related issues raised in this volume, such as the question of human procreation in high carbon footprint-societies). While it's debatable whether overpopulation in and of itself is an issue (Alberro, 2020), normalizing childlessness and providing universally available reproductive education and birth control would surely benefit everyone. However, it's also worth considering why people reproduce in the first place. Often, childbearing is driven by material and/or psychological scarcity. Among poorer populations, having large families can provide unpaid workers for family farms and businesses, childcare, eldercare, fetch a dowry price, provide additional income, compensate for the scarcity-driven deaths of other children, and defend the family from scarcity-driven invasions/theft (World Vision, 2020). More affluent populations often procreate to alleviate psychological scarcity through providing meaning and purpose in life, vicariously living out derailed dreams, preventing a partner from leaving, providing affection, validation, recognition and emotional support, increasing status, gaining demographic political leverage, and creating community in atomized societies. A directly democratic, non-hierarchical communalist system where everyone had equal political power, participation in meaningful work, communal support, and access to all necessities could empower people to make such decisions from a place of abundance, not scarcity-driven need.

That said, the greatest overpopulation problem by far today is force-bred "domesticated" animals. A mass transition to veganism would end that practice. However, other animals have similar procreation motivations to humans.

In an intriguing paper regarding the role of sanctuaries in the animal rights movement, philosophers Will Kymlicka and Sue Donaldson (2015) examine how other animals also desire offspring. Like us, they long to nurture others, enjoy the company of youngsters, and seek inter-generational relationships. Inspired by sanctuaries like V.I.N.E. Sanctuary, and Pig Preserve, Donaldson & Kymlicka (rightfully) challenge human entitlement to control others' reproduction, but also suggest sanctuaries meet nonhuman psychological needs by cultivating multi-generational populations and encouraging inter-species interactions, allowing residents to mix with and care for non-biological young. In short, their needs could also be met through communalism.

Humans' psychological needs could also be met through multi-species interactions. From the nurturing tendencies that maximum-security prisoners engaged in animal care programs exhibit (Leder, 2016), to the healing effects of nonhuman "animal therapists" on human trauma survivors (Zaiontz, 2021) and seniors (Bemis, 2013), evidence suggests bonding with other animals can help heal human psycho-pathologies—and by extension, potentially help heal the scarcity wound driving over-consumption in order to compensate for psychological lack.

In atomized societies, caregiving is often perceived as stressful and burdensome for caregivers, but research has shown that looking after others can improve self-esteem, self-worth, and feelings of social connection. Other animal species also experience reduced stress and anxiety through engaging in care-taking behaviors like grooming (Inagaki & Orehek, 2017). This poses compelling possibilities for cultivating a multi-species care ethic between humans and other animals as a form of psychological mutual aid.

It's also striking how nonhuman animal needs parallel human needs in other ways. Kymlicka and Donaldson describe sanctuary residents as exhibiting desires for belonging, non-hierarchy, self-determination, interdependence, and a supportive environment—essentially the same basic human needs identified by Fromm (1941). Although constrained by the current anthropocentric society, sanctuaries like V.I.N.E. attempt to fulfill these needs through creating semi-autonomous zones for animals to rewild themselves and cultivate conditions for sanctuary residents to intermingle with wildlife, teach each other which plants are edible and which to avoid, participate in enrichment activities, and even assist humans if they so choose. Animals learn to socialize with others unlike them, learning about themselves in the process.

Therein lies the potential for a multi-species communalist society in which humans co-exist with other animals as friends, equals, comrades and neighbors. Recently, interest has been growing in sanctuaries as potential sites of political resistance (see Meijer, 2021.) Donaldson and Kymlicka (2015) also question the paradigm in which humans "own" the land and either employ workers or recruit volunteers, rather than fostering a non-hierarchical model where humans live with each other and other animals in multi-species intentional communities. Additionally, they consider how such communities might impact and interact with surrounding area human and nonhuman residents.

This mirrors a key aspect of Murray Bookchin's communalist philosophy of social ecology (1993). Since ecosystems are interdependent and depend upon each individual organism's and species' well-being to flourish, whatever takes place within human society affects the surrounding ecosystem. Additionally, human society itself is also a (social) ecosystem of sorts. Thus, social ecology is centered on the idea of building an ecological society that recognizes that in order for both human society and the natural world to flourish, every individual and group within human society must flourish. Thus, social ecology prioritizes non-hierarchy, social justice, and shared political and economic power as ecologically essential (Bookchin, 1993). Since hierarchical control of nature is driving manufactured scarcity through blocking access to the means of life-sustaining production, and driving real scarcity through trashing the ecosystem for profit, dismantling hierarchy in favor of directly democratic control would alleviate scarcity on all fronts—benefiting humans, other animals, and ecosystems alike.

As an expanded sanctuary that explicitly connects its work to larger political structures and prioritizes connecting with the local rural community it resides within over veganizing visitors (Meijer, 2021), V.I.N.E. could be described as operating in a social ecological way. By cultivating a flourishing inter-species community of individuals within the sanctuary which then serves to positively impact both the greater social and natural ecosystem locally, and the broader movement for collective liberation, V.I.N.E. is an example of social ecology in action. V.I.N.E.'s example can set the foundation for broader questions about how the animal liberation/vegan movement might connect with the communalist movement.

Currently, organizations like Symbiosis Revolution and the People's Network for Land and Liberation are collectively building a network of grassroots mutual aid initiatives, semi-autonomous communes, neighborhood assemblies, and others aligned with the communalist vision to a create a challenge to Capitalism through providing an alternative system capable of meeting people's needs while also regenerating ecosystems (Akuno, 2023). Yet, among all the social justice movements involved in this new movement for "ecology, (direct) democracy, utopia" (Chodorkoff, 2014), the animal liberation movement is strikingly absent. A social-ecological approach to movement-building could involve the animal liberation movement connecting

with the communalist movement by forming its own, self-contained network of communalist-aligned initiatives. These could include vegan mutual
aid, expanded sanctuaries, animal rescuers and vegan community outreach,
and connecting that to the wider communalist movement. The creation of
a vegan social ecosystem within the broader communalist social ecosystem
diversifies both movements, and integrates the struggle for animal liberation
into a wider praxis of total liberation.

Connecting these movements makes sense in multiple ways. Creating
a veganarchist network which would then integrate into a bigger network
would increase communication, resource-sharing, and solidarity between
organizations and movements, building systems of mutual aid. If one sanctuary or organization needed help, it would have expanded, more diverse
channels of support. Our movement would also have access to ecological
regeneration skill-sharing—something that would enormously benefit nonhuman animals through habitat restoration—and information about how
to obtain land to create sanctuaries through community land trusts, fund
such initiatives through public banks, etc. Connecting with the communalist
movement would also enable us to share knowledge about veganism/ani-
mal liberation with a new population—one that already aligns with a Total
Liberationist vision in many ways.

Additionally, sanctuaries could potentially become microcosmic experiments in participatory multi-species democracy and post-scarcity veganarchism. Sanctuaries could provide homes not only to nonhuman "refugees"
(Meijer, 2021), but also to human refugees like undocumented immigrants
and unhoused people, as well as short-term and long-term residencies for
"academic researchers, artists, farmers, craftspeople, architects, teachers,
ethologists, and others who want to be part of an interspecies community,
and lend their skills to exploring the potential for intentional communities of
interspecies justice and flourishing" (Donaldson & Kymlicka, 2015, p. 68).
Sanctuaries could also arrange transportation and housing for low-income
city residents to visit and volunteer at the sanctuary and serve as gathering spaces for cross-movement idea generation and organizing. Additionally,
they might incorporate ideas from other communalist organizations, such as
Mississippi's Cooperation Jackson, a Black semi-autonomous community with
a visionary build and fight formula for overcoming and replacing Capitalism
through a strategy rooted in mutual aid, food sovereignty, neighborhood
assemblies, land reclamation, community-controlled production and cooperative economics to build Black autonomy throughout the U.S. South via its
Jackson-Kush Plan. Cooperation Jackson's food-producing community gardens, worker-owned farm-to-table vegan cafe, ecologically-restorative Green

Team, time-bank where local residents receive fresh produce in exchange for volunteering, and setting up an "eco-village" of co-ops engaged in green projects like solar installation, waste management, and community childcare, could especially benefit a multi-species community and make strides towards a post-scarcity reality for non/humans alike.

Additionally, joining forces with the communalist movement could help create the conditions for multi-species democracy. Kymlicka and Donaldson explored that possibility in their 2011 book *Zoopolis* which advocates switching from a "capacity contract"-based democracy, which only allows those capable of participating in the linguistic/rational decision-making process any political influence, to a "social membership" model that extends participation to anyone affected by political decisions. This expanded concept of democracy is echoed by Bookchin, whose expansive concept of citizenship proposes that all (human) area residents should be involved in determining not only political policies but also local company policies. Kymlicka and Donaldson (2011) argue that we owe animals we've domesticated the fullest political participation/representation possible. Some sanctuaries, like V.I.N.E., have begun implementing such practices, taking care to consider nonhuman perspectives and even creating policies like requiring animals to be physically present during decision-making meetings in order to remind humans whose fate is being decided upon (Donaldson & Kymlicka, 2015).

Additionally, communalism can strengthen the vegan movement more broadly. Often, the movement is criticized as being overly individualistic and consumerist in nature (Gelderloos, 2008). There is some validity to this, as the emphasis on converting individuals to veganism overlooks the structural nature of animal exploitation under Capitalism, and falsely equates "voting with your dollars" with real political power. Focusing efforts on electing vegan politicians is equally misguided; the issue is not individual politician's speciesism, but rather how globalized geopolitical and market forces subvert individual will. In the current paradigm, only oligarchs wield real individual power (Krugman, 2020). However, in a direct democracy, individuals would have the power to propose, shape, and collectively decide upon policies. In such a system, conversion efforts would make sense, because public opinion would directly translate into public policy. Thus, joining the communalist movement, which would strengthen the movement for direct democracy, would also empower efforts to achieve multi-species justice and post-scarcity for all.

In many ways, vegan advocacy is inherently communalist. Centered around education, cooking, food-sharing, caregiving, habitat restoration, and other forms of direct action, it aligns perfectly with communalist praxis like mutual aid, community gardens and food forests, neighborhood pot-lucks and film screenings, and neighborhood cleanup efforts. Some vegan organizations, particularly B.I.P.O.C.-led ones, have begun moving in that direction. Rooted in environmental, economic and racial justice, Thrive Baltimore provides healthy plant-based food, vegan education, and cultural events to the low-income Black community it resides within, while New York's Liberation Farm focuses on reconnecting Black people with the land, food, and each other. Gaza's Plant the Land combines vegan food distribu-tion with planting food on public lands and other community projects to build Palestinian food sovereignty and land reclamation. Formed in the after-math of Hurricane Maria to provide emergency aid to impacted humans and nonhumans, Puerto Rico's Casa Vegana de la Communidad offers weekly vegan events and runs a chicken micro-sanctuary. Mexico's Nahautl-led Faun Accion and El Mocajete combine anti-speciesist activism with global classes on emergent/alternative economies, and run a store where people can barter or get things for free.

After centuries of scarcity mentality-induced trauma endured by humans, other species, and earth itself, we might consider the research on environ-ments that foster post-traumatic healing and growth in humans and other animals, called Phoenix Zones (Ferdowsian, 2018), for their ability to help traumatized individuals "rise like phoenixes from the ashes." According to Ferdowsian, a medical doctor, human and animal rights activist, whether humans and nonhuman animals crumble or survive and thrive post-trauma is largely dependent on environmental factors. Phoenix Zones are places where survivors thrive and share certain identifiable characteristics. Importantly, the Phoenix Effect can affect not just individuals, but entire societies. This begs the question of how to create a world comprised of multi-species Phoenix Zones. When exploring how to cultivate these qualities in our spaces, we might consider architect Jennifer Wolch's ideas regarding re-enchanting cities by re-designing them to welcome animals back in. This re-naturalized city model, which Wolch christened "Zoopolis" in homage to Donaldson and Kymlicka's vision of a multi-species democracy, could both meet the psycho-spiritual needs of humans and other animals by reconnecting them with each other and with nature, and also serve to thwart Capitalist, colonialist, and consumerist impulses, as the constant presence of nature and other animals would serve as a constant reminder of who is harmed by such practices (Emel & Wolch, 1998). It may take bringing animals into our spaces to make us recognize and protect the abundance that surrounds us.

## Conclusion

Reflecting upon the scarcity monster, we might realize it is us. By alienating ourselves from each other, other animals, and our own animality, and creating false needs for false selves, Capitalism turns humanimals into monsters who then go on to "monsterfy" other animals and nature, creating real scarcity in the process. Transforming our relationships with other animals, and with ourselves *as* animals, can also help us transform our relationships with fellow humans, eradicate the internal scarcity driving external scarcity, and develop an internal abundance that radiates outward, then reflects back upon us.

Abundia Alvarado, a Nahuatl and Apache trans femme migrant community organizer, Weelaunee forest defender, co-founder of the aforementioned FaunAcción and El Molcajete, co-founder of the Atlanta, GA-based queer indigenous/Latinx gardening collective Mariposas Rebeldes, and co-founder of the annual money-free gift-economy Dandelion Fest, describes what she calls the "Sacred Web of Abundance" (Collective, 2023):

> The Sacred Web of Abundance is the sum of the vast, intricate system that sustains all life on this planet. Your Sacred Web of Abundance is the place that you live, the ways in which it sustains you, and the ways in which you sustain it. We are here to be part of this web and invite in others who are on the same land. What we have found is that the Sacred Web of Abundance, with her billions of years of wisdom, is there for us, waiting for our gratitude, delight, offerings, rituals, and ceremonies—waiting to build a relationship with us.

As earth's fate lies in the balance, Abundance awaits us to exorcise our internal scarcity-monsters and return to our rightful position within nature's Web. The time has never been more urgent, yet more pregnant with possibility, than now.

## References

Abdullah O. (2013). *Democratic confederalism*. International Initiative Ed.

Akuno, K. (2023). *Ecosocialism from below. Encounter videos.* Cooperation Jackson. https://cooperationjackson.org/blog/ecosocialismfrombelowseries

Bailey, V. (2022, May 5). *COVID-19 pandemic exacerbated healthcare workforce challenges.* RevCycleIntelligence. https://revcycleintelligence.com/news/covid-19-pandemic-exacerbated-healthcare-workforce-challenges

Baker, A. (2021, July 20). Climate, not conflict. Madagascar's famine is the first in modern history to be solely caused by global warming. *Time Magazine.* https://time.com/6081919/famine-climate-change-madagascar/

Bartal, I. B.-A., Decety, J., & Mason, P. (2011). Empathy and pro-social behavior in rats. *Science, 334*(6061), 1427–1430. https://doi.org/10.1126/science.1210789

Beyer, R. M., Manica, A., & Mora, C. (2021). Temporary removal: Shifts in global bat diversity suggest a possible role of climate change in the emergence of SARS-CoV-1 and SARS-CoV-2. *Science of the Total Environment, 767*, 145413. https://doi.org/10.1016/j.scitotenv.2021.145413

Bookchin, M. (1971). *Post-scarcity anarchism*. Ramparts Press.

Bookchin, M. (1993). *What is social ecology?* The Anarchist Library. https://theanarchist library.org/library/murray-bookchin-what-is-social-ecology

Bookchin, M. (2017, December 14). *Toward a communalist approach*. New-Compass.net. http://new-compass.net/articles/toward-communalist-approach

Casamitjana, J. (2021, November 19). *Single-issue campaigning and veganism*. Vegan FTA. https://veganfta.com/2021/11/19/single-issue-campaigning-and-veganism/

Chodorkoff, D. (2014). *Social ecology: An ecological humanism*. Libcom.org. https://lib com.org/library/social-ecology-ecological-humanism

Kim, C. J. (2015). *Dangerous crossings: Race, species, and nature in a multicultural age*. Cambridge University Press.

Collective, C. E.-W. (2023). *Defending abundance everywhere: A call to every community from the Weelaunee Forest*. CrimethInc. https://crimethinc.com/2023/03/02/defending-abundance-everywhere-a-call-to-every-community-from-the-weelaunee-forest

Cook, C. D. (2020, May 7). Farmers are destroying mountains of food. Here's what to do about it. *The Guardian*. https://www.theguardian.com/commentisfree/2020/may/07/farmers-food-covid-19

de Waal, A. (2018). The end of famine? Prospects for the elimination of mass starvation by olitical action. *Political Geography, 62*, 184–195. https://doi.org/10.1016/j.pol geo.2017.09.004

DeSilver, D. (2013, December 5). *U.S. income inequality, on rise for decades, is now highest since 1928*. Pew Research Center. https://www.pewresearch.org/fact-tank/2013/12/05/u-s-income-inequality-on-rise-for-decades-is-now-highest-since-1928/

Dominick, B. (1995). *Animal liberation and social revolution: A vegan perspective on anarchism or an anarchist perspective on veganism*. The Anarchist Library. https://theanarchistlibrary.org/library/brian-a-dominick-animal-liberation-and-social-rev olution

Donaldson, S., & Kymlicka, W. (2011). *Zoopolis: A political theory of animal rights*. Oxford University Press.

Donaldson, S., & Kymlicka, W. (2015). Farmed animal sanctuaries: The heart of the movement? A socio-political perspective. *Politics and Animals, 1*(1), 50–74.

Eisen, M. B., & Brown, P. O. (2022). Rapid global phase out of animal agriculture has the potential to stabilize greenhouse gas levels for 30 years and offset 68 percent of $CO2$ emissions this century. *PLOS Climate, 1*(2), e0000010. https://doi.org/10.1371/journal.pclm.0000010

Ferdowsian, H. (2018). *Phoenix zones: Where strength is born and resilience lives.* University of Chicago Press.

Fischer, D. (2022). Let nature play: A possible pathway of total liberation and earth restoration. *Green Theory & Praxis Journal, 14*(1), 7–29.

Fromm, E. (1941). *Escape from freedom.* Farrar & Rinehart.

Gelderloos, P. (2008). *Veganism is a consumer activity.* The Anarchist Library. https://theanarchistlibrary.org/library/peter-gelderloos-veganism-is-a-consumer-activity

Goodman, P. S., & Chokshi, N. (2021, June 1). How the world ran out of everything. *The New York Times.* https://www.nytimes.com/2021/06/01/business/coronavirus-global-shortages.html

Grant, L. K. (2011). Can we consume our way out of climate change? A call for analysis. *The Behavior Analyst, 34*(2), 245–266. https://doi.org/10.1007/bf03392256

Halakhe, A. (2022). *We were warned: Unlearned lessons of famine in the horn of Africa.* https://static1.squarespace.com/static/506c8ea1e4b01d9450dd53f5/t/63925bbe1c50666e23354126/1670536126785/Food+Insecurity+Report+-+December+2022.pdf

Hasell, J. (2018). *Does population growth lead to hunger and famine?* Our World in Data. https://ourworldindata.org/population-growth-and-famines

Hodson, G. (2012, June 19). The human-animal divide and prejudices against humans. *Psychology Today.* https://www.psychologytoday.com/us/blog/without-prejudice/201206/the-human-animal-divide-and-prejudices-against-humans

Inagaki, T. K., & Orehek, E. (2017). On the benefits of giving social support. *Current Directions in Psychological Science, 26*(2), 109–113. https://doi.org/10.1177/0963721416686212

Kenton, W. (2019). *Green Tech.* Investopedia. https://www.investopedia.com/terms/g/green_tech.asp

Kepner, V., & Cole, P. (2013). Green consumerism: A path to sustainability? In N. Karagiannis & J. Marangos (Eds.), *Toward a good society in the twenty-first century* (pp. 105–122). Palgrave Mcmillian.

Kropotkin, P. (2017). *Mutual aid: A factor of evolution.* Martino Fine Books.

Krosch, A. R., & Amodio, D. M. (2014). Economic scarcity alters the perception of race. *Proceedings of the National Academy of Sciences, 111*(25), 9079–9084. https://doi.org/10.1073/pnas.1404448111

Krugman, P. (2020, July 1). Opinion | Why do the rich have so much power? *The New York Times.* https://www.nytimes.com/2020/07/01/opinion/sunday/inequality-america-paul-krugman.html

Kymlicka, W. (2019, April 30). *Human supremacism: Why are animal rights activists still the "orphans of the left"?* New Statesman. https://www.newstatesman.com/politics/2019/04/human-supremacism-why-are-animal-rights-activists-still-the-orphans-of-the-left-2

Leder, D. (2016). *The distressed body.* University of Chicago Press.

Malinovskaya, A., & Sheiner, L. (2016, September 20). *Four ways to speed up productivity growth*. Brookings. https://www.brookings.edu/blog/up-front/2016/09/20/four-ways-to--up-productivity-growth/

Meijer, E. (2021). Sanctuary politics and the border of the demos. *Krisis Journal, 41*(2). https://doi.org/10.21827/krisis.41.2.37174

Okasha, S. (2013, July 21). *Biological altruism (Stanford Encyclopedia of Philosophy)*. Stanford.edu. https://plato.stanford.edu/entries/altruism-biological/

Park, W. (2022, May 5). *How companies blame you for climate change*. www.bbc.com. https://www.bbc.com/future/article/20220504-why-the-wrong-people-are-blamed-for-climate-change

Poore, J., & Nemecek, T. (2018). Reducing food's environmental impacts through producers and consumers. *Science 360*(6392), 987–992.

Reliefweb. (2022, October 19). *Central America's dry corridor: Turning emergency into opportunities*. Newsroom. https://www.fao.org/newsroom/detail/central-americas-dry-corridor-turning-emergency-into-opportunities/en

Schiermeier, Q. (2019). Eat less meat: UN climate change report calls for change to human diet. *Nature, 572*. https://doi.org/10.1038/d41586-019-02409-7

Schleifer, L., & Fischer, D. (2022). *Animal liberation is climate justice*. New Politics. https://newpol.org/issue_post/animal-liberation-is-climate-justice/

*The World Counts*. (2023). Www.theworldcounts.com; The World Counts. https://www.theworldcounts.com/challenges/planet-earth/state-of-the-planet/when-will-the-world-run-out-of-water

Wolch, J. R., & Emel, J. (1998). *Animal geographies: Place, politics, and identity in the nature-culture borderlands*. Verso.

*World Food Programme*. (2023). A global food crisis. www.wfp.org. https://www.wfp.org/global-hunger-crisis#:~:text=2022%3A%20a%20year%20o

World Vision. (2020, July 13). *Why do the poor have large families?* Www.worldvision.ca. https://www.worldvision.ca/stories/why-do-the-poor-have-large-families

Youness, M. (2015, December 10). *How climate change contributed to the conflicts in the Middle East and North Africa*. Blogs.worldbank.org. https://blogs.worldbank.org/arabvoices/climate-change-conflict-mena

# Afterword

Seven Mattes

"We are stuck with the problem of living despite economic and ecological
ruination. Neither tales of progress nor of ruin tell us how to think about
collaborative survival. It is time to pay attention to mushroom picking. Not
that this will save us—but it might open our imaginations."
—Anna Lowenhaupt Tsing, The Mushroom at the End of the World: On the
Possibility of Life in Capitalist Ruins

My reading of the chapters in this volume paralleled my viewing of a Netflix
series entitled "The Last of Us"—a mycological take on the zombie apocalypse genre. While the series itself is rife with multispecies entanglements
and posthuman insights, the relation that continuously came to mind as I
took in these chapters was that of the resiliency constructed from community
and connections. Mainstream visions of zombie apocalypses tend to focus
on rugged individualism, hypermasculinity, and rampant violence as a means
for survival. "The Last of Us" is causing a slight stir as it not only portrays
queer lives, but in that it demonstrates love, mutual aid, compassion, and
possibilities for flourishing—rather than mere "bare life" survival. More so,
these possibilities exist during a parasitic fungal pandemic and under the
dominating force of a militaristic fascist regime.

The world in which these chapters are born is, thankfully, less contentious
than a zombie apocalypse. However, they may crash against the zombie-like
force (often lacking deliberate thought) of conventional cultural values, norms
and institutions. It is here, too, that connections and communities actively
sought and constructed are necessary—solidarity leads to mutual growth and
new opportunities for awareness and direct action. Conscious of the audience
who will take in these works, these chapters urge our community to address

connections and be openly critical of our current positionality and actions—calling on us to come to terms with our own humanity via an *anthroponomy* perspective, for example. They challenge the audience to address those topics oft seen as too touchy to touch, such as the question of our growing human population, the impacts of flight, and veganism across socioeconomic classes and ability. Connections and cross-species camaraderie are sought in the *monstrosity* that are non-conforming bodies. The historical and current interconnections in African and Black Anarchism and Black Feminism links the struggles addressed in CAS to myriad other foundations and routes—making space for new lines of thought. Together and among others, these works not only make waves in their individual areas, but they build community—both in the action of writing the chapters as a connected cohort and in the bridges they deliberately forge.

Ida B. Wells states, "The way to right wrongs is to turn the light of truth upon them." These chapters shed light on topics that may be considered *underground*, given their topic or critical approach. Again, the mycological metaphor arises. Whereas such perspectives are underground in the sense that they are not centered in mainstream culture, they arise in vibrant bursts across the landscape. Whereas they appear alone, perhaps vulnerable or even radically out of place, they are connected to and supported by a complex network. And they are spreading. CAS is a part of this network and works of this type are contagious. Filaments will continue to reach out and expand—aiding structures already in place, tearing down where necessary, and moving forward in new trajectories. Now is the time for foraging.

# Notes on Contributors

**Charlotte Anne** is a white privileged migrant living in Athens, greece. they are a long term vegan, human traitor, anti-binary gender antagonist, confronting their position within a racialized hierarchy with as much humility and self-deprecation as possible. their anarchism is anti-work and seeks to support others in doing as little labor as possible. they live with two cats and in support of many more local street cats.

**Nandita Bajaj** is the Executive Director of Population Balance that advocates for reproductive autonomy, ecocentrism, and degrowth. She also co-hosts the popular interview series The Overpopulation Podcast at Population Balance. She is an adjunct lecturer at the Institute for Humane Education at Antioch University, where she teaches about the combined impacts of pronatalism and human expansionism on reproductive, ecological, and intergenerational justice. Her work has appeared in major news outlets including Canadian Broadcasting Corporation, The Washington Post, The Guardian, Newsweek, Ms. Magazine, The Globe and Mail, and National Post. She has Bachelor degrees in Aerospace Engineering and Education, and a Master degree in Humane Education.

**Jeremy Bendik-Keymer** works as Professor of Philosophy at Case Western Reserve University, Cleveland, Ohio, USA, rightful and sacred land of many older nations, and is a Senior Research Fellow with the Earth System Governance, Project, Universiteit Utrecht. Recent books include The Wind ~ An Unruly Living, Involving Anthroponomy in the Anthropocene: on Decoloniality, and a forthcoming open-access edition of The Ecological Life: Discovering Citizenship and a Sense of Humanity.

**Will Boisseau**, Ph.D., completed his doctorate at Loughborough University. His research focuses on the place of animal rights within the British left, particularly on the relationship between the anarchist/direct action and legislative wings of the movement. His work explores the class and gender issues influencing this relationship, the marginalization of animal rights in mainstream labour politics and a range of concepts including total liberation, speciesism, intersectionality, and critical animal studies. Will is currently involved in trade union politics in the UK.

**Francesca Corradini** is a Master's student in Environmental Humanities at Ca'Foscari University in Venice. She obtained a degree in Cultural Heritage from the University of Trento with a thesis on the role of sounds as a means of interaction with the environment and other non-human species, exploring the role of sound recordings as a way of collecting and preserving memories and traditions. Currently, in her Master's degree she is focusing on the fields of critical animal studies, indigenous studies, conservation biology, environmental anthropology, and environmental education. In addition, she is now involved in a project on soundscapes, sound maps, and multi-species encounters.

**Elisabeth Dimitras** obtained a BSc in Mathematics and an MSc in Biodiversity Conservation but works in neither domain since both are anthropocentric. She is an activist who advocates for total liberation through the Ethos and Empathy website, raising awareness on ethical issues involving non-human animals but also the planet and fellow humans. She works as a freelance researcher for vegan/antispeciesist organizations while she lives off the grid with her two dogs and one cat in Evia island, Greece – in a land which she hopes to slowly transform to a self-sustainable microfarm sanctuary based on vegan permaculture and regenerative agriculture.

**Amber E. George**, Ph.D., is an Assistant Professor of Philosophy and Diversity, Equity, and Inclusion at Galen College. Dr. George is an executive board member for Critical Animal Studies (ICAS) and chief editor of *Journal for Critical Animal Studies (JCAS)*. Dr. George most recently edited *Gender and Sexuality in Critical Animal Studies;* and *The Intersectionality of Critical Animal, Disability, and Environmental Studies.*

**Ezgi Karaoğlu**, born and raised in Istanbul, Turkey, is a Ph.D. candidate in Sociology at Michigan State University. Previously she worked with refugees in Turkey for UN Refugee Agency and implementing partners of

UNHCR. She takes a critical approach to migration research and humanitarianism, focusing on the macro-structural forces driving international migration. She seeks to answer the way paternalism and power relations operate in humanitarian interventions and the placemaking strategies of urban migrants through multiple exclusion and inclusion patterns. Her academic guilty pleasure is thinking, observing, and writing on street animals and interspecies interaction.

**Agnese Martini** graduated in Philosophy from the University of Bologna with a thesis on the history of madness, focusing on Foucault's analysis of the oppressive system of asylum and the discrimination generated by the medicalization of mental illness. She is currently enrolled in a Master's degree in Environmental Humanities at Ca'Foscari University of Venice and her academic interests revolve around Critical Animal Studies, Multispecies Ethnography and Environmental Anthropology. She is also involved in an ethnobiology research project regarding traditional ecological knowledge of fishermen in the Venice Lagoon.

**Seven Mattes** received her PhD in Cultural Anthropology from Michigan State University and currently serves as an Assistant Professor in the Center for Integrative Studies. Specializing in Japanese human-animal relationships, her applied research is aimed at improving disaster preparedness and resiliency for animals through policy change and direct action with non-profit organizations. In both research and teaching she emphasizes the significance of valuing and understanding human-animal entanglements across cultures.

**Zane McNeill** is the founder of the DEIJ organization, Roots DEI Consulting and Policy, and co-manager of the labor rights group, Rights for Animal Rights Advocates (RARA). They have published anthologies on anti-carceral veganism and queer and trans liberation with PM Press, Sanctuary Press, and Lantern Publishing and Media. They are also a contributing writer with Sentient Media and Law@theMargins.

**Nathan Poirier** is a professional tutor at Lansing Community College who has spent much time studying and critiquing in vitro meat from vegan and critical animal studies perspectives. Nathan also has graduate specializations in (critical) animal studies and women's & gender studies. Nathan was co-organizer for Students for Critical Animal Studies from 2019-2023. Nathan co-edited the book Emerging New Voices in Critical Animal Studies: Vegan Studies for Total Liberation (2022).

**Matteo Porazzi** is a Master's student in Environmental Humanities at University Ca'Foscari of Venice. Previously, he graduated in Language and Cultural Mediation from the University of Milan with a thesis that resonated on the ideas of identity, femaleness and blackness of the Nigerian author Chimamanda Ngozi Adichie. Currently, in his M.A.'s program he is focusing more on the field of Critical Animal Studies, Food Studies, and Environmental Sustainability. Alongside his university career, he is working for The New Institute Centre for Environmental Humanities (NICHE) and the European Centre for Living Technology (ECLT).

**Laura Schleifer** is a lifelong: artivist," an NYU Tisch graduate who's performed throughout the Middle East with a circus troupe, taught in China, Nicaragua, and at Wesleyan University, performed off-Broadway, and arts-mentored homeless youth. Her screenplay, The Feral Child, was a Sundance Screenwriters' Lab finalist. Her essays appear in New Politics, The Leftist Review, Forca Vegan, *Kropotkin Now!*, *Neoliberal Schooling of Selfishness and Exploitation, and Fever Spores; William S. Burroughs and Queer Letters*. Laura is also ICAS Total Liberation Director, a Promoting Enduring Peace Board member, and co-founder of Plant the Land, a Gaza-based vegan food justice/community projects team.

**Simon Springer** is Professor of Human Geography, Head of Discipline for Geography and Environmental Studies, and Director of the Centre for Urban and Regional Studies at the University of Newcastle, Australia. His research explores the socio-political exclusions of neoliberalism, emphasizing the geographies of violence and power. He cultivates a cutting-edge theoretical approach through a radical revival of anarchist philosophy. Simon's more recent books include, as author, *A Primer on Anarchist Geography, Fuck Neoliberalism: Translating Resistance,* and as (co-)editor, *The Anarchist Political Ecology Trilogy,* and the *Anarchism, Geography and the Spirit of Revolt* trilogy.

**Kirsten Stade** is the Communications Manager at Population Balance. She has worked for over two decades for nonprofit organizations focusing on conserving wildlife, challenging extractive industries on public lands, and protecting the integrity of regulatory science, and has published research on the impacts of livestock grazing on fire ecology and ecosystem health in the American west. She has a Master's degree in Conservation Biology from Columbia University and a Bachelor's in Earth Systems from Stanford University.

**John Tallent** is an independent scholar-activist who founded the social media page Veganarchist Memes: Breaking Leftist Speciesism on Facebook, Twitter, and Instagram. They hold a BA in Political Science, and a Master of Art in Applied Sociology degree from the University of Alabama at Birmingham. Their work tends to focus on dismantling speciesism within the political Left, bringing anarchism into the vegan community, and creating a universally practicable vegan praxis that is based in total liberation.

**Sarah Tomasello,** an independent scholar, received her B.A. in Anthropology and Religious Studies and an M.S. in Anthrozoology from Canisius College. Throughout her studies and publications, Sarah's work has focused on the intersections between decolonization, animal rights, and wildlife conservation. She is especially interested in improving conservation initiatives so that they are respectful and inclusive of Indigenous communities, as well as more compassionate towards the nonhuman individuals they impact.

**Cameron T. Whitley**, Ph.D. is an Associate Professor of Sociology at Western Washington University with expertise in environmental sociology, sociological animal studies, and transgender studies. He has published over 30 peer reviewed journal articles, 16 book chapters, and a co-edited book. To date, his work has appeared in journals such as the Annual Review of Sociology, Sociological Perspectives, Sociological Inquiry, Teaching Sociology, Proceedings of the National Academies of Sciences, Sex Roles, and Environment and Behavior among others and been featured in such outlets as the LA Times, New York Times, Washington Post, BBC, and The Guardian.

# Index

# RADICAL ANIMAL STUDIES AND TOTAL LIBERATION

Anthony J. Nocella II, S E R I E S E D I T O R

The **Radical Animal Studies and Total Liberation** book series branches out of Critical Animal Studies (a field co-founded by Anthony J. Nocella II) with the argument that criticism is not enough. Action must follow theory. This series demands that scholars are engaged with their subjects both theoretically and actively via radical, revolutionary, intersectional action for total liberation. Founded in anarchism, the series provides space for scholar-activists who challenge authoritarianism and oppression in their many daily forms. **Radical Animal Studies and Total Liberation** promotes accessible and inclusive scholarship that is based on personal narrative as well as traditional research, and is especially interested in the advancement of interwoven voices and perspectives from multiple radical, revolutionary social justice groups and movements such as Black Lives Matter, Idle No More, Earth First!, the Zapatistas, ADAPT, prison abolition, LGBTTQQIA rights, disability liberation, Earth Liberation Front, Animal Liberation Front, political prisoners, radical transnational feminism, environmental justice, food justice, youth justice, and Hip Hop activism.

To order other books in this series please contact our Customer Service Department:

PETERLANG@PRESSWAREHOUSE.COM (WITHIN THE U.S.)

ORDERS@PETERLANG.COM (OUTSIDE THE U.S.)

To find out more about the series or browse a full list of titles, please visit our website:

WWW.PETERLANG.COM

www.ingramcontent.com/pod-product-compliance
Lightning Source LLC
Chambersburg PA
CBHW050644280326
41932CB00015B/2774